2ND Edition

BUILDING READING COMPREHENSION HABITS

IN GRADES 6-12

A Toolkit of Classroom Activities

Jeff Zwiers

TERNATIONAL
Reading Association
800 Barksdale Road, PO Box 8139
Newark, DE 19714-8139, USA
www.reading.org

The International Reading Association attempts, through its publications, to provide a forum for a wide spectrum of opinions on reading. This policy permits divergent viewpoints without implying the endorsement of the Association.

Executive Editor, Books   Corinne M. Mooney
Developmental Editor   Charlene M. Nichols
Developmental Editor   Tori Mello Bachman
Developmental Editor   Stacey L. Reid
Editorial Production Manager   Shannon T. Fortner
Design and Composition Manager   Anette Schuetz

Project Editors   Charlene M. Nichols and Christina M. Terranova

Cover   Design, Six Red Marbles

Library of Congress Cataloging-in-Publication Data
Zwiers, Jeff.
  Building reading comprehension habits in grades 6-12 : a toolkit of classroom activities / Jeff Zwiers. -- 2nd ed.
      p. cm.
  Includes bibliographical references and index.
  ISBN 978-0-87207-506-1
  1. Reading (Secondary) 2. Reading comprehension. I. Title.
  LB1632.Z95 2010
  428.4071'2--dc22

                                                                                     2009048149

CONTENTS

PART I
Developing Instruction Using Comprehension Habits

PART II
Six Comprehension Habits

PART III
Ancillary Materials

ABOUT THE AUTHOR

Jeff Zwiers teaches at Stanford University, California, USA, trains teachers, and participates in education development efforts around the world. After teaching different grade levels for a decade or so, he began to work with teachers and schools on improving the teaching of diverse students' literacy, thinking, and academic language skills.

He has written two other books: *Developing Academic Thinking Skills in Grades 6-12: A Handbook of Multiple Intelligence Activities* and, more recently, *Building Academic Language: Essential Practices for Content Classrooms*. He has also written articles that focus on academic language, cognition, and using interactions to foster deep and lasting understanding.

Jeff has worked in Pakistan, Liberia, Macedonia, Turkey, and Ethiopia on fostering critical thinking, student engagement, language acquisition, and formative assessment. He currently works with teachers on using collaborative inquiry in their teaching and in their professional learning communities. His action research focuses on building students' conversation skills in the classroom to accelerate their development of content understanding, language, and higher order thinking skills.

Author Information for Correspondence and Workshops

Please send comments and suggestions about this book. Most teachers will modify the ideas in this toolkit to meet their needs, and I would like to hear about these modifications and any success stories. Please also feel free to contact me with questions about specific situations that relate to older students' literacy. My e-mail is jazwiers@ usfca.edu.

PREFACE

How can I help my students develop *enduring* and self-sustaining habits of comprehension for a wide variety of texts?

How can I meet the literacy needs of students with widely varied reading levels, cultures, and linguistic backgrounds?

How can I integrate *helpful* and motivating assessments into my instruction?

How can I develop reading lessons that not only provide extra help for my struggling readers but also benefit all my other students?

My guess is that you are reading this book because you are looking for answers to questions such as the ones above. These questions surfaced and led me to write the first edition of this book and still surface today when I work with teachers in my current roles as a mentor, consultant, and teacher educator. These questions are, in my opinion, four of the most challenging questions that we face in secondary education—not because the questions don't have answers, but because the answers are as varied as the students in our classrooms and the contexts in which we teach. This second edition succinctly describes practical ideas, including more than 15 new activities, which have been working in a wide range of middle school and high school classrooms. I have used the ideas, seen them used by others, and researched their effectiveness in a variety of settings.

When I say that all teachers need to be experts on teaching students how to read the texts of their disciplines, I often hear, "Why not just leave the teaching of reading up to the English teachers?" I explain how teachers of other content areas, especially lengthy text subjects such as social studies and science, are uniquely qualified to teach students how to actively think about the texts in their particular classes. For example, analyzing the causes and effects of historical processes differs from visualizing physical and chemical processes in science, which differs from interpreting character motives and figurative language in literature.

It is eye-opening for teachers to realize how reading differs in the other content area classrooms within the school. I give teachers the analogy of mental workouts: Many students have not given their brains the types of vigorous thinking workouts—cross-training, if you will—that teachers want them to have in different types of reading and learning. Once teachers see how the comprehension process differs among subjects, I then bring up comprehension similarities from subject to subject.

Academic reading (reading for school purposes) requires the use of what most literature on comprehension calls *reading strategies* (e.g., Pressley et al., 1990). However, I prefer to use the term *habits* rather than *strategies* because I feel that *habits* more clearly describes the automatic and unconscious processes that are involved in constructing meaning from text. (The distinction between habits and strategies is explained in more detail in Chapter 1.) This book, then, provides a crash course on reading comprehension habits. The upcoming chapters put the course material to work in the form of activities, or tools, for building comprehension habits in all classrooms. My goal with this book is to provide research-based, innovative, "for-tomorrow-morning-and-it's-midnight-now" activities that are adaptable to multiple grade levels and subjects. I don't want teachers to spend a lot of precious planning time sifting through anecdotes and long stretches of text to find the tools they need. Also, I hope that teachers will modify and create their own tools based on their students' needs using the tools presented in this book.

This book is intended for middle school and high school teachers of social studies, science, English, English-language development (ELD; also known as English as a Second Language [ESL]), and any other subject with challenging texts and classes with readers who struggle to understand them. The activities in the following chapters are especially meant to help readers who are below grade level to access and organize the content of grade-level texts. The needs of English learners were very apparent in the development of this toolkit. I work with several school districts that have large numbers of English learners who have been in the United States for more than three years. Even though these students' needs are not identical to those of native-English-speaking mainstream students, many English-learning comprehension issues can be addressed by the tools in this book. Of particular interest to teachers with struggling English learners will be the chapters on background knowledge (Chapter 4) and understanding word meanings (Chapter 7).

These activities are designed for struggling readers, yet teachers tell me that the activities have been effective and engaging for all students in their classrooms. This is probably due to the "multiple intelligences" nature of the tools, especially those that are based on visual and social intelligences. I chose to include as many extralinguistic (visual, kinesthetic, musical, etc.) activities as possible to reach students who have been "turned off" by traditional approaches to reading improvement. Whenever teachers can reinforce plain text with extralinguistic ways of learning, students' comprehension improves (Armbruster, Anderson, & Meyer, 1992). In other words, we need to show students—rather than just tell them—the habits that support comprehension. Following is a visual representation of the intended results of using this toolkit of activities.

Teacher Effects

Teacher uses tools and modifies curriculum with activities from this kit that develop comprehension habits.

Teacher better understands comprehension process and develops own tools to meet specific needs.

Teacher creates and uses authentic assessments to shape instruction and inform students about habits they need to develop.

Cause

Using this toolkit

Student Effects

Students understand and learn content at deep and enduring levels.

Students acquire comprehension habits and apply them to texts in all content areas.

Students meet and surpass standards by demonstrating learning and by succeeding on tests.

Overview of the Book

Following this Preface, you will find a Master List of Activities that lists all the activities in the book, first in order of appearance and then in alphabetical order. You can use this list to locate a specific activity by name or to see what activities are offered in a particular chapter. Similarly, a Master List of Reproducibles also is provided for your reference.

Part I discusses ideas for using comprehension habits as a foundation for developing literacy instruction. Chapter 1 provides a description of comprehension habits for upper grade teachers who desire a clear and concise foundation for building literacy in their students. The chapter also offers a practical explanation of the importance of student background, language, and thinking in developing literacy instruction. Chapter 2 reminds teachers of the key components of assessment and instruction as they relate to the development of comprehension habits.

Part II covers the comprehension habits themselves. Chapters 3–8 cover a separate comprehension habit, with each chapter giving a description of the habit followed by recommended activities that help develop it. The six comprehension habits are as follows:

1. Organizing text information by sculpting the main idea and summarizing (Chapter 3)

2. Connecting to background knowledge (Chapter 4)

3. Making inferences and predictions (Chapter 5)

4. Generating and answering questions (Chapter 6)

5. Understanding and remembering word meanings (Chapter 7)

6. Monitoring one's own comprehension (Chapter 8)

At the end of each chapter, you will find corresponding reproducible forms and worksheets that are used in certain activities in that chapter. Feel free to photocopy these pages to hand out to students or to make transparencies of them for use on an overhead projector during whole-class activities. You also can enlarge the pages to make posters to hang in your classroom. In this edition you will also find new reflection questions to help guide and deepen thinking about each habit.

Part III contains two appendixes with useful information to help you with some of the activities. Appendix A lists common multiple-meaning words and Appendix B lists affixes and roots (word parts). Both appendixes are particularly useful for building the habit of understanding word meanings (Chapter 7) while reading.

This second edition contains several new features. It describes the most recent research on comprehension habits, their instruction, and their assessment. There is a stronger emphasis on being strategic and using formative assessment over time to answer key inquiries about student learning. In addition, this edition clarifies how to gradually release ownership of the thinking over to students as they develop the habits. Chapters 3 through 8 are updated with new tools and variations for meeting the needs of English learners and other diverse groups of students. More explanation of diverse learners and their needs is provided in Chapter 1. Likewise, several visual tools have been refined and adapted based on input from teachers who have been using them.

So if you are up to the challenge of answering the four opening questions, becoming more of an expert in reading the texts that you teach, and fortifying your curriculum with effective and motivating literacy activities, then take a closer look at the following chapters. They will help you hone your knowledge about reading comprehension so you can make the teaching of it more effective and motivating for students. Then use the tools in this book as seeds for your own creative designs of instruction and assessment. Granted, it all takes time and energy. Yet the rewards of seeing students become better readers of difficult texts—while they deepen their content understandings—will be well worth the effort.

Acknowledgments

I am deeply indebted to the following people for their ideas, flexibility, support, patience, and creativity: Patricia Coccone, Shannon Potts, Laura Dequine, Jan Wright, and Marcela De Carvalho.

MASTER LIST OF ACTIVITIES

Activities in Order of Appearance

Activities in Alphabetical Order

MASTER LIST OF REPRODUCIBLES

Reproducibles in Order of Appearance

Reproducibles in Alphabetical Order

PART I

Developing Instruction Using Comprehension Habits

A Crash Course in Reading Comprehension

* * *

Reading is like rocket science—
only more complicated.

The purpose of reading is to construct meaning. To the average literate person, reading appears to be quite simple. We look at the letters to make sounds to make words to make sentences, and then we understand. However, even a basic understanding of text depends on countless invisible thought processes that work together at lightning speed.

The first step in understanding the nature of reading comprehension is to appreciate its complexity. Most educators are fortunate to have had a large array of varied and rich literacy experiences, many of which were facilitated by easy access to books, literate parents and caregivers, good teachers, or a combination of these. The vital thought processes of reading became automatic for us, and this automaticity, ironically, tends to hinder us from seeing how complex comprehension can be for struggling readers, particularly those in grades 6–12.

A helpful analogy for reading comprehension's hidden complexity is that of driving a car. Most adults consider driving to be second nature because of many miles and years of practice. We hop in, drive, and arrive, often without thinking about the many explanations (and perhaps expletives) that our driving instructors offered to us when we were learning. We have long forgotten the nervousness we felt and the huge amounts of information we had to store in our minds when we were learning to drive, venturing out on the road the first few times. Reading is similar to driving in that the brain, from processing pages and pages of text, develops a variety of strategies and connections that facilitate efficient comprehension. These strategies and connections, especially the automatic ones, are the habits this book seeks to build.

The Comprehension Habits

A wide range of books and articles on reading comprehension strategies exists. Palincsar and Brown's (1984) reciprocal teaching concept is based on four key strategies: questioning, clarifying, predicting, and summarizing. A large number of successful programs and activities were then founded on these strategies. Keene and Zimmermann (2007) added strategies of background knowledge and schema, inference, synthesis, and metacognition to the list. Other researchers created studies that showed the benefits of teaching reading strategies to students in explicit ways (Beck, McKeown, Hamilton, & Kucan, 1997; Ciardiello, 1998; Friend, 2001). In creating this toolkit of activities, I analyzed many resources on comprehension strategies and synthesized them into the following six habits:

1. Organizing text information by sculpting the main idea and summarizing
2. Connecting to background knowledge
3. Making inferences and predictions
4. Generating and answering questions
5. Understanding and remembering word meanings
6. Monitoring one's own comprehension

As stated in the Preface, I feel that the word *habits* more clearly describes the automatic and unconscious processes that are used in constructing meaning from text. Comprehension habits are the split-second thoughts that kick in constantly to help a proficient reader actively construct meaning. They make up the majority of the thinking processes we use during reading, even though we seldom notice them (Taylor, Graves, & van den Broek, 2000). For example, a good reader seldom stops and thinks, "I need to relate this to my background knowledge," "This would be a good time to predict," "A quick summary right now will help me comprehend better," or "At this point I should visualize." Rather, a good reader does these things in the blink of an eye without, in a sense, even thinking. Because they happen so quickly, automatic habits keep the reader from losing the flow of the meaning and from letting any important thoughts seep out of the "attention tank." Figure 1 shows the complexity involved in keeping track of cognitive processes, connections, and information during reading.

The habits work together and overlap as they construct meaning (Villaume & Brabham, 2002). They are highly intertwined. For example, just after reading the end of one paragraph, I might quickly summarize the last three sentences, question a character's motives, infer possible causes for an event, tweak my main idea, wonder about a word, and predict what may happen in the next section—all while I am reading the first few sentences of the next paragraph.

How the Habits Work

One of the most important habits of comprehension is mentally organizing a text's information to match what the author had in mind. This is the ongoing process of seeing and inferring logical connections between chunks of text and using them to create a coherent main idea (Taylor et al., 2000). Organizing, in a sense, *is* comprehension. The other comprehension habits support this process by adding and subtracting key information to and from the evolving main idea.

Here's how the attention tank works. While reading, a reader constantly tries to make sense of the information stated in the current sentence by connecting it to two other sources of information: (1) concepts found in preceding sentences and (2) the reader's own background knowledge (Alvermann & Phelps, 2001). Connections to previous concepts found in the text help a reader keep track of elements such as people, objects, ideas, and events while he or she reads. These connections, which are the comprehension habits discussed in Chapters

Figure 1. Attention in the Reading Process

Reading Progress

ATTENTION TANK
(Information Stored From Comprehension Habits)

Purpose for reading
Main idea

Summaries 1 and 2
Connections to prior knowledge and mental images

Prediction 1
Prediction 2

Inference 1
Inference 2

Question 1
Question 2

Unknown Word 1 guess
Unknown Word 2 guess

Overall monitoring of comprehension
(Am I getting this?)

Comprehension "Events"
(Comprehension Habits in Action)

Purpose being met? (Yes)
Main idea further sculpted from new information, summaries, and results of events below

Summary 3 generated
Mental image of main character changed, using new text info and own related experience

Prediction 1 confirmed
Prediction 2 disconfirmed and changed to Prediction 3
Prediction 4 generated

Inference 1 confirmed
Inference 2 confirmed
Inference 3 generated
Inference 4 generated

Question 1 not yet answered
Question 2 answered
Question 3 generated

Word 1 guess confirmed by reading on and using context
Word 2 meaning still unclear
Word 3 guess generated

Comprehension is adequate

ATTENTION TANK
(Modified)

Purpose for reading
More defined main idea

Summaries 1, 2, and 3
Revised connections to prior knowledge and mental images

Prediction 3
Prediction 4

Inference 3
Inference 4

Question 1
Question 3

Word 2 guess unconfirmed
Word 3 guess unconfirmed

Overall monitoring of comprehension
(Am I getting this?)

Comprehension "Events"

Purpose being met? (Yes)
Main idea slightly changed in light of new information and events

Summary 4 generated
Similar situation visualized that happened last year

Prediction 3 unconfirmed
Prediction 4 confirmed
Prediction 5 generated

Inference 3 not confirmed
Inference 4 confirmed
Inference 5 generated

Question 1 not yet answered
Question 3 not yet answered
Question 4 generated

Word 2 guess unconfirmed
Word 3 guess confirmed by using word parts and reading on
Word 4 guess generated

Comprehension has broken down: need to reread two paragraphs because they don't seem to fit

3–8 of this book, help the reader to identify how the different facts and events depend on one another to form the author's message. The second type of connection, background knowledge, helps a reader to visualize the text's descriptions and fortify his or her understanding of implicit and explicit ideas in the text.

Good readers use comprehension habits to add "branches" of key information to the main idea as they read. Then, they seek to either strengthen the branches or prune them by judging how logically relevant they are to upcoming text (Fletcher & Bloom, 1988). Strengthening branches is the process of finding text information that agrees with or repeats the original summary, prediction, or inference that supports the main idea. Repeated ideas or references in a text usually strengthen the main idea. Pruning, on the other hand, is the process of discarding or modifying a "wrong" or unimportant branch, such as a prediction that did not come true, a summary of irrelevant information, or a hypothesis that was disproved later in the text. For example, I recently read an article on space travel in which the title and pictures led me to predict that traveling the speed of light might be possible in the near future. I soon had to prune this assumption away, however, because of the author's arguments and the details presented in the article.

In order to create, strengthen, and prune the needed branches for sculpting the main idea, the reader must store and manage multiple thoughts at the same time (Taylor et al., 2000). These thoughts include facts, predictions, summaries, inferences, questions, word meanings, and the ever-evolving, overarching main idea. For this reason, good comprehension depends on the reader's ability to effectively allocate attention to multiple thoughts and textual details all at the same time. In other words, good reading requires effective mental multitasking. (See the Mental Multitasking Practice activity in Chapter 8.)

In Figure 1, notice the many thoughts being stored and processed in the brain's attention tank during reading. As we read, we retain and modify our collection of thoughts in a way that maximizes our ability to construct meaning. For example, yesterday I quickly used the title of an article to begin sculpting a main idea. Then, in the first paragraph I thought about a similar incident in my family, created a prediction about the rest of the article, and generated two questions that I hoped the article would answer. (All of this happened *as* I was reading the second paragraph.) I retained all of these thoughts as I read. Whenever a new piece of information confirmed or contradicted a thought, I made the necessary adjustments. My evolving main idea, predictions, connections, and questions were a few of the pieces that helped me construct a meaningful and organized mental framework for comprehending the text of the article. If I had lost track of these thoughts, my comprehension would have suffered.

For this reason, teachers must do more than merely teach the strategies; we must help struggling readers *automatically* and unconsciously use strategies, even to the point at which they cannot help but to use them. (A student once said to me, "I am trying not to predict and infer so much, but I can't help it.") Strategies will then become habits that allow the brain to do other things during reading, such as organize the details, concepts, and abstract ideas that are presented. The mental capacity to effectively remember, manage, and prioritize thoughts comes from years of reading millions of pages of a variety of narrative and expository texts— and from good teaching. Good teaching is where we come in. Many classroom activities, when effectively modeled, scaffolded, and practiced, can help struggling students make up for loads of lost time and pages.

Comprehension Habits for Expository Texts

Struggling readers tend to have trouble with the content vocabulary, background knowledge, abstract thinking, and habits necessary for organizing the large amounts of information found in middle school and high school texts. For this reason, high-quality literacy instruction in all content areas is vital for meeting the demands of increasingly complex expository materials in secondary curricula—not to mention the demands of high-stakes exams, college courses, and the real world of work. In my experience working in secondary schools, I have noticed that struggling readers benefit greatly from extra modeling, practice, and explicit literacy support, particularly with nonfiction texts. Why? Because in addition to the lack of emphasis in earlier grades on nonfiction comprehension, secondary classes often are taught by teachers who got into the exciting business of education in order to teach the ideas and concepts of their content areas—not to teach reading. Content teachers earnestly want their students to read better but are overwhelmed by the different reading levels among their students, the lack of appropriate materials, the pressure to cover a year and a half of content standards in one year, and the lack of time available for literacy training.

Students who struggle the most with reading and language tend to benefit significantly from teachers who are dedicated to building comprehension habits (Ryder & Graves, 2002). Many content area teachers (including teachers of English and ELD courses) do not realize that they can—and should—teach comprehension while teaching their content. *In fact, teaching rich content is one of the best ways to build comprehension habits—and vice versa.* In other words, when a topic is interesting or is taught in an engaging manner, students are more likely to put effort into actively thinking about the text (Guthrie & Wigfield, 2000). Active thinking is a catalyst for developing automatic comprehension habits. Worksheets, grammar activities, and "answer the 10 questions" exercises have become insipid and ineffective long before many of our struggling readers and long-term English learners reach secondary classes. Older students are ready for more respect as adolescent thinkers, and they are ready to be challenged to think in more complex ways than what many curricula currently offer. It is up to us to give our students the tools for such thinking and to model how they are used.

"Academifying" the Comprehension Habits That Students Already Use

Students already use these thinking skills for making sense of their world outside of school. We must help them transfer the use of these skills into academic tasks, such as reading. Some teachers have asked, "How can I teach inference to students who don't know how to infer?" I remind them that every student already uses, on a daily or even hourly basis, all the comprehension habits mentioned in this book. The comprehension habits are the integral thought processes we all use for making our way through each day of life—for reading the world, as Freire and Macedo (1987) say. For example, many students already interpret metaphors in songs, infer feelings from pictures, guess word meanings from posters, ask questions about movies, visualize stories read to them, predict the end of television shows, or summarize what they did last weekend. Our students simply need to transfer and extend the comprehension habits they already use outside of school to the comprehension of academic texts inside of school (i.e., they need to "academify" their existing habits). It is our job as teachers to create, model, and support experiences in which students can successfully do this.

The Comprehension Challenges of Linguistically and Culturally Diverse Students

Many struggling readers do not spend their childhood years in U.S. "mainstream" homes and schools. Many are linguistically or culturally diverse students who grow up in U.S. homes where a non-English language is spoken, and some grow up in households where a nonmainstream version of English is spoken. Most of our diverse students have not been privy to the large amounts of cultural, linguistic, and academic "capital" that the majority of mainstream students bring with them to school (Bourdieu, 1986; Delpit, 1995). This capital, as you might guess, plays a large role in comprehension. The more ideas, language, and thinking processes that connect and align with the text in your hands, the better your comprehension is.

Most of the ideas in this book were created with diverse students in mind, many of whom have different ways of viewing the world—views that might clash with the texts and teaching styles that we currently use in the classroom (Peregoy & Boyle, 2005). When this clashing occurs, comprehension suffers. Most teachers have U.S. mainstream backgrounds and, therefore, can find it difficult to empathize with the many academic and nonacademic differences of diverse students. When approaching a text, such students might lack the specific background knowledge, academic language, and culturally bound perspectives needed to make the connections and inferences that many mainstream English-using authors assume that their readers will make.

Diverse students also come to us with varying degrees of literacy in their native languages. It is much easier to teach students to read in English if they already know how to read in Spanish, Arabic, Russian, or Mandarin. Literate students already have built up many of the automatic habits of comprehension and have trained their brains to process written text (Urquhart & Weir, 1998). They have developed abilities in mental multitasking and hierarchically organizing written information. Reading in their first language has challenged them to think in complex ways and to process text quickly. Other English learners, however, come to us with limited literacy experience in any language, and these are the ones who struggle the most to catch up to those students who have had the opportunity to practice with words and written ideas since infancy.

Many older English learners can fluently read aloud words in English but do not sufficiently understand the text. They say the words and they might know the meaning of each individual word in the text, but they may lack the ability to put those words together the way the author intends. English learners often misinterpret dialogues, metaphors, slang expressions, and word variants, such as verbs or adjectives that have been turned into abstract nouns.

Unfortunately, many educators and authors are not sensitive to thinking patterns that differ from their own, and they have had little experience thinking outside their cultural–linguistic boxes. The majority of U.S. teachers have not had their thinking shaped by the many factors that have shaped the thinking patterns, habits, and attitudes of their diverse students. These factors may include war, culture shock, loss of family members, poverty, hunger, hard labor, leaving home forever, racism, linguistic prejudice, illness, differing religions, differing adult–child interactions, family illiteracy, caring for siblings, frequent moves, gang involvement, divorce, drugs, and pregnancy—just to name a few. Moreover, these factors may be compounded by radically different educational experiences that students may have had in the schools of their home countries.

We must strive to see classroom learning through the eyes of our diverse students and then provide texts and teaching that relate to their diverse backgrounds and interests. Even our teaching of expository text comprehension can be improved significantly by a better understanding of how linguistically diverse readers may relate to a topic (Gillet & Temple, 2000). Many of the ideas in this book equip the teacher to build text "scaffolds" with diverse readers in mind. These scaffolds are organizational frameworks onto which a student can build concepts and organize text information for the purposes of increased understanding of complex language, retention of the information, and development of comprehension habits to use for future similar texts.

One helpful way to engage diverse students is to show your thoughts as you read by using visuals, drawings, or graphic organizers. The use of visuals to show the connections and structures in varying texts is especially helpful to those learners who are still familiarizing themselves with the complexities (and inconsistencies) of English (Peregoy & Boyle, 2005). English learners, for example, encounter frustration much sooner if spoken or written words are the only medium used in a lesson or text. Visual aids extend students' mental endurance and more concretely communicate what the words mean in order to improve overall comprehension. This toolkit of activities contains many visual ways to organize information and build the habits that diverse and mainstream students alike can use to improve comprehension.

For students who lack academic English or reading experience, learning by immersion and osmosis isn't enough. They need extra and explicit support in order to develop grade-level comprehension abilities (Irwin, 1991). It is our job to provide this support in the form of extra modeling, practice, feedback, and scaffolding. These are a few of the essential elements of instruction described in the next chapter.

Reflection Questions

1. Describe what happens in the brain while you read.

2. In regards to comprehension habits, how do fiction and nonfiction reading differ?

3. Does growing up in a family with few books or a non-English home language make a difference? How?

NOTES: _____

_____

_____

_____

_____

_____

_____

_____

_____

_____

_____

_____

CHAPTER 2

Assessment and Instruction That Build Comprehension Habits

* * *

Teaching is the ultimate synthesis
of science and art, of organization
and improvisation.

The primary purpose of this book is to help teachers fortify instruction with activities that develop automatic reading comprehension habits in students. In a sense, we want to "soup up" current instruction with the best tools available in order to provide our students with ample modeling and practice in active text processing. We want students to be engaged, challenged, and saturated with academic thinking—without being overwhelmed. Unfortunately for many of our struggling readers, there often has been too little engagement and too much overwhelming. The first step in the process of enhancing our instruction is to find out what our students do as they comprehend and learn. This is what I tend to call *useful assessment*, also referred to as *authentic assessment*, which is assessment that informs how we teach and how students learn.

We must monitor student progress *while* students are comprehending, not just after. This helps us see students' strengths and weaknesses in using their habits to construct meaning. Many elementary teachers already do this informally in their minds. They usually know which students are struggling and in which areas. For example, a teacher knows that Ana doesn't use context very well to figure out new words, Robert doesn't connect to background knowledge very well, and Celia excels at making logical predictions. Yet in middle school and high school, with larger numbers of students and a focus on content, teachers are much more challenged to observe student comprehension and keep track of their observations. With some teachers having as many as 170 students to keep track of, this is understandable, but it also is rectifiable. The trick is to modify instructional activities so that they also serve as assessments. This book offers suggestions for doing this.

Assessing Reading Comprehension

Comprehension is a highly individual process, and assessing it is far more complex than many decision makers lead us to believe. To climb inside a reader's mind and accurately "measure" the quality, speed, and durability of the countless connections and processes that occur during his or her interaction with text is impossible. How can we see and measure the lightning-fast inferences that zip through readers' minds as they read? How can we measure the nature and quality of thinking itself? How can we see what the student is visualizing and how he or she is modifying that scene based on the text? Each student brings a different set of tools and materials (skills and background knowledge) to each text. All we can do is learn as much as we can from what we observe. To do this, we must sharpen our observation abilities and instruments.

What do we want to know about a student's comprehension? Table 1 deconstructs the six habits to help you create checklists or rubrics for observing students. You can then use this book's activities as lenses to see how well your students comprehend and in which areas their comprehension processes are breaking down.

Students must also develop abilities to self-monitor and self-assess their developing habits. Through the use of reading logs and other ongoing records of student thinking, students can keep track of their ideas and thinking processes. By allowing students to self-assess, students begin to own their learning more and become less focused on external rewards for learning. This ownership, coupled with a variety of practice activities with a wide range of increasingly difficult texts, causes the skills and strategies to become automatic habits. One student remarked, "I use to just wait and hope I would understand, but now all those thoughts (habits) keep popping up all the time as I read!"

Along the way, we must provide clear feedback to students with regard to their progress (Marzano, Pickering, & Pollock, 2001). Students want to know their academic strengths and weaknesses. A score of 84 on an essay or multiple-choice test provides little feedback, but the chances of learning improve when the assessments provide specific ideas on what to improve. Assessments that allow more choice, creativity of expression, and validation of original thought tend to be more motivating and informative (Wiggins, 1998; Zwiers, 2008). For these reasons, I work with teachers to create nontraditional and less "assess-y" assessment strategies such as graphic organizers, charts, checklists, matrices, and anecdotal records. These types of assessments are usually more engaging and helpful than many question-based forms of reading assessment. In fact, some of the best assessments I have used are ones that students don't consider to be assessments.

Every teaching activity can be a window into students' comprehension. Consider using the following steps to help you use the activities in this book as assessments:

1. Know what aspects of the comprehension habit(s) you want to assess. Refer to Table 1 for ideas.

2. Decide what type of evidence a student can provide to show the quality of the aspects in step 1. The evidence may be the information in a graphic organizer, drawing, discussion, written text, and so on.

Table 1. What We Would Like to Know About the Comprehension Habits

Comprehension Habit	We Want to Know How Well a Reader...
1. Organizing text information by sculpting the main idea and summarizing	• Recalls important details that relate to the author's purpose and main idea (i.e., the big picture) • Recalls sequence • Organizes the information hierarchically during and after reading • Uses textual aids and visual cues • Considers purposes—author's, teacher's, reader's
2. Connecting to background knowledge	• Connects to related background knowledge (cultural, experiential, cognitive) • Modifies background knowledge, using the text's descriptions in order to create new patterns of information • Combines previous experience with text descriptions to create useful pictures in the mind
3. Making inferences and predictions	• Stores inferences and predictions in short-term memory for later use during reading • Uses all aspects of text (e.g., visuals, headings) to create inferences • Reflects on previous texts or experiences to make a connection or assumption • Relates text to current events and classroom themes • Uses cause and effect and fact and opinion to infer and predict • Interprets figurative language • Generates relevant predictions with logical evidence that relates to main idea and/or author's purpose • Revises predictions based on new evidence in text
4. Generating and answering questions	• Generates relevant implicit and explicit questions to interact with the text • Generates questions that the author wants the reader to ask • Uses questions before, during, and after reading • Actively seeks to answer questions during reading
5. Understanding and remembering word meanings	• Uses sentence structure and semantic clues to predict word meaning • Uses context to figure out the meanings of multiple-meaning words • Uses knowledge of key vocabulary, prefixes, suffixes, and roots
6. Monitoring one's own comprehension	• Uses fix-up strategies when comprehension breaks down • Adapts reading and thinking to fit the type of text (narrative/poetry, functional, expository/social science, science, math)

3. If you have a few minutes, create a checklist (or rubric) that lists what is to be learned and how it is evidenced by the activity. These checklists also are very helpful for informing students about what they are expected to know, do, say, and think. You can even include a section in which to take notes on the specific evidence of the habit or skill. See the following example:

Prediction		Evidence Notes
Uses evidence from background knowledge to make prediction	1 2 3 4	
Prediction logically and helpfully relates to the main idea of the article	1 2 3 4	
Revises predictions according to new information in text	1 2 3 4	

4. If you don't have time for the previous step, pick one or two key aspects of comprehension that will show up in the activity and focus on them while discussing work with students or grading student work. For example, in the Prediction Chart activity (Chapter 5), I might focus on the quality of evidence for predictions, how well the prediction relates to the main idea of a text, or both. Then, I focus the discussion or my written comments on these aspects.

5. Share your observations and assessments with students as a whole class and then individually. (Hand out the checklist or rubric before teaching the activity so students know what is expected of them.)

Even though high-stakes tests are an ever-present influence on what we do in school, most reflective teachers are hopefully interested in taking their students much further down the road of reading comprehension than what is measured by such tests. Fortunately, improved test scores are a positive side effect of building comprehension habits (Marzano et al., 2001). Yet the enduringly valuable effects are students' improved abilities to reason, infer, judge, organize, interpret, apply, communicate, problem solve, and comprehend the world—abilities that are shallowly tested by the multiple-choice test experience but deeply tested by higher education, the working world, and life.

Instructional Habits

We should begin with clear content and comprehension goals in mind. We should also have a well-developed set of lesson elements and teacher behaviors (I call them *instructional habits*) that automatically kick in before, during, and after each lesson. The rest of this chapter briefly outlines several instructional habits and key components of instruction that should become a natural part of teaching, especially the teaching of comprehension habits that will form a foundation for students' lifelong learning.

Teaching Strategically Through Inquiry and Collaboration

A set of tools is one thing—but knowing which ones to choose, how to modify them, and when to use them is another. Randomly filling in lessons and units with activities will not work, as most teachers learn quickly. Being strategic means matching the teaching to student needs. Although this seems obvious, at times students are forgotten and narrow lists of practices deemed to be foolproof are mandated. Yet being strategic means closely observing and assessing student growth and needs, and then choosing, sometimes by trial and error, the most effective teaching practices. It means modifying the activities and using creativity to make things work for 29 very diverse learners.

Being strategic means collaborating with other professionals to ask and answer complex pedagogical questions over time. It means closely analyzing student work, reflecting, making changes to instruction, analyzing student work, reflecting, and so on, in a cycle of inquiry. A group of history teachers, for example, might observe that students are not asking deep questions when they read history texts. They craft an inquiry question that looks closely at how to build this habit during the year. They design their own assessments that effectively show student questioning, and then they choose several teaching strategies. They gather evidence of learning over time. They make adjustments to assessments and instruction. Over time, this cycle of teaching, assessing, and student learning evolves into a strategic approach. (See www.nsrfharmony.org/resources.html for teacher collaboration protocols.)

I encourage all teachers to take on this inquiry-based approach with all teaching strategies and assessments. See if it works for you and your students. Just because a famous consultant, well-known book, or teacher next door raves about the strategy doesn't mean it will work for you. Try it out, talk about it with other teachers, adapt it, ask students for their input, and make it your own.

Connecting the New to the Existing

We must provide teaching that helps students relate new concepts, skills, and strategies to what they already know (Gillet & Temple, 2000). Chapter 1 mentioned the importance of helping students build academic habits on the existing foundation of their knowledge and skills. If we don't help students make connections, they quickly lose interest and become overwhelmed with too much disjointed information. To combat this, we can do several things: (1) relate current learning to previous lessons, other courses, current events, school issues, or life outside of school; (2) incorporate familiar texts such as movies, songs, images, television shows, commercials, community issues, and controversial topics; (3) show students the similarities between thinking inside school and outside school by using a Venn diagram or T-chart; (4) fill in the necessary background knowledge before the lesson or reading, using pictures, stories, gestures, drama, and so on; and (5) try the activities in Chapter 4 of this book.

When students feel that they are not starting anew and that they already know something about a topic, they can build their understandings. And they will be much more likely to be interested in learning a little more about it—especially if they feel that it relates to their lives in some way (Delpit, 1995).

Modeling Comprehension

Modeling is a key component in learning (Vygotsky (1934/1978). Yet I have noticed a serious lack of modeling of reading comprehension in upper grades. Many teachers of grades 6–12 do not know how to model reading comprehension and, therefore, they do not do it. They assume that students already know how to read and just need extra time to figure out the meaning of texts on their own. When the many invisible thinking processes (habits) that facilitate comprehension of school texts do not occur to students, it is mainly because they have rarely seen or heard them applied to school texts by another person. They have not had the chance to be an apprentice, so to speak.

Even though teachers tend to assume that secondary students are beyond learning to read, most students *still* need to observe another person modeling academic skills many more times than once, especially with difficult texts (Wilhelm, 2001). Teachers are the best qualified people to show students how good readers think. For example, we should model our thinking when reading challenging content texts and performing tasks such as filling in graphic organizers, drawing mental images from a text, and creating written responses.

One powerful form of modeling is reading aloud. Reading aloud is highly effective for building fluency and language (Robb, 2003). Many struggling readers did not have this type of text-to-language modeling when they were young. They missed out on thousands of pages of rich vocabulary, pronunciation, thinking, and discussing stories and ideas in nonfiction texts. For these students, reading aloud becomes even more vital in middle and high school in all classes.

Think-alouds (Farr, 2001), which can happen during read-alouds, also are very effective ways to show students how proficient readers think while reading. By verbalizing our thoughts, we can make visible the many complex habits that help us comprehend a text, and we can show how much mental work it is to read for meaning. We can show how we also get stuck, figure out words, ask silly questions, make predictions, infer, and so on. Many think-aloud suggestions are found in the following chapters of this book.

Scaffolding Students' Comprehension

Students need to be given opportunities to do what the teacher has modeled, but with teacher assistance that gradually diminishes as students master the skill. "Just enough help to get them to the next level of learning" is one way to remember the term *scaffolding*, which is often seen as the gradual release of responsibility from the teacher doing the task to the student doing it independently (Alvermann & Phelps, 2001).

As an illustration of scaffolding, imagine a master artist with several apprentices. The master artist does not simply let her apprentices gather in the corner and create products on their own all day. She works with them, models various steps, voices her thought processes while she works, asks for comments, and provides clear feedback. On the other hand, she does not give a long lecture as the apprentices listen and take notes, with the goal of passing the multiple-choice test on sculpture the following Friday. The latter scenario would be similar to the teacher-centered formats sometimes used in modern schools, which tend to be too rigid and incomprehensible for struggling readers, not to mention boring and irrelevant to students' lives.

In scaffolding, the teacher does most of the task in the beginning and then uses scaffolding activities to build student abilities and independence at the task over time. For example, a teacher may start a lesson on figurative language with a popular song and then show students how to fill in a chart that helps them to analyze the relation between figurative and intended meanings (see FigFigs activity in Chapter 7). Gradually, the teacher allows students to fill in the chart, with less and less assistance, until eventually the chart is taken away and students can discuss figurative interpretations without extra support.

We need to keep in mind that we are striving to do far more than build student proficiency at specific tasks such as answering questions about a text or filling in charts—or doing well on tests. Rather, we intend for the thinking abilities required for success on such tasks to develop into mental habits that kick in automatically when students read any type of text in the future: DVD player instructions, newspaper articles, project reports, business letters, standardized tests, a long novel. The years between 6th and 12th grade are delicate and crucial years for strengthening, refining, and expanding the habits that facilitate comprehension (Robb, 2003). With sufficient scaffolding we can help our students to move on, prepared for any comprehension challenge that might arise.

Giving Minilessons

An important component of comprehension instruction is the minilesson—a short and targeted lesson that teaches a particular aspect of reading when the need arises (Lyons & Pinnell, 2001). For instance, a teacher might notice three or four students who struggle when asked to summarize. During an appropriate time, the teacher takes the students aside to provide a minilesson on summarizing. Steps for teaching the minilesson include the following:

1. Introduction—Let students know what they are about to learn. Connect the new material to students' prior knowledge and the text currently being studied.

2. Teacher modeling—Show students how to use the strategy. Teacher think-aloud techniques are effective for this.

3. Student modeling and guided practice—Have students gradually take charge of the strategy and begin to require less support from you.

4. Independent practice—Give the students opportunities to try the strategy in new situations and then to reflect on how it has been useful.

Table 2 shows some ideas for using minilessons with your class.

Building Academic Language to Facilitate Comprehension

For students to understand the concepts and content in their texts, they need to understand the academic language that authors use in these texts. Teachers must make this challenging language more understandable for struggling students, many of whom struggle because

Table 2. Minilesson Topics	
Reading	Writing
• Understanding unknown words in context • Classifying and categorizing information • Using the glossary or index • Making inferences and drawing conclusions • Identifying story elements (setting, plot, etc.) • Interpreting symbolism • Seeing Spanish-English connections • Using text structure to comprehend • Generating under-the-surface questions • Discerning fact from opinion • Identifying cause and effect • Taking multicultural perspectives • Interpreting idiomatic expressions • Using word parts	• Writing hooks and grabbers • Going from graphic organizers to written compositions • Taking different points of view • Considering audience and purpose • Using similes and metaphors • Writing business letters • Using appropriate words • Creating topic sentences • Using paragraphs • Using quotation marks • Using capital letters • Addressing counterarguments • Using appropriate words

of diverse language backgrounds. Some important ways to make academic language more comprehensible include the following:

- Clarify content and language objectives before, during, and after instruction.

- Take observation notes on students' language use in small groups and in pairs. Share academic language phrases that you hear from students by writing them on an overhead transparency or on the board. For example, you might write such phrases as "He is different from her because...," "I disagree because...," "This argument outweighs theirs because...," and "We should consider...."

- Provide wait time (five seconds or so) after you ask questions, in silence with no hands raised. This gives time for students with slower language processing to formulate answers. Also, allow students to provide answers nonverbally at times (e.g., thumbs up/thumbs down, shake or nod of the head, gestures).

- Ask questions that prompt critical thinking and allow for open-ended responses.

- Require students to support their answers, opinions, predictions, and inferences with evidence and examples from the text or real life.

- Model the use of academic language and show students how the language is used to describe comprehension. Use posters that show academic language.

- Use gestures for academic terms. For example, move your hands in a certain direction and then turn around in the opposite direction for the terms *however, but,* and *on the other hand.*

Table 3 shows some ideas for promoting academic language among your students and for specific language to associate with each comprehension habit. Use the table to create posters

Table 3. Examples of Academic Language Starters	
Comprehension Habit	**Academic Language That Expresses the Comprehension Habit**
Organizing text information by sculpting the main idea and summarizing	The part where...is important because.... The gist of it is.... The main idea is.... The key details that support the main idea are.... The purpose of this text is.... The author wanted to tell us.... It's about a...that....
Connecting to background knowledge	This relates to what I learned in my other class about.... I remember when I had a similar experience. Before I form an opinion, I need to learn more about.... In my family, we....
Making inferences and predictions	I think we could infer that...because.... I hypothesize/predict that.... Based on...I guess that.... The picture (or other graphic) means.... Given that...I bet that....
Generating and answering questions	Why...? How...? Would...? Should...? Could...? I wonder.... I found the information in (resource).... One answer might be.... What do you think about...? What is your opinion of...?
Understanding and remembering word meanings	The meaning that works best in this sentence is.... Because the prefix means...I think the word is.... I can remember this word by picturing a....
Monitoring one's own comprehension	I forgot who he was so I went back and re-read.... This doesn't seem to fit with the main idea. I think the author intended to teach.... My predictions and questions helped me understand....

from which students can borrow terms when they are developing the habit. You can also refer to the posters while teaching.

Using Graphic Organizers and Other Visuals

All learners have varying degrees of what is often called *visual intelligence* (Gardner, 1999). Visual intelligence is the mental skill a learner uses to organize and process information by seeing and creating images. Most authors of narrative and expository texts expect readers to visualize many concrete and abstract ideas while reading. Teachers must, therefore, be adept at developing visual lesson components that help students cultivate their visual abilities as they learn.

Visuals are summaries of the text's information that show, rather than just tell, what the words mean. For students who struggle with text language, visuals help make language stand still long enough to sink in and be understood (Hyerle, 2008; Urquhart & Weir, 1998). Visuals are helpful in all of the three stages of reading: before, during, and after (Alvermann & Phelps, 2001). The most common visuals are pictures, videos, maps, and graphic organizers such as diagrams, charts, and tables.

Pictures, videos, and maps show physical descriptions of a text's information and images. Graphic organizers, on the other hand, are drawings that use geometric shapes or tables to show connections between pieces of information (Hyerle, 2008). For many learners, seeing the connections in a visual and organized way helps them to better comprehend and remember information. Graphic organizers also can make invisible and complex comprehension strategies more explicit, visible, and tangible to students (Merkley & Jeffries, 2001). When teachers and students see and understand their own thinking processes while reading, they internalize the comprehension habits found in Chapters 3–8 of this book.

One of the most important features of graphic organizers is their ability to help a reader create a mental picture of the text's information (Hyerle, 2008). This allows the reader to clarify and keep track of the relations, sequences, and important concepts in the reading. Ideally, the process of using (i.e., designing, filling in, studying) visual representations of text will eventually develop into an automatic habit that no longer necessitates the use of the actual graphic organizer. For example, I have used Venn diagrams so often that now, when I am reading a text that compares two concepts, I picture the two intersecting circles in my mind, which helps me retain the information. This process is now a constructive mental habit for me.

As you develop your own expertise and insights as a builder of graphic organizers, you should pass on these tips to students. Provide a hefty supply of varying models and explain why they are made the way they are. Ask students for other ways of graphically showing different types of information beyond the Venn diagram or semantic web.

Students who learn to make their own graphic organizers are far better at remembering and understanding the information in texts than those students who just fill out a graphic organizer made up by the teacher (Peregoy & Boyle, 2005). When students construct and use graphic organizers during learning, they must mentally manipulate and organize the information that they are reading. For example, most graphic organizers give much-needed practice in identifying key elements of text and reducing (i.e., summarizing) them to fit in the spaces provided for writing.

For students, the process of designing the graphic organizer reinforces their understanding of the material by requiring them to reconstruct the information in their own words and to create connections that you or other students may not have noticed. This creative design process gives them more ownership of their learning and of their interpretations of the text. This ownership translates into better comprehension and retention (Hyerle, 2008). And the more students enjoy a task and find it relevant, the less they mind the extra thinking.

Maximizing the Visuals. I have seen many teachers put up a wonderful visual and then use it only once. Remind yourself to use each visual to its maximum potential in all stages of the lesson. Refer back to it often. Add to it. Have students add to it and teach others from it. Use it as an anchor for the concepts in the lesson. Finally, use it to review key concepts before giving summative assessments.

Assessing With Graphic Organizers. As discussed in the beginning of the chapter, graphic organizers can give you the chance to informally assess how students are understanding text information. Students' ways of thinking, interpreting, and organizing text information into graphic organizers often prove to be very innovative and insightful. You can make simple rubrics or checklists that go with the graphics to be used. For example, for a Venn diagram, you could use the following checklist:

☐ Correctly identifies four shared features

☐ Correctly identifies three contrasting features on each side

☐ Uses examples and evidence from text to support statements

☐ Makes valid inferences and hypotheses

☐ Summarizes using own words

☐ Effectively explains to partner how to use the graphic organizer

---

Putting More Movement, Hands-On, and Music Into Lessons

Movement includes drama, kinesthetics, gestures, and hand motions; hands-on includes real objects, manipulatives, and arts-crafts projects; and music includes chants, rhymes, songs, and rhythm. These are all extraverbal, nontraditional methods that reinforce content learning and make language comprehensible. These techniques can be especially helpful when teaching new vocabulary and concepts (Marzano et al., 2001). Unfortunately, I have noticed that the quantity and quality of such techniques seem to decrease each year from grades 1–12. By high school, many classes are seriously lacking in these extraverbal techniques, which consequently deprives many struggling students of optimal learning conditions. These engaging methods are helpful for teaching all students, but they are especially helpful (even vital) for reaching those students who struggle with reading comprehension and the processing of academic language (see McLaughlin & Vogt, 2000).

Some activities, such as hands-on science experiments, already have several of these techniques. But, we might ask, will every student adequately learn the standards for a given lesson? And if not, could additional extraverbal techniques (e.g., chants, objects, or role playing) be used to improve learning? The answer is almost always *yes.* This is because many students need to learn the same concept in more than one way. Often it is the nonverbal way that clarifies the verbal learning and makes it stick in the brain. For this reason, the more standards there are the more beyond-verbal techniques we should use. I strongly encourage middle school and high school teachers to use these techniques more than they already do. Unfortunately, many teachers consider techniques such as chants and hand motions to be a waste of time or too juvenile for their students and, therefore, do not even attempt them. Yet I have had numerous teachers come to me and say something like, "I thought my students would boo and hiss as if I were treating them like babies, but they loved it! And they still know the content after three months!"

Table 4.	Questions and Examples for Integrating Movement-Hands-On-Music Techniques	
Technique	**Reflection Questions**	**Examples**
Movement	• How can some kind of movement, either with hands or the whole body, show this concept? • Can students come up with their own motions?	• Hand motions for comprehension habits and thinking skills • Moving to sides of the room depending on which side of controversial issue the student takes • Mime, skits, drama, role play
Hands-on	• How can I bring in or create objects or simulated objects that show concepts? • How can students manipulate things to show learning and remember concepts?	• Clothes, sticks, clay, cardboard, index cards, sentence strips, posters, models, dice, instruments, tools
Music	• How can I, the students, or both create a song that embodies the learning that needs to happen? • Is there a song already out there that can serve our purposes? • What vocabulary should be in the song? • What instruments might be fun to use with the song?	• Chants, songs, raps, poems

Perhaps the biggest gap that movement, hands-on, and music strategies fill is the need for spicing up boring teaching. The next six chapters have a number of extraverbal techniques that can be used to enrich content and comprehension learning in the pre-, during-, and postreading stages. Gradually, we should make them a natural part of our teaching; Table 4 shows some ideas for how to do this.

Facilitating Meaningful Academic Communication

The act of communicating a concept to another person helps students learn it better (Lyons & Pinnell, 2001). When we communicate, we are forced to organize and clarify our thoughts into coherent sentences before we speak. This process makes an imprint on the brain, creating ownership of the information and, subsequently, facilitating more enduring learning. The process of discussing ideas with other people also forces us to challenge our own preconceptions, negotiate meaning, and sharpen our thinking. Several types of activities are helpful for promoting interaction in classrooms:

- Students teaching other students—Students learn a lot when they can effectively teach the target concepts to other students. This is especially true when the other students being taught do not already know the information. Jigsaw Summaries are good examples of this type of learning (see Chapter 3).

- Pair activities—Pair activities are effective because they can be constructed quickly (e.g., "Turn to a partner..."), and anxiety is low because only one other person is listening. See Think-Pair-Share and variations (Chapter 4) and Academic Conversations (Chapter 8).

- Group projects and discussions—Groups of three to five students can provide powerful learning experiences when handled correctly. Students need to have their roles clearly defined. Initially, teachers should model what to say and how to say it by using minilessons and a lot of guidance during the process. Academic Conversations (Chapter 8) and Socratic Sessions (Chapter 6) are examples of cooperative group work. Following are a few of the possible group roles:

Clarifier	Graphic designer	Presenter
Comparer	Inferrer	Problem solver
Discussion director	Notetaker	Questioner
Encourager	Predictor	Summarizer

Caution: Use most roles sparingly because students should actually be playing all roles (using all habits) all the time. That is, one student should not be the only predictor; all students should be predicting, questioning, summarizing, and so on.

Promoting "Minds-On" Reading in All Stages of Reading

Active reading means struggling, connecting, reflecting, organizing, note taking, and *thinking hard* in order to create an accurate representation of the text. "Minds-on" reading means comprehending a text before, during, and after reading. Using these pre-, during-, and postreading stages, which also boast an array of fancier names (into, through, beyond; initiating, constructing, extending), is, in a sense, a separate habit. If we can get students to build the habit of actively processing text in all three stages, comprehension will improve. Refer to the reproducible Comprehension Bookmark (see page 198) to see possibilities for each stage. Copy it and give it to your students for ongoing reading. You can even laminate it and have students use it as a checklist over and over.

These three stages are important because struggling readers often view reading as just a "during" process (or worse, just a decoding process). Comprehension increases drastically when students develop their pre- and postreading habits, which are teachable and need to be taught. Using these stages is particularly effective with expository readings, which tend to be the texts that give students the most trouble (Brown & Stephens, 1999). So we must provide plenty of support during all three stages, especially in the prereading stage. Students should rarely "go in cold" to a reading assignment without some kind of brain warm-up or content preview (Alvermann & Phelps, 2001).

Why should we spend time on pre-, during-, and postreading activities? Prereading activities do the following:

- Introduce focal lesson concepts and important words and terms
- Build foundational background knowledge
- Provide motivational "hooks" for reading
- Make connections to prior lesson content, activities, and readings

During-reading activities do the following:

- Coach students through various stages of reading a text
- Model and build reading strategies so they become habits
- Help students to organize and retain the information
- Help build ongoing assessments of strategy use and comprehension
- Allow for student-centered and collaborative learning

Postreading activities do the following:

- Model different ways of summarizing and synthesizing information
- Help to organize and retain information
- Allow students to apply the text to their lives
- Help students to reflect on the readings and bring closure to the prereading and postreading activities

Table 5 is a list of selected activities from this book that particularly lend themselves to one or more of the three reading stages. They are listed under pre-, during-, and postreading categories, but most are very effective in more than one stage of reading. You can cross-reference this list to find activities that meet your needs. In each of Chapters 3–8, there is a similar chart that helps you see which activities are especially helpful for different content areas. In Table 5, the chapter numbers indicate where each tool is found in this book. The symbols tell which comprehension habits are emphasized; see the key at the end of the table for an explanation of the letter symbols. You also can refer to similar tables in each chapter that show when and in which content areas the tools are best used.

Using Powerful Practices Every Day

We must fill our lessons with activities that maximize learning and the building of good academic habits for our students. Powerful practices can be used all year long with a variety of subjects and texts. I often tell teachers who are reluctant to change teaching practices to start with one or two activities and to keep doing them throughout the year, adding one more each month. By the end of the year, the powerful practices will replace most of the mediocre practices. (And you'll enjoy teaching even more.) I suggest creating a literacy binder for quick reference while lesson planning. One teacher created the following chart in order to catalog the powerful practices that she used consistently each week:

Prereading	During Reading	Postreading
Anticipation Guides (+ Why)	FigFigs	Quickwrites
K-W-L Plus	Read-Aloud Think-Aloud (RATA)	Semantic Webbing
Quickwrites	Semantic Webbing	Think-Pair-Share
Think-Pair-Share		
Word Bank		

Getting the Most Standards and Habits Out of Each Minute

Given our limited time and resources, we should strive to foster the most learning possible with each activity. So take a critical look at the teaching activities you use and notice which ones address more content, literacy, and thinking per hour. For example, a diorama or a map-coloring activity may take up more precious time than they are worth in terms of standards achievement and thinking practice. On the other hand, a group activity that generates a matrix with information from a social studies text might address multiple objectives at once (e.g., organizing information, categorizing, summarizing, learning content, discussing, figuring out vocabulary).

Table 5. Activities and the Habits They Emphasize		
Activities	**Comprehension Habits Emphasized**	**Chapter**
Academic Conversations	B, M, Q, S	8
Anticipation Guides (+ Why)	B, I, P	4
Background Knowledge Backpack	B	4
Big Questions	Q, M, I, C	6
CATAPULT Into Literature	B, M, P, Q, W	4
Cause and Effect Timeline	I, P, S	5
Central Question Diagram	B, C, M, Q, S	6
Character Report Card	I, S	5
Closed Eyes Visualize	B, I, P, S	4
Comprehension Target Talk	B, I, P, S, Q, M	8
Concept Poster Preview	B, M, P, S	4
Connect the Words	M, S, W	7
Critique Chart	B, M, Q, C	4
Dialogue Comic Strip	I, M, S	5
Evolving Main Idea Three-Column Notes	C, M, S	3
Example Webs	W, S, Q	7
FigFigs (Figuring Out Figurative Language)	I, Q, W	7
Genre Transformation	C, M, S, B	8
Give One–Get One	B, M, Q	4
Guess and Adjust	I, M, P, W	7

(continued)

Table 5. Activities and the Habits They Emphasize (*continued*)

Activities	Comprehension Habits Emphasized	Chapter
Hot Seat	I, M, Q, S	6
Image Inferences and Predictions	I, P, S	5
Inference Advertisements	I, M, P, Q, S	5
Jigsaw Summaries	M, S	3
Keyword Construction	M, S, W	3
K-W-L	B, P, Q, S	4
List-Group-Label Plus	W, S, C	7
Main Idea Formula	C, M, P, S	3
Main Idea Memory Storage	C, M, Q, S	3
Matrices	M, Q, S	3
Mental Multitasking Practice	C, M, S	8
Multiple Meanings Table	W	7
New Words in Context Chart	I, Q, W	7
Outline-ish Thoughts	I, M, S	3
Podcasts	M, S	3
Prediction Basketball	I, P	5
Prediction Chart	I, P, Q	5
Prediction Path	C, M, S	5
Prediction Signals	I, P, W	5
Pro–Con Improv	B, C	4
Question the Author	I, P, Q	6
Question Tree and Sea	I, Q, S	6
Quickwrites	B, I, M, P, S, C, Q, W	4
Quotation Café	I, M, P, S	5
Read Aloud Everything	B, C, M, S, P, I, Q, W	8
Read-Aloud Think-Aloud (RATA)	B, C, I, P, S, W	8
SCUBA Diving Into Word Meanings	I, W	7
Semantic Webbing	M, S, W	3
Socratic Sessions	C, I, M, Q, S	6
Sorry, I Lost My Headings	M, Q, S,	3
Sticky Note Snapshots	B, C, I, P, Q, S	4
Story Map	I, M, P, S	3
Student-Created Quizzes and Tests	Q, M, S, W, C	6
Students Get to Teach	M, S, Q, W	3
Summarizing Training Camp	M, S	3
T+B=I Inference Machines	I, P, S, W	5
Talk Show	Q, M, S, B, C	6
Text Structure Graphic Organizers	B, M, P	4
Theme Possibilities Visual	M, S, Q	3
THIEVES	B, M, P, Q, W	4
Think-Aloud Note Grids	C, I, M, P, Q, S	8
Think-Pair-Share	B, I, P, S, W	4
Two-Word Sentence Stickies	W, S	7
Vocabulary Bank Notes	W	7
Webpage Creation	B, I, M, Q, S	3
Word Bank	W	7

B = Background Knowledge Usage; C = Comprehension Monitoring; I = Inferring; M = Main Idea Sculpting;
P = Predicting; Q = Questioning; S = Summarizing; W = Word Meaning Interpretation

Building Textbook Reading Habits

Many students in upper grades do poorly in school because they cannot read their thick, imposing textbooks. However, this can be prevented by taking the time to show students how to *strategically* read their textbooks (Alvermann & Phelps, 2001). Most content area teachers have not devoted much time or reflection to their own reading or to their teaching skills that develop reading in their content area.

Content area teachers (especially in science and social studies) should commit to extensive teaching of expository reading habits, especially because English classes do not have time for it. Content teachers are experts at the thinking needed to comprehend their content material. They can effectively model the ways in which historians, mathematicians, and scientists actually think as they read a text. Ultimately, content teachers usually discover that building comprehension habits is well worth the extra time when students, as they improve their reading, excel at learning and retaining more content. To aid this process, many of the activities in the following chapters are geared toward nonfiction and textbook reading.

Developing Literacy Teacher Habits

To teach the "rocket science" of reading comprehension, simply pulling ideas from books and workshops and then stuffing them into the curriculum is not enough. There is too much going on in the thick of each lesson to plan everything beforehand. For this reason, we need to develop automatic literacy-related instructional habits that engage every time we make instructional decisions. The following list shows just a few of the important habits of a literacy-minded teacher, some of which are borrowed from the points previously discussed:

- Teach to different learning styles (beyond verbal methods only).
- Model your thoughts, questions, confusion, and problem-solving steps.
- Clarify objectives (know, do, say, think).
- Relate learning to real life.
- Maximize student interaction and use of academic language.
- Provide useful feedback that directly relates to higher success on assessments.
- Take notes on behavior and individual student progress during learning activities.
- Creatively tap into learning from previous lessons and from students' lives.
- Draw, doodle, and act to make language and concepts comprehensible.
- Strategically move around the classroom to observe and support learning.
- Strategically design lessons and assessments based on student needs.

The suggestions in this chapter for building comprehension habits are just starters; they are meant to be adapted by you to fit your needs. The next six chapters provide a variety of tools for building these good habits in any class where students read.

Reflection Questions

1. Why is assessment covered so early on in this book?

2. Why is reading comprehension so difficult to assess?

3. What do we want to know about what is happening in a student's brain before, during, and after reading a text?

4. What does it mean to *strategically* develop comprehension habits?

5. How does building language help students to comprehend?

6. Which "literacy teacher habits" are the most challenging to develop?

NOTES:
_____

_____

_____

_____

_____

_____

_____

_____

_____

_____

_____

_____

PART II

Six Comprehension Habits

Organizing Text Information by Sculpting the Main Idea and Summarizing

* * *

If you don't stop at times and get
your bearings, you get lost.

Finding the main idea has never been fun for most struggling readers. They have been asked to find it countless times and have produced inadequate answers. After repeated failures, many students just give up on the search altogether. They figure out how to work the system instead, most often by searching for answers to questions or by copying.

Unfortunately, getting the main idea is the most vital type of thinking readers can do to comprehend a text. We cannot sidestep it. It is why the text exists. Nor can we avoid the related habit of summarizing along the way, because it supports the main idea. For these reasons, this chapter provides a variety of ways to help students develop better text organizing abilities in engaging ways.

Have you ever started reading a book that was just too stuffed with information to absorb it for more than five minutes? You either take lots of breaks or choose not to read it. Our students do not have these choices. We ask them to read and learn it all, but the texts are overloaded with information. What does a good reader do? A good reader reduces text to just the essentials. The good reader then proceeds to organize the essentials by using a process I call *sculpting the main idea*—the process in which a reader looks at emerging clues and develops the text's core information *before and during* reading, not just after.

The good reader uses this evolving main idea to decide what to store in the smaller summaries. Summarizing is the process of reducing a just-read portion of text into a manageable chunk of important information. This chunk, in turn, helps guide the reader in sculpting the overall main idea. As one can see, this becomes a codependent cycle: As the main idea becomes more defined, the reader can more effectively decide which information goes into the summaries that support the main idea. As the summaries increase in number, they help the reader sculpt a better defined main idea.

This chapter offers ideas for helping all students to develop these symbiotic organizing habits:

- Identifying, generating, developing, and sculpting the main idea of the passage

• Summarizing portions of text to strengthen, change, and challenge the evolving main idea

Sculpting the Main Idea

"What's the main idea?" might be the most popular question asked by teachers and tests. Yet many students have never been directly taught how to figure out the main idea of a text. This is because secondary teachers tend to assume that the students learned such a basic skill in previous years of schooling. However, getting the main idea is a complex and challenging habit to develop, and it gets more challenging as texts become more complex in middle school and high school. Thus, sculpting the main idea is a habit that we cannot afford to stop developing in our students (Baumann, 1986; Wormeli, 2005).

Main Idea Components

Sculpting the main idea is the process of creating a compact chunk of information that includes the topic, what is said about the topic, and, usually, the text's purpose. These items can be shortened to the What? What about it? and Why? components to help students remember the process. Starting with the text's title and other initial visual clues, we begin to formulate the main idea. Some titles are misleading, however, and we must test our hypotheses about the main idea and look for evidence as we read. If evidence comes along that contradicts our existing main idea, we must "trim" away pieces and "attach" new ones that align with the text.

Topic (What?). The topic is a word or phrase that describes what the text is about. It usually is a main subject, process, or event. Sample topics include "a quest to destroy a ring," "ionic and covalent bonding," and "unsung heroes of the American Revolution." Students should develop the habit of generating a topic every time they see a title and then to use it with other prereading clues such as visuals, charts, subtitles, boldface words, and so on. Fortunately, in most expository texts the topic can be found in the title of the passage. But if it is not so obvious, we need to train students to generate it. This can be done in two ways: (1) Show students how to focus on repeated references, that is, ideas that are central and repeated throughout the text (Friend, 2001); and (2) "Be the text's author at a party," a thinking activity in which the student thinks like the author in order to come up with answers to cocktail party questions such as What's your writing about? (see the Hot Seat activity in Chapter 6). For example, if asked the above question about my book, I might answer, "Reading strategies." The next question partygoers might ask is, "What does your text say about that?" This second question is the "what about it?" component of the main idea, discussed next.

Description (What About It?). We must train students to dig a little deeper into what *this* specific text says about the topic. Think about the many times we have asked students the question, What does the text say about [the topic]? What important ideas did this text offer to further describe [the topic]? This step is key because it helps (forces) the student to find that just-right area between too broad a topic and a description that is too detailed. Following are some examples of What About It? responses:

- The main characters sought to destroy the ring because if it fell into the wrong hands, the world would be overcome with evil.
- These types of bonds between atoms are different in that covalent bonds share an electron and ionic bonds are created by attraction between positively and negatively charged atoms.
- Many people, even though they didn't become famous, helped to produce food and weapons in order to make the American Revolution a success.

Text Purpose(s) (Why?). The text has a reason for which it was written—and for which it is read. The more effectively a reader figures out these reasons, the better he or she will comprehend the text. Knowing the first two components just discussed can help a reader figure out the text's purposes. Then again, knowing the purpose(s) can significantly help a reader generate the first two components. For example, knowing that the teacher is trying to teach me about the influence of Confucius on Chinese politics, I will approach the text by focusing my summaries and main idea on this "influencing." Following are three types of purposes that help shape main ideas and summaries.

Author's Purpose. Knowing why the author wrote the text gives us immediate clues to help us organize and gather information from it. For instance, if we quickly guess that an author of an editorial about deforestation is trying to convince us to take her side, we can better organize the article's contents in our minds. If we figure out that a history textbook author wants to inform us about the hardships of the Great Depression, we have a good start on the main idea. Good readers automatically ask themselves questions such as, Why did the author write this? or What does the author want me to get from this?

Struggling readers who improve at asking and answering these questions become better readers. We need to train students to ask such questions as they look at the initial text clues—and not just wait for teachers to ask them such questions. Remind students to engage a portion of their brain to keep track of the author's purpose while they are reading because it may change, particularly in works of fiction. Readers need to be flexible and ready to reshape their main idea at each turn of the page.

Teacher's Purpose. For most of the reading done outside of school, the reader gets to choose the text, and he or she chooses it for a purpose already in mind. For instance, an engineer reads a manual to learn a new computer language, a counselor reads the recent psychology journal article that relates to a current case, a college student reads the requirements for a scholarship application, and so on. School tends to turn this practicality around and assign texts because the state, the school, or the teacher have purposes for reading that they impose on students. Students who understand these purposes usually exhibit better comprehension and perform better on assessments (Readence, Bean, & Baldwin, 2001). Teach students that one great way to learn these purposes is to ask, because most teachers are happy to respond.

Reader's Purpose. We might be surprised—even shocked—to find out how many of our students don't have a real reason for reading. The most common reason that arises, which is not a good one, is that the teacher requires it as a way to answer questions or respond to a writing prompt. Yet, even faced with this external pressure, good readers will ask, What will I get out of this? and then generate a working answer as they begin to read. Readers who use the author's and teacher's purposes to help form their own purposes improve their comprehension. Teachers can model this habit with think-alouds (see Chapter 8) to show how expert readers establish purpose. For example, you can say, "Looking at the title and pictures, the author probably wants me to learn...," or "If I look at the objectives for the lesson that the teacher put on the board, this text will help me...."

Consider putting up a copy of the Steps for Purpose poster (see page 62). Model the steps for students and then have them do the steps in pairs or groups. After reading, have them check to see if the purposes were fulfilled.

The Role of Flexibility

The reader must be flexible when forming and refining the main idea. The main idea generated in the beginning of a reading may be very different from the main idea at the end of a reading. Perhaps the beginning of a text is so difficult or unfamiliar that the reader can only form a very generalized main idea. For example, I may start off thinking that *Moby Dick* is going to be about a great whale hunt. Then, as I look at the style of writing and the emphasis on character actions and thoughts, I realize that it is much more about the human psyche. We must, therefore, be willing to adjust our expectations during reading in order to effectively use each new section of text. In other words, readers must be open to sculpting major changes in the main idea along the way, particularly when the text contains new concepts and unfamiliar vocabulary.

The Role of Memory

A good reader monitors the quantity and quality of information that goes into his or her memory (Taylor et al., 2000). In the beginning of a reading, there is more room in the memory, and, therefore, more extraneous information can fit. Gradually, the less important details are discarded to make room for the more important ones. A reader must decide if each piece of current information is important enough to store; the reader does this by deciding how well it supports (or changes) the evolving main idea. The reader also continues to monitor how well the key information is supported throughout the text. Gradually, as the important details that need to be stored accumulate, the brain consolidates them into summaries. Refer back to Figure 1 (see page 5) to see the many pieces of information that need to be stored in memory as we read. Also see the Mental Multitasking Practice activity in Chapter 8 for a way to help students improve their memory of the thoughts they have during reading.

Components in Summarizing

The "clay chunks" of information that we gradually add to sculpt the main idea as we read are the summaries. Summarizing happens when we employ a portion of our thinking cells to condense and trim a portion of text into a manageable chunk. You will probably summarize this paragraph when you reach the end of it.

Why do we summarize? The main reason is brain capacity. Let's say, for example, that we can hold only seven separate pieces of information in our brains at one time. (I chose the number seven because it is the quantity of digits of many phone numbers. It could be any number over two.) Many texts have a lot more than seven pieces of information. So what do we do when we hit the limit of seven (or whatever the number may be)? We group several related pieces together into one category and give it a name, which is actually a summary (Baumann, 1986). This makes room for other important pieces that may come up. This process is similar to putting files into folders on a computer, which then fit into other folders, and so on. Imagine a computer with every single file sitting individually on the desktop. They would not all fit and, therefore, must be organized.

Teaching summarizing can help students improve their grasp of the main idea and, subsequently, their comprehension of the text (Friend, 2001). Now it's time to dig a little deeper into the thinking that goes into summarizing: Two key components of summarizing are categorization and classification.

Categorization

Categorizing is the process that occurs when a reader has a category name, such as title, main idea, or summary, and then finds information to fit underneath it. This type of organization is common in textbook chapters, but it does not help if students do not look at or think about the category name and how it connects to the text that follows. The mental process of categorizing may look similar to the steps shown in Figure 2.

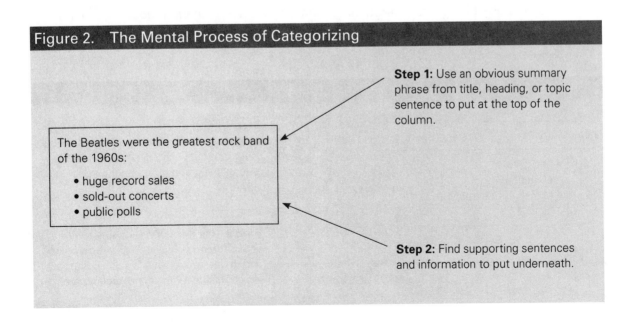

Figure 2.   The Mental Process of Categorizing

The Beatles were the greatest rock band of the 1960s:

- huge record sales
- sold-out concerts
- public polls

Step 1: Use an obvious summary phrase from title, heading, or topic sentence to put at the top of the column.

Step 2: Find supporting sentences and information to put underneath.

Classification

Classifying is even more useful for summarizing. Of the two components of summarizing, classifying is the more inductive and, hence, the more challenging habit for struggling readers to develop. As Jaworski and Coupland (1999) state,

> Academic study, but in fact all aspects of experience, are based on acts of classification, and the building of knowledge and interpretations is very largely a process of defining boundaries between conceptual classes, and of labeling those classes and the relationships between them. (p. 4)

To classify while reading, the reader analyzes the details, such as words, sentences, or paragraphs, and then looks for what they have in common. The reader then groups them by their possible commonalities. Often the reader will need to generate a rough category name for this group that describes why they are together (e.g., "These sentences all describe how atoms attract to make molecules."). This category name is the summary phrase under which the reader will continue to classify future sentences. The mental process of classifying is shown in Figure 3.

A big help for summarizing is being able to recognize topic sentences in a paragraph. The topic sentence tells the reader what the whole paragraph is trying to say, and, therefore, indicates the main idea or the summary category under which we can organize the paragraph's details. However, we should avoid teaching students that the main idea is usually found in the first sentence of a paragraph. Baumann (1986) found that only about 15% of paragraphs in adult expository material have the topic sentence in the initial position. He also found that only 30% of the paragraphs have the main idea explicitly stated anywhere in the paragraph. These findings strongly suggest that we must teach students to overcome the lack of an explicitly stated main idea and learn to generate their own summaries and main ideas. The rest of this chapter contains activities for building main idea and summarizing habits in all content area classes.

Remember, we are not teaching a *new* habit here. We are expanding in our students their existing habit of organizing information into summaries, teaching them to do it in academic ways. In each activity found in this chapter, start with the ways in which students already use

Figure 3. The Mental Process of Classifying

Summary Phrase
- title of text
- sentence 3
- phrase from sentence 4
- picture 1

Step 1: Fill in the column with sentences and pieces of information that seem to be important to overall text meaning and to belong in a group because of similarities.

Step 2: Use the analysis of similarities and differences to establish a topic phrase and to determine what is said about that topic. This becomes the category name, or main idea, of those sentences.

this organizing habit in nonacademic contexts. Start with the concrete and familiar; then move to the more abstract and academic. For example, in Main Idea Formula, you can start with common texts such as movies, television shows, websites, posters, songs, and so on. Point out to students how easily they can generate main ideas and summaries from this material. Then, transfer this activity to the topic or text of the upcoming lesson.

Tools Chart for Organizing Text Information

Table 6 shows the appropriateness of this chapter's activities for various content areas. On the left side of the table, a √ in a column indicates that the activity is useful in that stage of reading. On the right side of the table, a √ in a column indicates that the activity is helpful for comprehension of common texts used in that content area. A √√ on the right side of the table mean that the activity is especially useful for texts in that discipline. Take some time to look at all the activities and spend a few moments thinking about how you might use and adapt them in your teaching. I have been impressed at the variety of creative ways that teachers have adapted these activities and organizers. (Each chapter has a similar chart of activities.)

Table 6.	When and Where to Use the Activities in Chapter 3					
Before Reading	During Reading	After Reading	Activity	Social Studies	Science	English/ EL
	✓	✓	Evolving Main Idea Three-Column Notes	√√	√√	✓
	✓		Interpretive Drawings	✓		√√
	✓	✓	Jigsaw Summaries	√√	√√	√√
✓	✓		Keyword Construction	√√	√√	✓
	✓	✓	Main Idea Formula	√√	√√	✓
	✓		Main Idea Memory Storage	√√	√√	✓
	✓		Matrices	√√	√√	√√
✓	✓	✓	Outline-ish Thoughts	√√	√√	✓
	✓	✓	Podcasts	√√	√√	✓
✓	✓	✓	Semantic Webbing	√√	√√	✓
✓	✓	✓	Sorry, I Lost My Headings	✓		√√
✓	✓	✓	Story Map	✓		√√
		✓	Students Get to Teach	√√	√√	√√
✓		✓	Summarizing Training Camp	√√	√√	✓
✓	✓	✓	Theme Possibilities Visual	✓		√√
	✓	✓	Webpage Creation	√√	√√	✓

Don't forget to apply the general teaching suggestions from Chapter 2 to the activities in this chapter. When you find an interesting activity, refer to Chapter 2 and ask how you can best integrate its instructional suggestions into the activity to meet your specific needs.

Activities for Organizing Text Information

EVOLVING MAIN IDEA THREE-COLUMN NOTES

This activity helps students to build the habit of sculpting the main idea and using key details to create summaries while reading. The summaries are based on the detail notes that are placed in the far right column of the page. This process (main idea to details to summary to main idea) is a written approximation of how a reader's brain processes text information. This is an adaptation of two-column notes, also called Cornell notes (Pauk, 2001), a note-taking technique found in many curricula and teacher resources (e.g., Buehl, 2009; Wood, Lapp, Flood, & Taylor, 2008).

Procedure

1. Create three columns on the board. (When students do this activity by themselves, they will do it on a sheet of paper.) The left column is labeled "Main Idea," the middle column "Summaries," and the right column "Details."

2. Based on the title of the text to be read, generate a possible main idea with the students and write it in the "Main Idea" column. This main idea can and may change throughout this process.

3. Read the first paragraph aloud, and take notes in the "Details" column. Details include keywords, phrases, and examples that relate to the main idea.

4. Use these detail notes to create a one-sentence summary to go in the middle column. Create several one-sentence summaries of different sections or paragraphs of a text.

5. Connect, mentally or with arrows, the summaries to the main idea.

6. Show students how the process went from column 1 to column 3, then to column 2 and back to column 1.

7. Refine and rewrite the main idea in the left column as it evolves.

INTERPRETIVE DRAWINGS

In this activity, students pick an important part of the text (or use the main idea) and create a drawing or visual representation of it. With expository texts, these can be in the forms of graphic organizers with connecting arrows. Emphasize that the drawing is meant to help students understand and remember the text better. Students also can think of it as a way to teach others about the text without writing an essay.

For narratives, this activity can be very effective at getting students to think at deeper levels than just the literal meaning (Hibbing & Rankin-Erickson, 2003). Analogies, symbols, and metaphors can be interestingly portrayed in drawings. This activity also is effective for building habits of generating inferences and visualizing.

Procedure

1. Offer plenty of visual examples: previous student drawings, modern artwork, textbook pictures, cartoons, and so on. Some examples can be very simple or basic, to show students that they do not have to draw well to do this activity.

2. Think aloud what you would do to create a drawing that summarized a text. Pick different texts and show how you would draw something to fit each one's information and remember it. For example, you might draw a raft on a river for a story about Huck Finn. You could draw a map with symbols on it to show different groups involved in or events of the Spanish conquest of Mexico. You could sketch a comic strip with a cell's comments for a text on cell division.

3. Give students an easy text for their own interpretive drawings. Remind them that there are no wrong "answers" and that they do not have to be artists. Remind them that some very expensive abstract art does not necessarily fit what they would think of as an attractive look. Tell them to be artists who try to capture the moment, mood, meaning, symbolism, importance, or purpose of the text.

4. Optional: You could call this activity "Picture Cheating" and tell students to pretend they are artists who need to create a picture that gives away the meaning of the text to unmotivated students who do not want to read it.

5. Optional: Have students write their explanation of the drawing's meaning on the backs of their papers. This is a subtle way to get them to verbalize and write a summary and main idea.

6. Put students into pairs or groups and have them respond to one another's drawings. Point out that responding entails guessing the meaning, praising the work, and asking questions; remind students not to be critical.

7. Have students share their own drawings with the class and explain them.

JIGSAW SUMMARIES

Jigsaw groups (adapted from Aronson, 1978) provide students with a way to build summarizing habits while also pushing them to communicate meaningful messages with other students. Students in one group become experts on a portion of the text and the experts then teach that text to a different group.

Procedure

1. Divide the chosen text into three to five sections. Plan to have the same number of students in each group as there are text sections.

2. Prepare an expert sheet or study guide that will help students become experts as they summarize a section of text. The sheet may have questions (open-ended or under-the-surface), a task, or a graphic to fill in, and so on.

3. Use a pocket chart, random numbers, or some other method to create home groups. Then assign each student a letter that corresponds to his or her expert group and the text that the group will study. (See Figure 4.)

4. Have students with the same letters get together in expert groups and read (silently) their assigned section. Then, have them discuss their conclusions, summaries, opinions, answers, task, or graphic organizer and how they will teach it to their classmates in the home groups.

5. Have the experts report back to their home groups to summarize and teach the important parts of their text sections.

6. Hold a class discussion about the text, perhaps with graphic aids that you have created to organize the information.

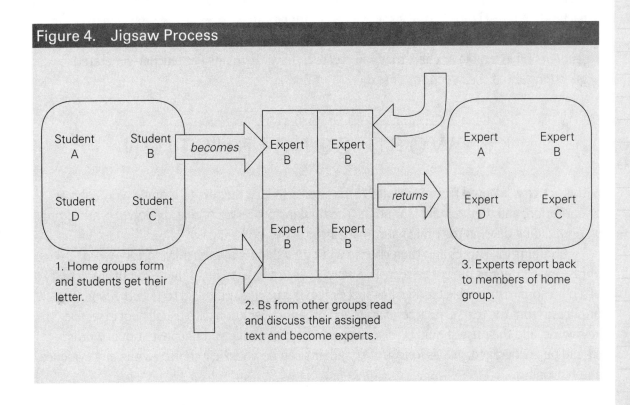

Figure 4. Jigsaw Process

1. Home groups form and students get their letter.

2. Bs from other groups read and discuss their assigned text and become experts.

3. Experts report back to members of home group.

Figure 5. 4 × 4 Jigsaw Circle

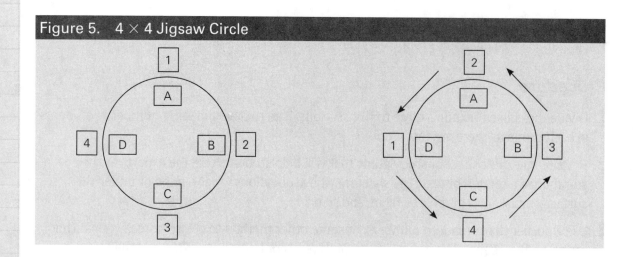

Variations

- **Expert Panel:** Have each group prepare for a question-and-answer session with the rest of the class about their topic after they become experts on it. They can try to predict the questions they might get and discuss them before fielding questions from the class.

- **4 X 4 Jigsaw Circle:** Have eight students each read a different section of text. Then, put four of the students in an inner circle and four in an outer circle. Each student in the inner circle exchanges information about what he or she has read with a partner in the outer circle, and then one circle rotates. The students repeat the process with a different partner, then rotate again. This process repeats until all four pairs have shared their reading with each other. (See Figure 5 for a visual representation of the process.) You may want to give the students a time limit—say, five minutes—for each partner session. You also can have students fill in a table or chart that you create or have them answer teacher-generated questions about their sections of text.

KEYWORD CONSTRUCTION

In this activity, adapted from Bleich (1975), students reduce the text to a single word, phrase, or quotation, and then rebuild from that. The thinking processes of tearing down, synthesizing, and rebuilding develop the brain's summarizing muscles, so to speak.

Students take notes and then choose what they think is the most important word, phrase, or concept of the entire text. The word does not have to be in the text, but the activity often is more manageable (and just as successful) if students are asked to take the word or phrase from the text. Character names and other proper nouns are usually not effective keywords, and their use should be discouraged. Use of creative and unconventional words should be encouraged, just as long as the students can defend their choices with valid evidence and reasoning.

Procedure

1. First, model this activity for students. Choose a text and use sticky notes to write down important information, doodles, and summaries from the text. Place the sticky notes on the boxes in the top half of the Keyword Construction form (see page 60 at the end of this chapter).

2. Verbalize how you choose your own keyword for the text. Have students discuss your decision, if desired. Refer to specific evidence in the text that supports your choice. Let students hear how you chose your word over other options. Use the Keyword Construction form as a scaffold.

3. Now, begin to scaffold the activity. Choose a new text and repeat the process, this time inviting the class to participate. Have students discuss and choose several keywords as a class. You can keep them from using certain "obvious" words that might limit their thinking by making a "no-use" list.

4. Now, let students in pairs or small groups read a new text and choose a keyword. Have them write their keyword in the key-shaped area at the center of the page. In the bottom section, they can write their reasons for the word's importance—reasons that come from the text and their ideas of the purpose of the text.

5. Have students use the keyword and build a summary of the text from it. The summary should include several reasons why the keyword is important. The sentences should connect the keyword with the purpose of the section and the current content being learned.

MAIN IDEA FORMULA

We need to train students' brains to sculpt main ideas and create good summaries. By using a formula, I have seen many students perk up because they like math and want to know how math and reading connect. The formula is a visual way to show how readers think when they generate main ideas.

Procedure

1. Bring in, and have your students bring in, "texts" such as videos, taped television shows, photos, songs on cassette tape or CD, and so on. Ask the question, What was it mainly about? for these and other well-known texts. Then, discuss the purposes for reading various texts. Many narratives, for example, have a plot that carries the author's message or purpose.

2. Ask students why teachers think the main idea is so important. Why should we train our brains to know the main idea? Highlight student answers that emphasize that the main idea gives the direction, foundation, or purpose.

3. Explain the parts of the formula and have students generate answers.

Topic + What is said about the topic + Purpose = Main Idea

Topic +	The discovery of North America by the Chinese
What is said about the topic +	Historical Chinese maps and documents show the arrival of the Chinese people on the west coast of North America 70 years before Columbus's first voyage.
Purpose =	To challenge people to consider evidence of early Chinese contact with Native Americans and to show how history is up for continual debate
Main Idea	Based on evidence from accurate Chinese maps and documents, the Chinese may actually have landed on North American soil before Columbus did. This should cause us to rethink our traditional accounts of history and even question how history is written.

Other examples of the formula equation include the following:

- A high school student + he goes back in time, messes up his young parents' lives, almost preventing his own birth, and then fixes it + purpose of entertaining people with a story about time travel and courage = the movie's main idea

- Space travel + not worth the cost to taxpayers + attempts to persuade readers to stop paying taxes and to vote for a certain person = the article's main idea

- A child dying + the horrors of war and the innocent victims + showing viewers the smaller stories of war the television does not highlight = the picture's main idea

4. Now show how the main idea can change during reading. The second and third parts (variables) of the equation often change as one reads. Think aloud (i.e., verbally model for the students) how to identify or generate a main idea with a variety of texts. Use interesting material to make the process engaging. Also, throw in some texts that challenge *you* (e.g., song lyrics or articles provided by students) to offer a more genuine sense of how a teacher also might struggle with text and think about how to understand it. Model the following processes for students:

a. Think about the title. What does the author think the text is about? Why might the author have written it?

b. Skim the text. Notice the text structure. Is it a narrative, description, list, sequence of events, comparison/contrast, opinion, or other type of text?

c. Read the first paragraph or two. Ask yourself, Why did the teacher assign this text? What can I, or should I, get out of reading this?

d. Use steps (a) through (c) to create a rough draft (mental or written) of the topic of the text plus what is written about that topic and a possible author's purpose. This draft must be short.

e. Read the rest of the text:

- Look for the most important information from each paragraph or section of text, and relate it to the rough draft main idea. For example, while reading a paragraph, always think, "This is about..." or "This strengthens or changes the overall main idea because...." (Use a sticky note to jot down the idea.)

- Notice highlighted and repeated words, subheadings, diagrams, and other clues that signal importance; these might be words such as *important*, *relevant*, *in conclusion*, *that is*, *ultimately*, *main problem*, *for example*, and so on.

f. During reading, makes notes of key points in the margins or on a separate piece of paper.

g. Sculpt the main idea to accommodate new pieces of important information.

h. Go back and skim or reread the text, and use your notes to finalize the main idea.

5. Have students practice the previous steps with you as a guide. Provide feedback as you gather glimpses of student thought processes. In longer passages, you can lead the students through a passage, pausing to give the students a chance to summarize each manageable section. Ask the students if the summary still supports the overall main idea of the passage. If not, then ask students to resculpt the main idea.

6. Allow students more independence in their practice as you give them increasingly challenging texts. Have them compare their main ideas with others, working in pairs and groups.

MAIN IDEA MEMORY STORAGE

This activity is a visual and kinesthetic simplification of the active thinking we use to comprehend. It is based on research related to semantic organizers and their positive effect on comprehension and retention (Marzano et al., 2001). Main Idea Memory Storage gives students practice in keeping one "mental hand" on the main idea and the other "mental hand" on the summary chunks of information that relate to the main idea. This can be done alone or in pairs, and silently or as a think-aloud. As always, you should model the activity sufficiently before the students take over.

Procedure

1. Choose a narrative or expository text that is challenging to the students.

2. Think aloud about the process of using initial clues to form a rough main idea. Write the main idea on a sticky note (use clear ones if you are working on an overhead projector) and place it in the top box of the Main Idea Memory Storage form (see page 61 at the end of this chapter). Then explain to students that you will modify the main idea while you read. You can even assign the left hand only to the main idea and say that the summaries can be touched only by the right hand.

3. Read aloud from the text and stop at an appropriate point to summarize. Create a summary note (use a different color sticky note than the main idea note, ideally) and place it on one of the six boxes under the main idea note. Discuss with students whether the summary requires you to change your main idea note. If so, write a new main idea note and replace the old one. The old one can go down on the lower right stack. Repeat this step six times.

4. When your six summary boxes are full, explain aloud to students as you shuffle the boxes around based on importance, the upper three being more important than the lower three, and explain how you can consolidate two or more notes into one (e.g., by classifying and categorizing). As you run out of spaces in the six boxes, you can move old or less important information to the four boxes on the lower left of the diagram.

5. As you read the text, continue to use sticky notes to modify the main idea and move around the important information found in the text.

6. When a revised main idea forms, move the former main idea to the bottom right space on the diagram.

7. Notes that hold important supporting information can be shuffled around to fill the six spots along with the most important supporting summaries.

8. When students understand what to do, have them go through the process in pairs as you assist them. They can then share their diagrams with others and defend their choices.

Variations

- Students can use a 5" × 7" card instead of the head diagram for the main idea, writing the main idea in the center of the card and then attaching the sticky notes all around the sides of the card.

- You also can fold an 8½" × 11" sheet of paper horizontally and, using a pencil, write the main idea above the fold and the smaller summaries below. Then, simply erase as you need to change the information.

MATRICES

A matrix (grid, table) allows a student to organize various categories of information according to different variables that are placed in columns and rows. Using matrices for organizing information is an adaptation of a well-known vocabulary strategy called *semantic feature analysis* (Johnson & Pearson, 1984). It is an effective way to get students to analyze ideas, reduce information to the minimum, and then rebuild it in their own words.

For many expository descriptive texts, particularly in science and social studies, a matrix is an effective way to organize important information. Matrices help students to compare characters, solutions to problems, symbols, wars, policies, time periods, and so on. More than just a "data entry" tool, matrices can be used as springboards to discussion, inference, and further research.

Procedure

1. You or the students examine the chosen text and find the categories to put in the left-hand column of the matrix. Then decide which variables (often these are adjectives) to put across the top row, such as in the following example:

War	Cause	Effect	Cost
WWI			
WWII			
Vietnam			
Gulf			

2. Model the process of filling in some of the cells as you read and think aloud. Show students how to self-question in order to fill in answers: What were the effects of the Gulf War?

3. Model finding evidence from the text(s) to support your entries.

4. Have students finish the matrix in pairs or individually. Working in pairs offers students a chance to talk and academically argue about what they include and why. Remind students to give evidence for some of their answers.

5. When finished, students analyze the grid for patterns and relations. With these patterns and relations, they can generate hypotheses for discussion or research.

6. Have students write a conclusion based on the information on the matrix. (You can model this the first few times.)

OUTLINE-ISH THOUGHTS

They may not seem exciting, and they aren't, but outlines are some of the most prevalent and powerful types of texts around. Sooner or later, their time must come. Cute graphics and semantic maps will not serve our students forever. Students will see information organized in outline form their entire lives (e.g., in articles, tables of contents, webpages, directions, textbook chapters, study guides, and more). Most authors think in some kind of outline-ish way. If readers think "outline-ishly" too, then comprehension improves. Hence, teaching outlining skills can be very helpful for developing the lifelong habits of organizing, summarizing, prioritizing, and subordinating information (Readence et al., 2001).

Procedure

1. Show students a wide variety of outlines.

2. Dissect the outline and discuss why headings and subheadings are named the way they are. Does every detail fit underneath the correct subheading? Ask students why a detail fits under a heading. Ask how the same level of details is related and see if they refer to the heading.

3. As a class, generate outlines of everyday and relevant things: school, sports, food, friendship, music, weather, war, art, parents, cars, movies, television shows, and so on.

4. Have students work together to create an outline of a recent topic discussed in class. Share all the ideas generated and create a whole-class outline on an overhead transparency or on the board.

5. Model how to use ideas from a text to create an outline. Use titles and subheadings.

6. Provide a partially filled outline or semantic web of a longer passage that contains supporting details and paragraphs but no paragraph summaries or main idea for the text. (Many study guides for textbook chapters are in the form of partially filled outlines.)

7. Have students fill in the blanks and discuss their results with other students.

Variation

Show students how to create outlines from semantic webs (see the Semantic Webbing activity in this chapter on page 49) and vice versa.

PODCASTS

Podcasts are oral recordings that are easy to manage and take up little space on computers. They are effective at building students' oral language and articulation skills and usually are more motivating than writing. They also are ways to take advantage of all the technology hidden away in students' pockets and backpacks. While students can (and do) record a variety of ideas, here I emphasize the recording of ideas that help students summarize texts and sculpt main ideas. Such podcasts can take a number of forms: news brief, book review, movie review, interview with an author, current event overview, opinion column, and so forth.

Most computers have built-in sound cards, which allow you to use inexpensive microphones to record directly into the computer using software such as Audacity for Windows (www.audacity.sourceforge.net) or Garageband (www.apple.com/ilife/garageband/) for Macintosh. You can also purchase microphones that attach to Apple iPods and other MP3 players.

Procedure

1. Remind students that their podcasts might be heard around the world, so they must think of who will listen to it (audience) and why they are creating it (purpose). For example, they might create a summary of a science textbook chapter for next year's students of the same class.

2. This will determine the type (format) of podcast. They should also keep it short because it is a summary.

3. Student pairs read a text and take notes on the most important parts that they will include in their podcasts. If groups are large, students can prepare different parts of the podcast.

4. Students can write their podcasts, but they should practice enunciating and using animated voices because reading aloud can sound flat. Ideally, students should practice going from notes or drawings straight into speech. They can practice this, of course, in front of other students and adults before recording, to get feedback.

5. Students record their podcasts and make them available online and so forth. Students can comment on one another's podcasts and even assess them with a checklist or rubric that they create, similar to what they do with written essays. The checklist or rubric might have elements such as the following: content is appropriate to task, sufficient detail and explanation, voice is animated and interesting, ideas supported with evidence, and so forth.

SEMANTIC WEBBING

Semantic webs and organizers have long been used effectively for hierarchically organizing information. They actually are outlines presented in visual form. Many semantic organizers have a central concept, surrounded by key supporting concepts that increase in level of detail as you move away from the central concept. For the purposes of reading comprehension, the central concept usually is a main idea, key question, or the author's purpose. As one moves outward from the main idea, the next spaces shape headings and key supporting concepts, then subheadings, and finally, key details. Semantic target and semantic web organizers, which are easily drawn as follows, can both be used for this activity:

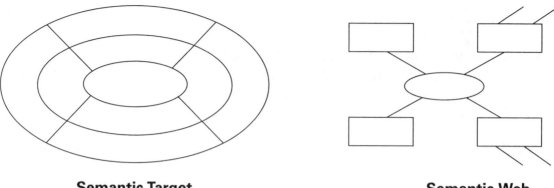

Semantic Target   **Semantic Web**

Procedure

1. Choose a text that lends itself well to semantic webbing. (Most knowledge is organized hierarchically with categories, under which fit discrete pieces of information depending on their characteristics. Therefore, texts that compare, persuade, analyze, describe, classify, and interpret all lend themselves well to semantic organizers.)

2. For prereading, on the board write a topic or a preview question that relates to the text's key ideas, and underneath it list some key vocabulary terms. Nearby, draw a simple semantic organizer on the board or on a separate poster sheet. Ask students to guess which terms might be grouped together and which terms might go in the organizer's boxes (or other shapes). Fill in the boxes' headings during class discussion. Eventually, students will fill in the boxes without your help.

3. After filling in the main headings (categories), students will have a general idea about the text and can summarize what they expect the text to cover (perhaps in a Quickwrite or Think-Pair-Share activity found in Chapter 4).

4. During reading, have students read silently as they fill out their own organizer. For some groups, you can read the first part of the text and even model the building of the organizer on the board. Emphasize the use of key words and phrases that are in the words of the student, rather than sentences copied from the text. Students also can draw symbols or images in the boxes to better remember the information.

5. Using the semantic organizer as an aid, have the students retell (to a partner or small group) the important points of the text. Then, the listeners can remind the teller of any important information not included. Putting the pieces of the text back together in their own words helps students take ownership of the information, which solidifies it in their minds. The semantic organizer also helps the brain build more lasting visually based connections.

6. The semantic organizer provides a helpful framework for writing that is based on the text. The boxes can help a student get ideas for appropriate paragraph separations. Give students a list of transition and connector words to choose from, depending on the style of the writing they are doing. Have students help you create a paragraph on the overhead to model how to transfer the semantic web into written text. Students can write along with you.

Variations

- **Details-First Webbing:** This type of semantic webbing starts with the details of a text and organizes them into categories, which then helps students discover the main idea or central theme. The best way to generate the details list is to pick out keywords from the unit you are teaching. (Figure 6 provides a sample details-first web for an exploration unit.)

- **Main-Idea-First Webbing:** This variation is effective when students have a good grasp of the main idea and the categories that form it—when the ovals and boxes of the semantic web organizer are mostly filled in. Main-Idea-First Webbing helps to generate and organize the details, along with any further categories that might arise. Figure 7 shows a sample main-idea-first web for the topic of *war*. In this example, the class started with the topic in the center. Students worked in pairs or groups to generate possible main categories and then generated details for the other column. There was ongoing discussion about the web elements and how to organize them.

- Show students how to go from a semantic web to an outline (see Figure 8). The central concept is the main idea; the next boxes out become the headings numbered I, II, III, and so on; and the branches are the A, B, and C, and so on.

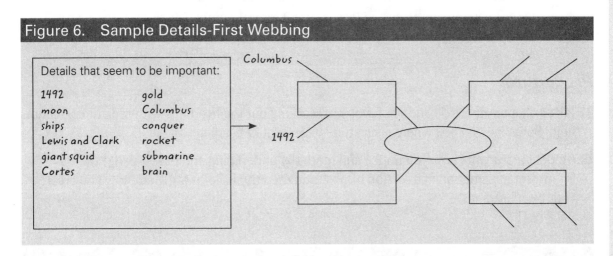

Figure 6.   Sample Details-First Webbing

Details that seem to be important:

1492	gold
moon	Columbus
ships	conquer
Lewis and Clark	rocket
giant squid	submarine
Cortes	brain

Columbus

1492

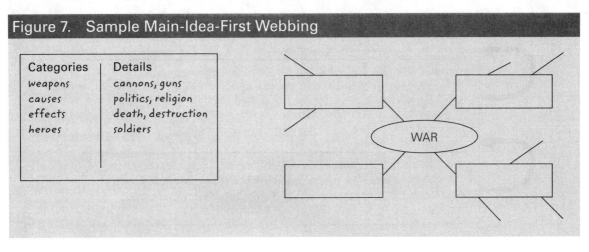

Figure 7.   Sample Main-Idea-First Webbing

Categories	Details
weapons	cannons, guns
causes	politics, religion
effects	death, destruction
heroes	soldiers

WAR

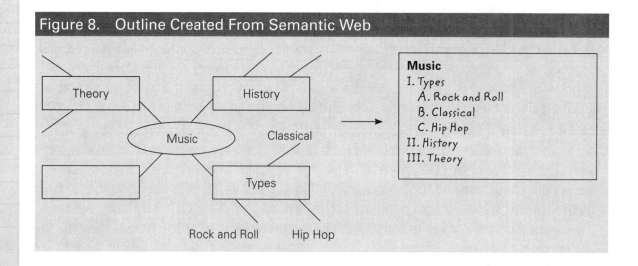

Figure 8.   Outline Created From Semantic Web

SORRY, I LOST MY HEADINGS

This activity encourages students to read text sections and generate a tentative heading or subheading for a section's information (see Figure 9 for an example). It also gives effective practice for text-marking and note-taking.

Procedure

1. Take a chapter or article and photocopy it, blocking out the headings with tape or correction fluid. Put a line or a box where each student-generated heading will be.

2. Model for students how you notice and mark (by underlining and note-taking) the important information in a section of text, and then think aloud for them how you create your own headings.

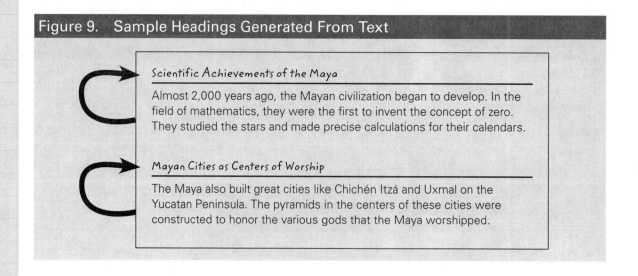

Figure 9.   Sample Headings Generated From Text

3. Discuss with students whether each of your headings is too general or too specific. This can be a very useful and powerful step. It helps students to refine their thoughts to be clear and focused and to see ideas at the right "distance." It will help students in writing as well.

4. Have students work in pairs or individually to fill in the rest of the headings and discuss them with others before sharing all the headings as a class.

STORY MAP

The story map is a tried-and-true way to show the important elements of narrative text (Buehl, 2009; Johns & Berglund, 2001). It also can be used with history texts as an outline of an important event, with supporting events leading up to the climax (perhaps for a war). Different versions of this graphic abound, so feel free to adapt this one to suit your needs. Science teachers have even used it successfully.

Procedure

1. Model on the overhead or board how to fill in the story map (steps 2–8) for various texts such as short stories, songs, fables, television shows, movies, and any novels that you already have read in class. (A full-size story map to photocopy for this activity is provided at the end of this chapter.)

2. First, fill in the character names around the oval in the bottom right corner. You can add doodles or notes, such as *protagonist* and *antagonist* labels, next to the names.

3. Fill in place and time. Discuss why the author might have chosen this setting.

4. Put the main problem or conflict in the large diagonal box. If you are filling in the map during reading, emphasize the use of pencil because the conflict may change.

5. On the left-hand lines, put the important events that lead up to the final climax or resolution of the problem. This is great practice for summarizing because the lines do not allow much space.

6. Summarize the climax or resolution in the banner box at the top.

7. Put the final events on the "ending events" and "changes" lines at the right. These are the important events and changes in the characters or situations that resulted after the resolution.

8. Discuss the message or lesson that the author might have intended when writing the text. Consider historical, moral, social, political, and entertainment purposes. Write the theme, message, or lesson in the box on the right.

9. Have students use the map with additional texts on their own.

Variation

Analyze stories from different cultures and compare their "maps" to the one used in this activity. Have a discussion on why stories with very different structures might be popular in their settings.

STUDENTS GET TO TEACH

The act of teaching a concept to another person helps us learn it better (Lyons & Pinnell, 2001). Think about how much you know about what you teach! Teaching also forces us to summarize, focus on main ideas, and determine what is important. Most of us have seen how well students learn through the process of teaching other students. They learn much more in depth when they effectively teach the target concepts to others. In this activity, they become teachers of the moment. This gives them a more genuine goal for learning the material than simply regurgitating it out on a test or in an essay. This activity works best when the other students being taught don't already know the information.

Procedure

1. Explain the purpose and methods of teaching. Describe for students what you think about when you prepare a lesson or when you are teaching in front of the class. Using an example, model by thinking aloud how you summarize and focus on key points to teach. Explain the importance of modeling thinking and focusing on main points as you teach.

2. Brainstorm various ways students have learned in the past, in your class and from other teachers. Show students various ways to teach a concept. Teach them to be teachers.

3. Explain to students the ideas of multiple learning styles and multiple intelligences. Brainstorm additional activities that they might choose from—for example, they can create a summary poster or a skit that summarizes the text. Tell them to think of ways that students can participate such as pair shares, brainstorms, movement, and so on.

4. Place students into teaching pairs and give them a section of a reading or a concept to teach. This should be new material. In a class of 30, this makes 15 ideas to be taught. I often gain some keen teaching insights from my students.

5. Lead a brief summary discussion as a whole class to solidify the main concepts learned.

SUMMARIZING TRAINING CAMP

Good readers do not tend to go back over a section several times in order to produce the needed summary. Good readers summarize in a split second and move on. This "training camp" helps readers to quickly see what's important, reduce it to a memorable chunk, and relate it to the main idea.

Procedure

1. Pull a paragraph or passage from an article or textbook chapter, or use other types of text such as a webpage, painting, cartoons, or so forth. Let students know the title of the text from which the selection was taken.

2. Put the selection on the overhead projector or the board. Remind the students that the author included this paragraph or passage for a reason and point out that it is important to find out what that reason is.

3. Read aloud the selection to the students. (Try to use paragraphs without obvious topic sentences.) Model how to be on the lookout for topic or summary statements to save time in summarizing.

4. Underline details, phrases, and words that are important to the topic as you read.

5. At the end of the selection, quickly write a summary of why it is there. You can ask the following questions:

   • Is the author describing a thing, person, process, story, or event?

   • Is the author describing something by using literary devices such as metaphor, analogy, hyperbole, and so on?

   • Is the author explaining a cause and effect or a problem and solution?

   • Is the author comparing or contrasting two or more things?

6. Practice makes mostly perfect. If we model the process and then give students a variety of interesting texts to break down, students can build summarizing skills without even realizing it. On a regular basis, give students a short paragraph, article, picture, video clip, poem, song, or other type of text for which they can generate a possible summary. Ideally, the text will be interesting, motivating, and standards based. Some teacher resources contain ready-made passages and even include summaries to compare with student responses.

   Here are some tips for good summaries:

   • Use your own wording, but don't include your opinions.

   • Don't repeat ideas or distort the author's meaning.

   • Use summarizing lingo: *The author says that, states that, explains that, points out that, mentions that, emphasizes that, argues that, maintains that, highlights the fact that,* or *concludes that....*

THEME POSSIBILITIES VISUAL

This activity develops students' habits of thinking more deeply about the underlying themes and lessons in texts, including nonfiction texts. One of the most important side effects of reading is the extra thinking that we do. As we read and keep track of the main ideas, plot, and so forth, we also form other hypotheses, connections, and ideas that the author may or may not have intended. In narratives, in particular, the text often has several themes or lessons. These themes might be different and have different effects on different readers. What we want students to do is be in the habit of noticing and generating themes and using parts from the text to logically support their interpretations. This will also serve them well when they write responses to literature.

Procedure

1. Model for students, using a text or video, how you hypothesize a theme. Using the Theme Possibilities Visual at the end of this chapter, put the short version of the theme in the little oval on the cloud. Model the process of finding evidence from the text to put in the arrows below. Then create a sentence that explains the theme a bit more: "This story shows how it is important to be honest, even if it seems counterproductive at first."

2. Have students work in pairs to read silently and discuss possible themes as they stop periodically. They can have different ideas but should be able to put at least two supporting points in the arrows below and connect them to the theme.

3. Students then pick a theme (or two, if they disagree on what to write about), and collaboratively create a paragraph that explains the theme, its importance, and how it is supported in the text.

WEBPAGE CREATION

This activity provides an effective way to see and develop the nonlinear and hierarchical connections that are so vital in the comprehension of difficult material. Creating webpages builds habits of summarizing, sculpting the main idea, categorizing, identifying the author's purpose, and classifying. Using simple (and free) webpage creation sites and tools such as webs.com, Microsoft Word, or bravenet.com, students can summarize a text or content area concept. Even creating a paper copy of the webpage can be effective and engaging for students.

Procedure

1. Show students at least six exemplary webpages with varying content. Explain the parts and possible variations. Use a computer projector, if possible. Work with students as a class to create their own rubric for this activity (see Chapter 2). Have students use the sample webpages and the rubric to guide them during the process of creating a webpage. They can then ask you what score they would receive on the rubric during the creation process in order to make corrections as indicated by the criteria in the rubric.

2. Optional: Put a webpage's contents into a semantic web or outline to show how the hierarchical relations can be represented.

3. Discuss with students how creating a webpage helps to build habits such as organizing information and summarizing. Use a Think-Pair-Share activity (see Chapter 4) if there is time.

4. Use a short reading sample and show students how you take notes on the following comprehension processes: summaries, questions (answered and not), visualizations, (realized and not), connections to prior knowledge, and so forth. Take notes in a two- or three-column format or use a semantic web.

5. On the overhead or a computer screen, quickly design a webpage with a column on the left and a bar across the top. Show how you take the summaries and turn them into one- or two-word headings for the category buttons in the left column. For example, the Webpage Template (see page 65) has buttons with causes, effects, people, places, and purpose from my notes on the history chapter that they will read. In the center space, create a brief overview in your own words that describes the text's main idea. Finally, model how to create the subpages, the pages to which the buttons on the main page will point. You can color code these pages.

6. Students create a similar layout because they will read the text and fill in the details for the button headings on separate pages.

7. Eventually, students can create category names that will become the buttons for the webpages. Students can put these on the paper draft and also can draft the pages (on a different color of paper) that will connect to the buttons. These "branch" pages will contain the details.

8. Optional: Extend the webpage beyond summarizing to include other habits and content area concepts. Suggest the following buttons or images that will connect to other pages:

- Suggestions to help readers read this text
- Prior knowledge that helped me
- Things I visualized while reading
- Questions answered and not
- Predictions realized and not
- Elaborations on the text, alternate endings, or subplots
- Purposes of the author, teacher, and me
- New words from the text
- Information from prereading

- How the webpage could have been better
- Inferences

9. Use a word-processing program to enter the textual information that will be contained in the webpage. (This does not have to be complete before students begin the webpage creation.)

10. Optional: Publish the webpage on a school or public website.

Reflection Questions

1. How do the habits of summarizing and sculpting the main idea work together?

2. Choose a text that you will teach in your course. Now discuss different purposes it might have (author, teacher, reader). What do you do with this knowledge?

3. How does the skill of classification play a role?

4. Write an inquiry question for this chapter's habit and a teaching activity. Gather evidence over time and make adjustments based on student work (e.g., How can I best help students summarize complex history texts, evidenced by quick-writes and quiz scores, using the keyword construction activity?).

NOTES: _____

_____

_____

_____

_____

_____

_____

_____

_____

_____

_____

KEYWORD CONSTRUCTION

Important Notes, Quotes, Images, and Possible Keywords

What do all these notes share?

This is the key term for understanding this text because...

MAIN IDEA MEMORY STORAGE

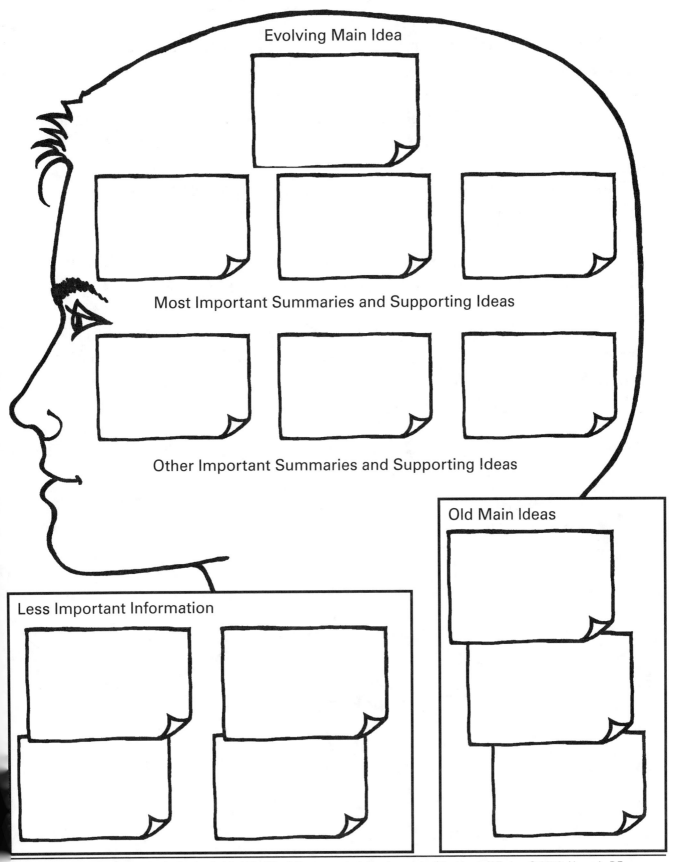

Evolving Main Idea

Most Important Summaries and Supporting Ideas

Other Important Summaries and Supporting Ideas

Old Main Ideas

Less Important Information

STEPS FOR PURPOSE

☐ Look at text clues: title, summaries, subtitles, introductions, pictures, and so on.

☐ Listen to the **teacher's** explanations for why you are reading the text. (Hot Tip! Directly ask the teacher's purpose for assigning the text.)

☐ Think about current lessons and objectives and about how this text might fit into what you are learning.

☐ Think about why the **author** took the time to write this text. What does the author want readers to know or do as a result of reading it?

☐ Use the above steps to help form **your own** purpose for the text. What might you get out of reading this text? What could be interesting about this? Ask yourself, "Why am I reading this?" and have at least one answer that keeps you going.

☐ The purpose may change while reading. Be ready and flexible.

Teacher's Purpose   Author's Purpose

My Purpose

STORY MAP

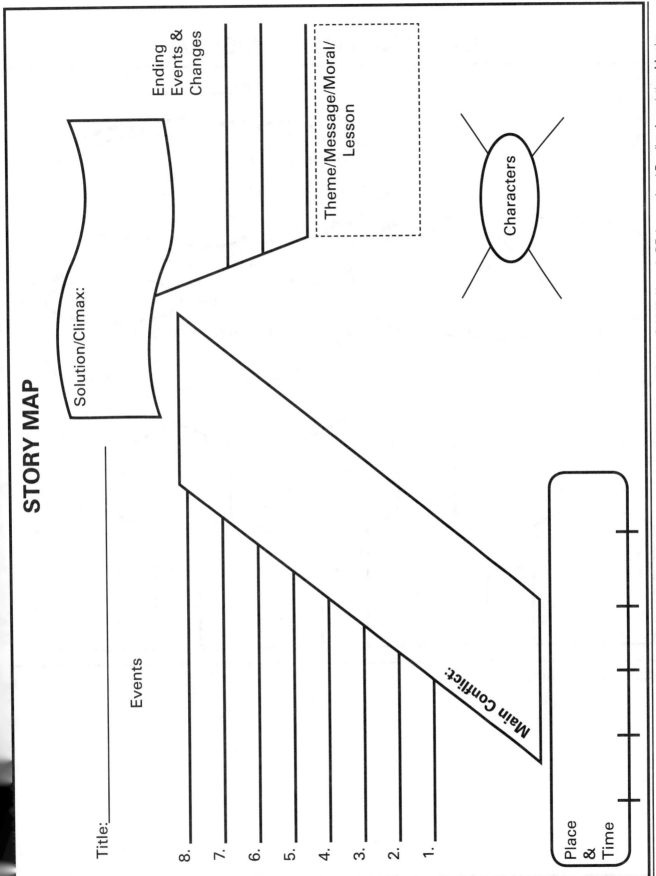

Title: _____

Events

8. _____
7. _____
6. _____
5. _____
4. _____
3. _____
2. _____
1. _____

Main Conflict:

Place & Time

Solution/Climax:

Ending Events & Changes

Theme/Message/Moral/ Lesson

Characters

THEME POSSIBILITIES VISUAL

Text Title:_____

Possible ideas for themes

Theme/lesson/topic:

Theme in complete sentence:

Theme/lesson/topic:

Theme in complete sentence:

Theme/lesson/topic:

Theme in complete sentence:

Key parts or quotes that might support themes

Negotiated paragraph

WEBPAGE TEMPLATE

Title:

Main Idea | Connections to My Life | Questions

Causes

Effects

People

Places

Purpose

Connecting to Background Knowledge

* * *

I am a collage of all
that I have heard, seen, wondered,
and dreamed.

Background knowledge is like a backbone for comprehension. For this reason, I sometimes call it *backbone knowledge*. We can't do without it. Why? Because as we read, we must connect the text's information to related knowledge and experience in our brains that we, in a sense, use as raw material to construct meaning as the text dictates. We compare this evolving meaning with each successive piece of text and we modify or discard any inconsistencies (i.e., we "prune away" the less useful information).

Authors expect readers to possess and use certain pieces of background knowledge. This fund of background knowledge often consists of facts, concepts, experiences, values, and ideas (Alvermann & Phelps, 2001). An author will use idioms, analogies, technical words, and descriptions that the readers of the text are supposed to understand already; the author does not take the extra time to elaborate on what he or she considers to be common experience or knowledge shared by most of the prospective readers. For example, an author might omit common details about a typical ocean beach. When the text deviates from this common fund of background knowledge, however, then the author must take the time to describe how it differs from readers' common expectations (e.g., an ocean beach with mounds of red seaweed and pink sand). The problem for many struggling readers and English learners is that their funds of background knowledge and vocabulary are not what the authors of middle school and high school texts expect them to be.

A useful analogy for using background knowledge in reading is that of constructing a house. (Of course, it helps for you to have background knowledge of house building in order to read and understand this analogy.) The builder must bring a variety of materials to the building site. The builder looks at the plans (the text, in our case) and then searches for the materials that the plans require. If the materials are not handy, the builder goes to the store to obtain them (a reader refers to other resources). Perhaps a substitute material can be used (related background knowledge) that is modified to fit the needs of the plan. Sometimes the builder brings prefabricated sections to the job (background knowledge patterns or schemata). These

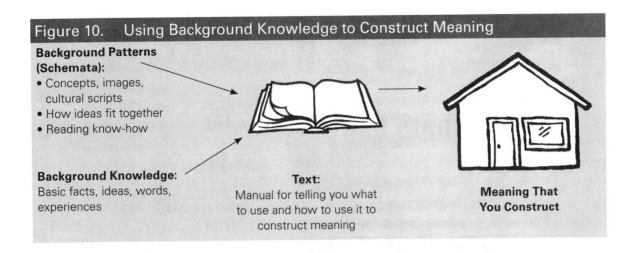

Figure 10. Using Background Knowledge to Construct Meaning

Background Patterns (Schemata):
- Concepts, images, cultural scripts
- How ideas fit together
- Reading know-how

Background Knowledge:
Basic facts, ideas, words, experiences

Text:
Manual for telling you what to use and how to use it to construct meaning

Meaning That You Construct

save time by avoiding the need to put many separate pieces together. For example, if a reader already knows what a typical U.S. wedding ceremony entails, the author does not need to spend pages on common details that the reader can fill in with cultural background knowledge. But when that background knowledge is not there (e.g., for a recent immigrant from Laos), the knowledge needs to be built up in some way or comprehension will suffer. Refer to Figure 10 for a visual representation of how this process works.

Using and Developing Background Knowledge Patterns

Background knowledge patterns, also called *schemata*, are the larger chunks of information that a person uses to make sense of text. Background knowledge patterns tend to be complex concepts of culture, beliefs, expectations, values, and past experiences that we use to comprehend the nature of things and events. For example, if you read "I found coal in my stocking, knocked over the tree and started a fire, and smiled at my grandfather who was wearing a red suit," readers with the cultural schema of Christmas morning in the United States would quickly *get the drift of it*. Others might *scratch their heads* in wonder, even though they *grasped* the meaning of each individual word in the sentence. Additional examples of background knowledge patterns include common ideas about restaurant settings, greetings, sports, hobbies, politics, rural and city scenes, human behavior, and emotions in response to certain situations, and idiomatic expressions such as the italicized phrases in this paragraph.

Here is another example of a text that may stump some readers who do not have the matching background knowledge pattern already in mind as they read:

> The process is actually quite simple. First, you separate them into several piles according to shape and color. Then you separate them again according to their age. The oldest ones need the most cleaning. After they are clean, you carefully look for the spot where each one belongs. Then you write down which ones are still missing so you can search for them. You look in drawers, under furniture, and inside the pockets of old clothes.

Some reading teachers probably saw the first line of the text above and immediately skipped the whole passage, thinking it was the same vignette (about laundry) that they have seen in many literacy trainings. Others read on and realized that this was a different text and proceeded to connect the clues to fit background knowledge. Some eventually figured out that the text was about coin collecting by using text clues and background knowledge. (If you didn't, now you know.)

We have countless background knowledge and cultural patterns that we use to organize how we think and live. These include patterns for hygiene, eating, romance, religion, communication, work, relaxation, and how people behave or learn in a given context. We need these patterns to make quick sense of a current situation. For example, if I read that a young girl is heading off to her first day of school, my background knowledge kicks in and I picture her walking into a sunny classroom, with students seated in perfect rows as a teacher smiles and introduces her to the class. The text may drastically change this image, but at least I have a starting point. Remember that diverse learners who did not have mainstream upbringings in the United States may have background knowledge that is much different than what mainstream American authors envisioned when they were writing their texts (Peregoy & Boyle, 2005). In such cases, it is even more important to predict what kinds of background information diverse students will need in order to comprehend successfully.

Background knowledge significantly influences other comprehension habits such as inferences, predictions, questions, and visualizations. In making inferences and predictions, we mix our knowledge of what we know has happened or what normally happens with what is said in the text in order to create meaning that is not directly stated (Keene & Zimmermann, 2007). In creating questions, we have certain areas of knowledge with holes in them and the text piques our interest to fill those holes with a question. We then use the text to construct an answer.

Visualizing

When we use background knowledge to create mental images and associations that aid us in comprehension, we are visualizing. Proficient readers routinely create a variety of mental pictures during reading. We use the text's information to bring up prior mental images that we obtained from life, photos, movies, television, or other sources. We adapt the images as we read in order to fit what the text says. The more vivid the mental pictures we can create, the more comprehensible and memorable the text tends to be (Hyerle, 2008).

Why is visualizing so important? When we visualize, we use mental energy to create meanings and connections that form the images. It is this mental organizing that helps the images and their information stick in our brains. In reading, as in most learning situations, we are more likely to learn something if we take control of the learning process and are active constructors of meaning, not just passive receivers. Research has shown that when students are taught to visualize text images, they experience better recall and are better able to make helpful inferences and predictions (Gambrell & Bales, 1986; Keene & Zimmermann, 2007). In the case of narrative text, we make a "mental movie" of what is happening in the story. Think about scenes from books you have read and how they are still in your mind even after many years. Sometimes the images stick so well that we think we saw them in a movie or even that we actually experienced them.

For expository materials, such as those in science or economics, we can make mini-"movies in the head" (e.g., of the water cycle or cell division) or concept posters (e.g., of a supply–demand chart or a Venn diagram) in our minds. In science, I might visualize a scene of two atoms sharing an electron or a graph of cell division rates. The quality of these images, of course, depends on my prior experience with texts and images containing atoms and graphs. In social studies, I might visualize ships setting sail for Africa or a Mayan woman grinding maize for the next meal. For math, I might picture the accelerating vehicles described in a word problem before I begin working the problem.

We often begin to create mental pictures from the very start of a reading session. We use the title or first sentences of the text, create rough mental images, and continually revise them according to each new sentence. Table 7 shows how this process works. Read the passages in the left column of the table and notice how the reader's mental pictures on the right change with each sentence.

A reader who makes similar visualizations while reading the sentences in Table 7 will better remember the main idea that being an astronaut is very demanding. In my observations of many struggling readers, I have noticed positive comprehension results when teachers (a) used images to provide background knowledge, (b) trained students to actively process images already in the text (they sometimes skip them without this training), and (c) trained students to create their own mental images as they read. Activities in this chapter that are particularly helpful for visualization include Background Knowledge Backpack, Closed Eyes Visualize, Concept Poster Preview, Sticky Note Snapshots, and Text Structure Graphic Organizers.

Drawing while reading also helps students to actively and visually comprehend, provided that the drawing is accurate enough and does not use too much time. If we train students to create symbols or doodles while reading, they will tend to better remember the information they read. This should not surprise us because the process of visualizing and then drawing

Table 7. Visualization Example

Science Paragraph Sample	Images Visualized by Me
Astronauts do much more than just float around in space and smile for cameras.	A smiling astronaut in a spacesuit, with the Earth in the background
They learn how to eat, sleep, and exercise while being weightless.	Several astronauts in gray shirts, inside a cramped ship, one using a rowing machine
For example, you can't just set your sandwich down and expect it to stay on the table!	Bread, cheese, meat, and tomatoes floating around inside a space shuttle
Astronauts also perform a large number of work tasks, such as spacecraft maintenance, testing, and experimentation.	An astronaut outside with a big wrench; other astronauts inside looking at computers
They even study the effects of life in space on the human body, in order to see how we might do on trips to other planets.	Someone taking a blood sample from an astronaut to see any changes
So if you sign up to be an astronaut, remember that it is more work than any job you may ever have on Earth.	Me in a spacesuit taking in the view of the Earth, and the boss astronaut yelling, "Get back to work!"

what we see requires active thinking. We must, of course, extensively model for students how to make quick and accurate drawings and doodles. One suggestion is to use a piece of paper with four television screens drawn on it (see the Visualization Stations form at the end of this chapter on page 98). Students can be given a short amount of time to make sketches on the four screens to depict what is happening in the text while they read or listen to someone read aloud (Hibbing & Rankin-Erickson, 2003). Activities such as this also can give you a quick view into what is happening in a student's brain while he or she is reading. If the student is way off the mark, you can provide feedback.

Movement, or kinesthetics, also can help students develop their background knowledge and visualization habits. When students see you act out an idea (character, scene, or process) or, even better, when students also do the movements, these actions become imprinted in the brain as background knowledge. The ideas are easier to visualize and recall when a text refers to them.

How Students Use Background Knowledge

Every student has stores of background knowledge and experience just waiting to be tapped in order to improve his or her comprehension of school texts. Every day, students connect experiences to their background knowledge in order to communicate, learn, and carry out life tasks. Our task is to build on the ways in which students already connect to and use their background knowledge outside of school and our classroom in order to meet the academic comprehension needs in our classroom setting. For example, a student may draw from his or her experience working on a farm when describing hard work to a friend, but may not yet connect to this experience when the topic of feudal systems is introduced in social studies or when learning about animal adaptations in science. It is our job to see that this "extra" connecting happens—and then becomes a habit.

We are not teaching a new habit here. We are developing in our students the existing habit of using background knowledge in more academic ways. In each activity found in this chapter, I recommend starting with the ways in which students use the habit in nonacademic contexts. Start with the concrete and familiar and then move to the more abstract and academic. For example, in the Pro–Con Improv activity, you can start with common topics such as soccer, school, music, friendship, food, cities, or cars. Point out to students how easily they categorize and classify the pieces of their background knowledge. Then, transfer this activity to the topic of the upcoming text or lesson.

Tools Chart for Background Knowledge

Table 8 will help you figure out when to use this chapter's activities in which content areas. On the left side of the table, a √ in a column indicates that the activity is useful in that stage of reading. On the right side of the table, a √ in a column indicates that the activity is helpful for comprehension of common texts used in that content area. A √√ on the right side of the table means that the activity is especially helpful for that type of text and that you should try it as soon as possible.

Before Reading	During Reading	After Reading	Activity Name	Social Studies	Science	English/ EL
			Table 8. When and Where to Use the Activities in Chapter 4			
✓		✓	Anticipation Guides (+ Why)	✓✓	✓✓	✓
✓		✓	Background Knowledge Backpack	✓	✓	✓✓
✓			CATAPULT Into Literature			✓✓
✓	✓		Closed Eyes Visualize	✓✓	✓✓	✓✓
✓			Concept Poster Preview	✓✓	✓✓	✓✓
✓	✓	✓	Critique Chart	✓✓	✓	✓✓
✓		✓	Give One–Get One	✓	✓✓	✓
✓	✓	✓	K-W-L	✓✓	✓✓	✓
✓	✓	✓	K-W-L Plus	✓✓	✓✓	✓
✓		✓	Pro–Con Improv	✓✓	✓✓	✓
✓	✓	✓	Quickwrites	✓✓	✓✓	✓✓
	✓		Sticky Note Snapshots	✓✓	✓✓	✓✓
✓	✓	✓	Text Structure Graphic Organizers	✓✓	✓✓	✓
✓			THIEVES	✓✓	✓✓	
✓	✓	✓	Think-Pair-Share	✓✓	✓✓	✓✓

Activities for Background Knowledge

ANTICIPATION GUIDES (+ WHY)

Anticipation guides (Tierney & Readence, 2000), also known as prediction guides, activate a student's prior knowledge and set a purpose or framework for the reading. They are most useful when the text contains controversial issues, problems, or opinions that do not have one easy answer. The guides serve as springboards for modifying beliefs and opinions about a topic (Duffelmeyer, Baum, & Merkley, 1987). They can be used to bring up and examine commonly held assumptions such as "The Earth is round" (actually, it isn't) or "an animal is a bird if it has a bill" (not the platypus). Figure 11 shows a sample anticipation guide for a text on computers.

Procedure

1. Identify major concepts in the reading or lesson.

2. Create statements that question certain notions, beliefs, or opinions or that may challenge what students already know. You can use the reproducible Anticipation Guide at the end of

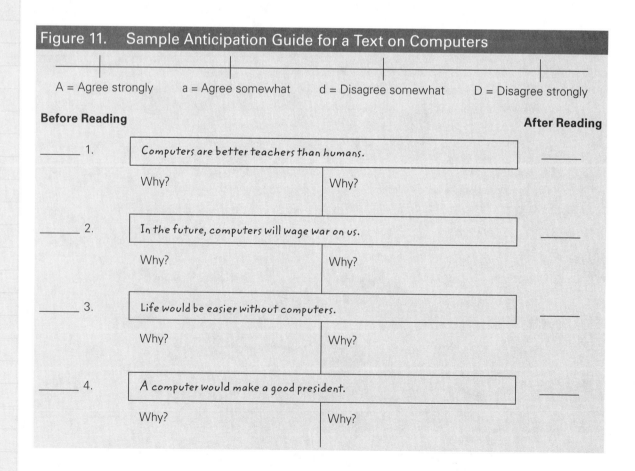

Figure 11. Sample Anticipation Guide for a Text on Computers

A = Agree strongly   a = Agree somewhat   d = Disagree somewhat   D = Disagree strongly

Before Reading   **After Reading**

_____ 1.   Computers are better teachers than humans.

Why?   Why?   _____

_____ 2.   In the future, computers will wage war on us.

Why?   Why?   _____

_____ 3.   Life would be easier without computers.

Why?   Why?   _____

_____ 4.   A computer would make a good president.

Why?   Why?

this chapter on page 93 to save time; write your questions or statements in the numbered boxes and then make a copy for each student.

3. Hand out the guide and briefly explain the statements. Have students mark their responses of agreement or disagreement in the "Before Reading" column.

4. Have students give reasons for their opinions by answering the "Why?" question on the left under each statement.

5. Have students read the text. During reading, the students can refer to the guide and take notes.

6. After reading or other follow-up activities, have students mark the "After Reading" column and fill in the "Why?" section on the right under each statement.

7. Conduct a discussion comparing the before and after results. Your discussion should refer to evidence in the text and should cover students' reasons for changes in their before and after answers.

Variation

Anticipation Questions: You also can have students answer several questions before the reading or lesson. Then, they read the text and answer the questions again after reading. For an activity for generating good questions (which can, in turn, be used for this activity), see Chapter 6.

BACKGROUND KNOWLEDGE BACKPACK

The Background Knowledge Backpack is a simple way to help students build the habit of accessing different types of background knowledge for comprehension.

Procedure

1. Use the reproducible Background Knowledge Backpack form at the end of the chapter on page 94. Read aloud a text to the students and stop several times to fill in the "pockets" in the backpack. Model this activity many times so students can see the different types of useful background knowledge that can be used. Figure 12 shows a sample of the completed form.

2. Have students read the text from where you left off and pause at times to fill in the pockets. (They can do this in pairs as well.) Let students know that there is no set order and that all three types of background knowledge listed on the sheet can be used for the "My BK" pockets.

3. Have students (either in pairs or in groups) explain their "Text" pocket responses and how their background knowledge helped them to understand the material.

4. Have students share with the entire class as you write a similar diagram on the board or overhead.

Figure 12. Sample Background Knowledge Backpack

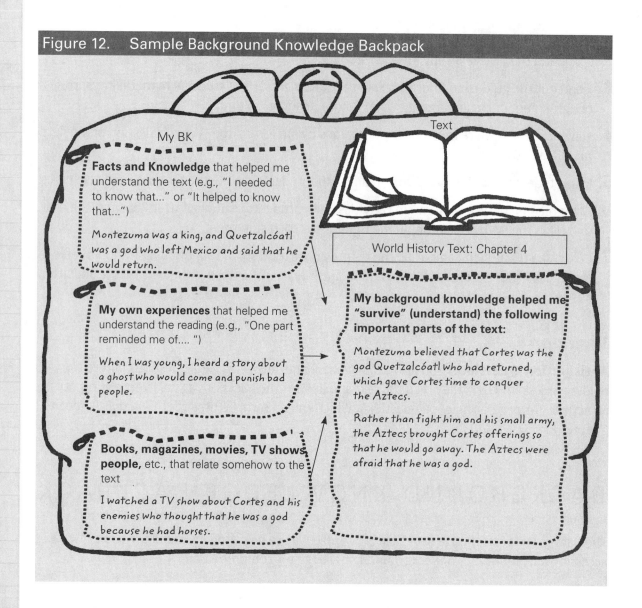

My BK

Text

Facts and Knowledge that helped me understand the text (e.g., "I needed to know that..." or "It helped to know that...")

Montezuma was a king, and Quetzalcóatl was a god who left Mexico and said that he would return.

World History Text: Chapter 4

My own experiences that helped me understand the reading (e.g., "One part reminded me of.... ")

When I was young, I heard a story about a ghost who would come and punish bad people.

My background knowledge helped me "survive" (understand) the following important parts of the text:

Montezuma believed that Cortes was the god Quetzalcóatl who had returned, which gave Cortes time to conquer the Aztecs.

Rather than fight him and his small army, the Aztecs brought Cortes offerings so that he would go away. The Aztecs were afraid that he was a god.

Books, magazines, movies, TV shows, people, etc., that relate somehow to the text

I watched a TV show about Cortes and his enemies who thought that he was a god because he had horses.

5. As a slight variation, students can create a similar diagram that has "What I didn't understand" on the right and "What I needed to know" on the left side.

CATAPULT INTO LITERATURE

A prereading activity, CATAPULT (covers, author, title, audience, page 1, underlying message or purpose, visuals, and time) Into Literature is useful for getting students to survey and "launch" into works of literature. CATAPULT and THIEVES (this chapter, p. 87) give struggling readers some tricks of the book reading trade. If we can get students to mentally prepare as many ideas about the content and theme as possible before they read a text, they will have a much better framework on which to attach the details and ideas of the text. Students will be less likely to get lost in what they are reading.

Table 9. CATAPULT Process Steps

Covers (front and back)	What does the front cover show us about what we might visualize in the story? What does the back cover tell us about the story (the words, pictures, or both)?
Author	What is the author's background? Has he or she written any other stories that might be like this? What were they about? Are the same characters in this story as in the others?
Title	What does the title lead us to predict about the story? Let's hear some possible predictions.
Audience	For whom was this story written? Old, young; male, female; city-dwelling, country-dwelling; past, present, or future readers?
Page 1	Read page 1 and think about what the story might be about.
Underlying message or purpose	With what we have thought about so far, what message or purpose might the author have for the readers?
Look at visuals, maps, or sketches in the text	As we look through the story, what do the pictures, sketches, diagrams, or maps tell us? How will they add to our ability to visualize events and characters?
Time, place, characters	From clues so far, what can we say about when the story takes place, where it takes place, and the characters? What can we guess might happen to the characters?

Procedure

1. Model and scaffold the use of the steps shown in Table 9. Tell students to take notes during this discussion.

2. Create a half-sheet worksheet to remind students of the CATAPULT steps as they read (a reproducible CATAPULT Into Literature Practice form is provided at the end of this chapter on page 95).

3. If there is time, have students share their CATAPULT notes in pairs, groups, or with the whole class.

Variation

CATAPULT Prereading Web: This is a modification of the CATAPULT acronym-based activity, done in the form of a semantic web in order to give more visual emphasis to prereading. In the boxes around the text's title, put whatever prereading elements from CATAPULT that you want to emphasize, as shown on page 76.

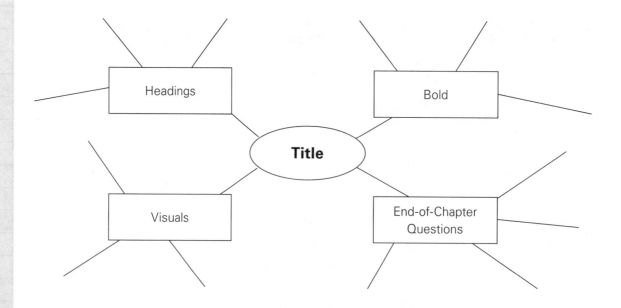

Have students use the web to fill in information that connects to each box. Students can then compare notes or you can have a whole-class share time to discuss the results. (Note that this modification is also effective for the THIEVES activity that appears later in this chapter.)

CLOSED EYES VISUALIZE

Visualizing is vital for comprehension. It is similar to painting a picture or making a movie in your mind. Readers need to use mental pictures from television, books, movies, and their own experiences to create the pictures that the author expects a reader to create while reading (Hibbing & Rankin-Erickson, 2003). For example, the book I am reading might be about a desert in Texas, and although I have never been to Texas or even to a desert, I have seen deserts on television and I have a rough mental image of dry sand, cacti, and lizards. So, as I read, I modify this mental image into what the author intends for me to picture and to know.

Procedure

1. Explain to students that picturing text in their minds is vital for understanding it.
2. Show students a series of three or four pictures (or show short video clips).
3. After each picture, have students close their eyes and visualize what was in the picture. They also can write down words to describe the images if they want.
4. Tell students to visualize a variation of each picture. For example, if you showed them a picture of mountains, have them modify this mental image to have several mountain climbers on the cliffs in a snowstorm.
5. Tell the students that this is what happens during reading: We start with a rough image, and the text makes us modify it with other details.

6. Have students visualize and imagine that they are in situations similar to those that will be encountered in the text they are about to study. (You can have them put their heads down if they do not like closing their eyes.)

7. Next, move to written text. Read aloud a text and stop after the initial clues are given. Allow students to form an initial picture. Then read on and stop at appropriate times to allow students to modify their mental images. You also should model and describe your visualizing processes while reading aloud.

8. As an option, play sound effects or music if appropriate.

9. Finally, have students visualize while they read their own texts. During and after reading, they can keep a "visualizing log" by writing how the text caused them to modify their initial images and scenes. The following sample should give you an idea.

Initial Visualization	Modified Visualization After Further Reading
A small town with old cars and poor people	A village with no cars, dirt streets, brightly colored houses, and no people
An army with tanks, green uniforms, and missile trucks	An army with cannons and soldiers in red uniforms, all mounted on horses

Variation

Have students read a text section silently, or even aloud, and then give them time to visualize what happened or what was described in the text. They should close their eyes to do this. Next, have students draw the scenes they visualize. They should modify these scenes as they read the text. They can verbalize their mental scenes to other students. This process will show on paper how they modify scenes in their minds, which strengthens the mental flexibility needed for learning new concepts.

CONCEPT POSTER PREVIEW

Based on research that has shown positive effects from using advance organizers and building background knowledge before reading (Marzano et al., 2001; Stone, 1983), a Concept Poster Preview is a short teacher presentation that uses a large poster that you create with markers while you explain the concepts to be learned from the text. It is a powerful way to build background knowledge and vocabulary, and it can be an excellent form of comprehensible input for English learners.

Procedure

1. Decide which key points you want your students to get from the text. Think about how you can draw these points on one or two large posters. Examples include an illustrated timeline,

a diagram, a story map, a character description, a Venn diagram, a cause and effect chart, a map, and a drawing of a scene.

2. Lightly sketch in pencil the main lines, symbols, and words you will cover when you fill in the poster for the class. A little bit of forethought can make a huge difference in learning with this activity.

3. Mount the poster on the wall. In class, draw over the pencil lines with a thick marker as you preview key concepts in the text and draw symbols to illustrate key vocabulary. You can even use props, drama, and physical objects if they fit the discussion. Students can take notes, if needed.

4. The teacher talk time during this activity should not last longer than 10 minutes. Have students do one or two Think-Pair-Shares (about 2–3 minutes each; described later in this chapter in detail) during that time in order to process the information. The whole activity, including the Think-Pair-Shares, should not last longer than 15 minutes.

5. Keep the poster on the wall for reference during the lesson or unit. Refer back to it often.

CRITIQUE CHART

The process of critiquing and evaluating a text uses students' background knowledge of how information should be communicated. Critiquing puts more ownership and engagement into the hands of the students. In this activity, they are not just required to learn what is in the text; they get a chance to evaluate it, improve it, criticize it, and challenge it. As they fill in the chart and discuss it with partners, students use their knowledge of the subject and ways of communicating that work best. This activity overlaps significantly with skills of questioning and monitoring comprehension (see Chapters 6 and 8).

Procedure

1. Model the process of critiquing a text using the chart below. This could be a textbook chapter, an article, a novel, story, advertisement, painting, and so on. Write in your ideas as you think aloud about the different boxes in the chart. Emphasize how the six boxes should support the author's overall purpose. Emphasize how you connect to your experiences and knowledge of what kinds of writing best communicate to you.

2. Go through the chart with students and have them add their input.

3. Have student pairs or groups read a text with the critique chart in mind. They can stop and jot down notes in the boxes if they want. They jot down positive and negative aspects of the text.

4. Students discuss their notes and what they want to put in the final chart to turn in.

5. Encourage them to be critical and not to accept just any text that gets put in front of them.

6. As a whole class, share final thoughts and suggestions for the author.

Overall Purpose(s) of Text

Organization of text	Examples and explanations	Missing voices and points of view
• How could the text have been organized differently?	• Were the examples helpful? • What other examples might have helped? • Were some parts too long?	• Whose voices were missing? • Were any other points of view missing?
Visuals and data	Importance of topic	Other suggestions
• Were the images and visual aids helpful? • What could have helped? • Did some parts need to be supported by data?	• Was this topic important enough to publish? • Is the topic important for us to read about and learn?	

GIVE ONE–GET ONE

Give One–Get One (Kagan, 1997) is a social way for students to tap into and build background knowledge for a text. It is similar to a brainstorm session but has a more communicative twist.

Procedure

1. Generate a topic idea from the text and put it on the board. Some examples are as follows:

- What I know about whales
- Examples of sacrifice
- Keywords for studying space
- Reasons to exercise
- Favorite idioms, metaphors, or sayings
- What we learned last month about electricity
- What will the text teach us about gravity?

2. Have students fold a piece of paper in half horizontally and number 1 through 4 above the fold and 5 through 8 below, as shown.

3. Have students write down ideas related to the topic.

4. Have students circulate throughout the room and exchange their ideas for at least three different ideas from other

```
Ideas I will give:
1. _____
2. _____
3. _____
4. _____

Ideas I got:              From
5. _____        ____
6. _____        ____
7. _____        ____
8. _____        ____
```

students, which go on lines 5 through 8. They need to get the student's name for each corresponding idea and write it in the "From" column.

5. After several minutes, have students regroup and share with the class the ideas they heard from other students.

6. Have students use academic language such as "Julie had a similar thought," "Manuel predicts that…," or "Katia differs in opinion because she…."

7. Discuss all the responses and then introduce the text.

K - W - L

K-W-L (Ogle, 1986) has a long and effective history in the scaffolding of expository texts. Basic K-W-L uses three columns in which to write down information that we Know (background knowledge), Want to know (establishing purpose and asking questions), and have Learned (main idea). In addition to teaching students to connect to background knowledge, this activity also can develop habits of summarizing, questioning, predicting, inferring, and figuring out word meanings.

Procedure

1. Create three columns on the board and head them with "What we know," "What we want to know," and "What we learned."

2. Ask students what they know about the subject or text you are about to study. Prompt the students with pictures, titles, or subjects to fill in the first column (some teachers put "What we *think* we know" in the first column to avoid confusing students with potentially incorrect information).

3. Ask students what they want to know and fill in the second column with their questions.

4. Have students read the text or do research on the topic.

5. In the third column, have students answer their questions from the second column in groups, add any key information that they learned, and share to fill in the third column.

Variations

Many teachers have successfully adapted K-W-L to expand its effectiveness for teaching comprehension. Following are some ideas.

- **Extended K-W-L:** Sampson (2002) creates more accountability for obtaining information in the K-W-L process. Six columns are used in this variation: the three traditional K-W-L columns, a column for checking off whether the text(s) confirmed the information in the "What we think we know" column, and two other columns for noting the sources of the information (see the example).

What We Think We KNOW	Confirmed?	Source	What We WANT to Know	What We LEARNED	Source

When using this activity, remember that not all the items in the first or second columns will be confirmed or answered.

- **K-N-L:** This variation uses content standards in the second column (what students *need* to learn) rather than items students are curious about (see example). You will need to help students with the second column, writing in content standards and taking time to explain them.

What We KNOW and Can Do	What We NEED to Learn	What We LEARNED (and/ or What We Can Do)

- **K-W-H-L-S:** In this version, you add two extra columns (see example), one for how students will learn the information and one for how they will show what they learned.

What We Think We KNOW	What We WANT to Learn	HOW We Will Learn It	What We LEARNED	How We Will SHOW That We Learned

- **K-W-L-U-M:** For this version, you can add either or both of the last two columns shown in the example.

What We Think We KNOW	What We WANT (Need) to Learn	What We LEARNED	How We Will USE (Apply) What We Learned	What MORE We Want/Need to Learn

- **W-W-W-W:** You might want to include other columns in K-W-L such as What the Teacher Wants Us to Learn, Why We Should Learn It, Who Needs to Know This in Life, and What Other Points of View There Are.

K-W-L PLUS

K-W-L Plus (Carr & Ogle, 1987) uses graphic organizers (within the context of a K-W-L chart) to help students further organize information into additional categories before, during, and after reading.

Procedure

1. Give students an initial topic or some clues, such as a text title or pictures, and ask students to think about what they might know that might relate to the topic. Have students brainstorm in order to fill in the step 1 area of the graphic organizer (see Figure 13 for a sample).

2. Have students generate several categories under which each of their responses can fit. Put these categories into the boxes of a semantic map that they will draw in the step 2 area. The first several times you use this activity with your class, you should think aloud when modeling and scaffolding the process of generating categories, sorting, and creating the graphic organizer.

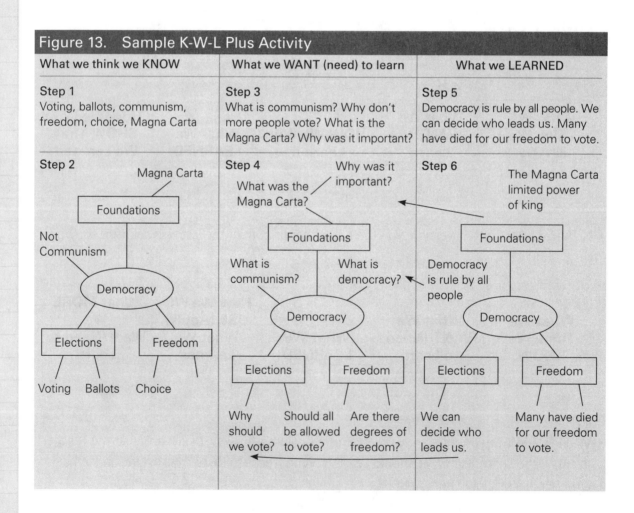

Figure 13. Sample K-W-L Plus Activity

What we think we KNOW	What we WANT (need) to learn	What we LEARNED
Step 1 Voting, ballots, communism, freedom, choice, Magna Carta	**Step 3** What is communism? Why don't more people vote? What is the Magna Carta? Why was it important?	**Step 5** Democracy is rule by all people. We can decide who leads us. Many have died for our freedom to vote.

3. Have students generate questions, with some guidance from you, for the step 3 area in the second column. They can relate their questions to information in the first column; you can even draw arrows across the columns to show how their questions in step 3 relate to their ideas in step 1.

4. Have students create questions that correspond to the boxed categories in step 2. Have them create a new semantic map in the step 4 area that has these questions around it.

5. Now have the students study the text. As they read, have students take notes on what they learn and write them in the step 5 column or on sticky notes. Students also can draw arrows from the answers they found to the questions in steps 3 and 4.

6. Have students use the original semantic map from step 2 as a template that they now change to fit what they learned. Have them write that information in the semantic map in the step 6 area, including any answers to the questions in step 4. They also can generate new categories here, if any should arise.

7. Students can compare their final graphic organizers with those of other students, in pairs or groups, and discuss the information, any differences in categories, and the importance of the information included.

PRO–CON IMPROV

This activity, adapted from Duffala (1987), helps to build oral language skills and abilities to think about the pros and cons of topics. It helps build up background knowledge for texts that deal with different perspectives and problems with multiple solutions. It then helps students to be critical readers, thinking about multiple points of view as they read. Pro–Con Improv can become an effective foundational activity for variations that you can use throughout the year as the complexity in subject matter increases.

Procedure

1. First model this process for the class by making a student your director. The director picks a topic from a list and says "Pro!" while clapping. As the speaker, you say one or two convincing reasons for the topic. Then the director says, "Con!" and you immediately switch to the negative aspects of the topic, using an academic transition such as *but, however, on the other hand, yet,* and so on. Then try Pro–Con Improv two or three more times.

2. Give students a list of possible topics that lend themselves well to this activity. Some good beginning topics include camping, rain, shopping, movies, the beach, watching television, dogs, parents, traveling, exercise, driving, computers, dating, cars, and fast food.

3. Next, put students in pairs and let them decide who will go first and then alternate between director and speaker. Encourage students to show the pro and con not only with their voices but also in body language and movement. The director then begins by saying the topic. The speaker, if uncomfortable, can tell the director to choose another topic, but

just once. When the director claps and says, "Pro!" the speaker begins. The director can respond by nodding his or her head, showing engagement in the monologue.

4. Ask for some volunteers to do a sample in front of the class. It is good to have a director say (after asking if the speaker wants to perform up front), "My speaker did an amazing job! We would like to go!" This validates the speaker's performance.

5. Students perform in front of the class and then discuss what they liked about the performances on a verbal and nonverbal level. What did they like about the communication on the part of the speaker? Did he or she make a smooth transition from pro to con and back? You can also comment on good use of academic language and transitions.

6. Finally, give students topics that pertain to the text they will read, such as the brain, the Vietnam War, Albert Einstein, Thomas Jefferson, laws, technology, democracy, nuclear power, Napoleon, radiation, anger, education, history, or oil. This will allow them to generate ideas and opinions before they read the text and will allow them to connect to such thoughts as they read.

QUICKWRITES

Quickwrites require each student to reach inside his or her mind and pull out something related to a prompt and organize it on paper. They are informal and low-stress ways to jump-start the brain of each student, particularly those who may not share in a whole-class brainstorming session. They are a way for students to connect to what they already know or just learned and to organize their thoughts enough to write them down. They are a great way to get students to focus and to formatively assess ongoing learning.

Procedure

1. Give the students a question or prompt related to the text about to be read, and have students write down whatever comes to their minds without organizing it too much or worrying about grammar. The topic should relate to the text being studied in some way: connection to background knowledge ("Describe a time when..."); a controversial topic or question that relates to student life; explanation of content concepts or vocabulary; or predictions, summaries, inferences, hypotheses, and so on. Give them a couple minutes of talk time before writing. All students should be able to write something.

2. You may need to offer some students extra support, particularly those with limited experience or knowledge about the topic. There often will be students who say, for example, "I don't have problems with friends," "I don't want to go anywhere," or "I've never seen a...." Be ready to modify the prompt to get all students to participate and to model a response for them with academic language.

3. Quickwrites can become a part of a student's journal and be used for assessment, especially if the student so chooses. They also can be used during Think-Pair-Share activities

(explained later in this chapter) or even as a Ticket Out the Door, in which each student writes a summary of what he or she learned and hands it to you on the way out of class.

Following are some sample Quickwrites:

History: I think wars start because people want to take over people's lands and control them. I'm not sure why people want to take over lands or control people—maybe because of selfishness or greed, maybe because they want to make people convert to their religion. The war in my country hurt many people who were innocent and just wanted to have a normal life.

Math: First, you have to get the similar terms together, but they have to have the exact same variables and exponents. Then you get the variable you want to solve on one side and the numbers on the other. You need to make sure to do the same thing to one side that you do to the other, like two sides of a seesaw. Then I get the variable all by itself by multiplying or dividing and that is the answer.

Science: The Punnett square helps you figure out the chances of a plant being tall or not if two parent plants have a dominant and recessive gene mix. It is a 75% chance that the plant will be tall because it shows in 3 out of 4 boxes. It will be short 25% of the time because the tt is only in one box. I think this works for humans but not sure because we have much more complicated DNAs and genes to mix.

Variation

Pen Go–Pen Stop: In this variation, students are given a prompt and a minute to think, and then they write as much as they can when you say "Pen go." A few minutes later, you say "Pen stop" and the students must stop writing. This variation helps students to challenge themselves to write as much as possible—while also making sense.

STICKY NOTE SNAPSHOTS

This is a visualizing activity for both fiction and nonfiction texts that uses 3" × 3" sticky notes. It is effective because it allows students to move the images while creating them to meet the specific needs of the text. Other habits that are developed with this activity include inferring, predicting, and summarizing.

Procedure

1. Tell students that they are to draw either pictures or diagrams that are created in their minds as they read a section of text. For example, you can assign one sticky note snapshot per page of text. You should use this activity to build the habit of choosing the most important information to visualize. Tell students to draw the most important concept that the author tried to teach on each page (or in each section). They should not copy any visuals that are already in the text. (Students who do not like drawing can describe what they see in their minds with written words.) Figure 14 shows a sample sticky note snapshot with a corresponding section of text.

Figure 14.   Sample of a Sticky Note Snapshot With a Science Text

Escape Velocity

Suppose you walk outside your space station on Mars. You throw a baseball straight up into the air. If you are not superhuman, the ball will rise for a while and then fall because of the planet's gravity. If your arm were strong enough, however, you could make the ball escape beyond the pull of gravity and it would continue out into space indefinitely.

The speed needed to throw a ball so that it can escape a planet's gravity pull is called "escape velocity." This velocity is related to the mass of the planet. If the planet is very massive, then its escape velocity is high because the gravity is strong. A less massive planet wouldn't require as much force to defeat gravity's pull. For example, you don't need to have a strong arm to throw a ball out into space from an asteroid.

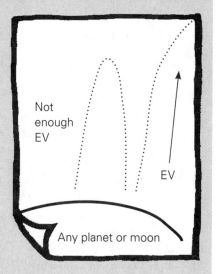

The escape velocity of the Earth is around 25,000 m.p.h., whereas that of the moon is only 5,300 m.p.h. You would need a strong arm on both the Earth and the moon to launch a ball into space. Another factor influencing escape velocity is how far you are from the planet's (or moon's) center. The further away you are from the core, the lower the escape velocity.

2. Students can include a brief written explanation on the front or back of each sticky note snapshot. If there is time, have them share with a partner what they drew and why.

3. When they finish reading, have students place their snapshots in a photo album (or on a poster) dedicated to that text, with captions written below or above the snapshots.

4. Use the snapshots to scaffold writing responses.

TEXT STRUCTURE GRAPHIC ORGANIZERS

This activity trains students to recognize the common forms of text structure. Good readers automatically consider how the text is structured in order to improve comprehension (Alvermann & Phelps, 2001). Even a quick glance at the title and headings of a text often can tell a reader how the author constructed the text. Yet many texts do not give obvious clues, and the reader has to take a closer look at embedded clues to help figure out the structure.

Remind students that a text may contain more than one (or even all) of the types of text structures that follow. The author, for instance, could describe a problem and then its causes with a cause-and-effect paragraph, then compare and contrast possible solutions, and then persuade the reader to lean toward one solution.

Procedure

1. Show students grade-level reading samples that have the text structure you wish to teach.

2. Circle the signal words and phrases that indicate the type of text structure.

3. Model how to fill in the graphic organizer for the text. (See Table 10 for samples and ideas.)

4. Have students help you fill in the boxes and outer details of the chosen graphic organizer. Discuss the hierarchical nature of most texts: overall purpose or main idea, then supporting main points, and finally details to support the main points.

5. Give students another text to read and another organizer that they can fill in while working in groups or pairs.

6. Optional: Have students use the graphic organizers to write their own texts based on the structures. The more familiar students are with the structures in their own writing, the better they can use them for reading (and the better they get at writing, too).

7. Give students a choice as to how they want to organize and visualize their thoughts. It might be one of the graphic organizers in Table 10, a sketch, or even an outline.

THIEVES

Many teachers employ the services of rather intimidating textbooks to provide instructional support in the classroom. These books are difficult for many students to read. THIEVES, CATAPULT Into Literature, and Text Structure Organizing activities give struggling readers some tricks of the textbook reading trade. Eventually, these activities can build prereading habits that will remain with students for as long as they read textbooks.

THIEVES (adapted from Manz, 2002) is an acronym that helps students go through all the necessary prereading steps before diving into a textbook chapter: title, headings, introduction, everything they know, visuals, end-of-chapter materials, and "so what?" It is a way to get students to build extensive knowledge of the text even before they read the first "normal" words of a chapter.

Procedure

1. Tell students something such as "We now get to become information 'thieves.' Let's see how much information we can 'steal' from the chapter before we actually read it."

2. Model how to go through each of the items in Table 11 as you look at the chapter. Use an overhead to write down the information. You can use the reproducible THIEVES Practice form (at the end of this chapter on page 97) with boxes for each letter, and can give students a THIEVES Bookmark (page 96) to fill in as they read.

3. After going through steps 1 and 2, have students use the THIEVES Practice form in pairs with another section of text.

Table 10. Organizing Text Structure

Text Structure	Purpose	Features	Key Terms	Graphic Organizer
Description	To explain an idea, person, place, or thing	Focus on one thing and its components	• is, are • consists of • also • this, that • in fact • for instance • most important	
Sequence	To describe the order of events or how to do or make something	The specific order of events or steps	• first, second • then, before, now • not long after • while • finally	
Cause and Effect	To explain why something happens or exists	Reasons and results	• so • so that • because of • as a result of • since • in order to	
Persuasion	To get the reader to act or to agree with one side of an issue or argument	Both sides presented; one side is favored; counterarguments addressed	• granted, despite • you must admit • then again • we should • it is important • therefore, even though	
Compare and Contrast	To show how subjects are alike and different	Two or more items with similarities and differences	• differs from • similar to • by contrast • unlike • similarly • yet, although, but, however, on the other hand • either...or, not only... but also	
Problem and Solution	Presents a problem situation and possible solutions	A problem, along with pluses and minuses of all solutions	• the main difficulty • one possible solution is • one challenge • therefore, this led to, so that • if...then, thus	

Table 11. THIEVES Sample Session

Component	What the Teacher Says and Does to Model
Title	What does the title tell us? Let's think of all the possibilities.
Headings	What do the headings tell us? They are the minititles of each section. What questions can we make from them that we think the section will answer? Let's also look at the table of contents, ask some questions, and make some predictions.
Introduction	Read the chapter introduction if there is one and think about it. Read the first paragraph of normal chapter text as well. Why do we think the author wrote the text?
Everything I know	Jot down all the facts and ideas about the topic that you think will be helpful for understanding. Create some questions about your own knowledge that you think the text might answer. Use the back of your paper, if needed.
Visuals	Let's look at all the diagrams, charts, and pictures. Let's read the captions. Why did the author include them? Can we think of any questions about them?
End-of-chapter material	Let's look at the end of the chapter to read any summaries (Don't ever forget to read the summary! It will save a lot of time.) and to see which questions the author thought were important. This can help us focus on what the author's purpose is. Let's try to guess the answers to a few questions using the information we have gathered so far. Write down a couple questions that look important. Also, we should notice every boldface or italicized word, especially if it is a new word or has a new meaning in this subject area. Look at any other text clue that might strengthen your initial idea (i.e., make you a richer thief).
So what?	Now, let's ask why we are reading this text. Why might I be interested in it? How might it connect to my life? Why does the teacher or our state want me to know this? Why did the author take the time to write this? For money? To teach us about the topic? For artistic expression? To improve my life somehow? For future classes?

THINK-PAIR-SHARE

A Think-Pair-Share (TPS) is a quick (2–5 minutes) verbal interaction between two or three students that allows them to quickly process the academic language and content being learned. TPS is not just a background knowledge activity, so also keep it in mind for building other habits and for the during- and postreading stages. TPS can be very effective during teacher presentations for creating "breaks" that push students to organize thoughts well enough to verbalize them. TPS also allows a student to hear how another person is processing the learning, which further builds background knowledge.

You can use TPS in many different areas of instruction, such as vocabulary, content concepts, opinions, compare-and-contrast activities, sharing parts of homework, summaries of text or visuals, connecting to background knowledge or other classes, making predictions or inferences, and solving problems.

Procedure

1. Create a question or prompt that will get students to use their background knowledge and experience to answer it. Table 12 offers tips for generating Think-Pair-Share questions or prompts.

2. Have students think in silence for 30–60 seconds to mentally prepare what they will say. They can also write down thoughts.

3. Put students into pairs. During the pair work, students should do the following:

- Face their partner, show interest, and listen actively. They can even take notes.
- Take turns talking.
- Stay on the topic.
- Remember what their partner says in order to share it with the class later.

Table 12.   Tips for Generating Think-Pair-Share Questions or Prompts
1. Create questions or prompts that zoom in on key content concepts in the text and relate to previous learning: • What was the Magna Carta and why was it important?   • Why do authors use metaphors to enhance a story? Give examples from our last book.   • Draw and explain how the circulatory system interacts with the respiratory system.   • Explain how a certain quotation from the story proves that the character fits your description.   • Explain how to divide fractions.
2. Create open-ended questions or prompts that connect to students' lives and allow for personalized, divergent responses: • If you were a colonist, would you have...? Why?   • How does our community deal with waste and pollution?   • Describe how acids and bases are used at your house.   • If you found a wallet with no ID, what would you do? Why?
3. Create questions or prompts for academic skills and other habits that you want to emphasize while reading and throughout the presentation, lesson, unit, or year. These skills might include generating questions, summarizing, predicting, inferring, classifying, persuading, evaluating, analyzing, comparing, and so on: • How might this war be similar to the Civil War?   • What were the causes and effects of the first Gulf War?   • Generate two below-the-surface questions about molecular bonds.   • Summarize how to solve equations by using the substitution method.   • What can you infer about the character's feelings from her actions?
4. Focus and Connect (FoCo): Create questions or prompts that focus students back on the author's purpose and connect the text to the essential standards for which you are using it: • What does this have to do with our goal of learning the many ways in which different people helped in the war?   • How does this connect to our objective of learning how to persuade others?

- Give reasons for any opinions, such as evidence from the book, class discussions, or one's own life.

- Use the vocabulary and academic language that you have modeled.

- Ask their partner questions that call for clarification and evidence: Do you mean that...? Why do you think that? Where does it say that? (Caution students to be polite and respectful in their questioning of one another.)

4. After pair time, ask students to share with the class what their partners said. This forces them to listen and also publicly validates what each partner has said.

Variations

- **Double Prompt Pair-Share:** Create two different questions for the TPS, one for each student, so they cannot simply say things such as "ditto" or "I agree" or "you said my answer."

- **Think-Pair-Square:** After pairs are done sharing with one another, have them turn to another pair to share. This gives students a chance to share with three people instead of the entire class. It also gives students a chance to compare and synthesize ideas as a group of four.

- Insert various reading and writing components. For example, you could have TWPS (Think-Write [Quickwrite]-Pair-Share), TPWS (Think-Pair-Write-Share), RPS (Read-Pair-Share), RWPS (Read-Write-Pair-Share), and so on.

Reflection Questions

1. Why do connecting to background knowledge and visualizing matter so much in reading? What kinds of background knowledge are most helpful?

2. Choose a short text that you will teach. Write down your connections and visualizations as you read. Were they helpful? How?

3. What are the challenges that diverse students might face in connecting to background knowledge?

4. Write an inquiry question for this chapter's habit and a teaching activity. Gather evidence over time and make adjustments based on student work (e.g., How can I best help students develop visualization habit, evidenced by quickwrites and lab write-ups, using the .... activity?).

NOTES: _____

_____

_____

_____

_____

_____

_____

_____

_____

_____

_____

ANTICIPATION GUIDE

Topic/Text

Before reading, look at each statement and decide whether you agree or not. Put the letter that corresponds to your opinion on the line on the left side. Write your reason under "Why?" After you read the text, do the same on the right side of the page.

A = Agree strongly   a = Agree somewhat   d = Disagree somewhat   D = Disagree strongly

Before Reading   After Reading

_____ 1.

Why?   Why?

_____ 2.

Why?   Why?

_____ 3.

Why?   Why?

_____ 4.

Why?   Why?

Building Reading Comprehension in Grades 6–12: A Toolkit of Classroom Activities (second edition) by Jeff Zwiers © 2010. Newark, DE: International Reading Association. May be copied for classroom use.

BACKGROUND KNOWLEDGE BACKPACK

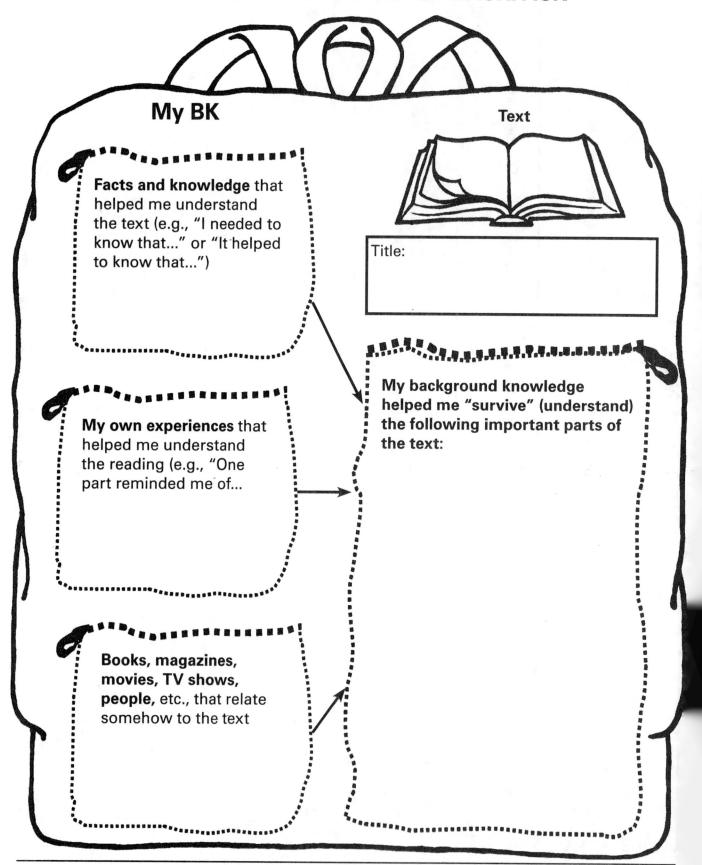

My BK

Facts and knowledge that helped me understand the text (e.g., "I needed to know that..." or "It helped to know that...")

My own experiences that helped me understand the reading (e.g., "One part reminded me of...

Books, magazines, movies, TV shows, people, etc., that relate somehow to the text

Text

Title:

My background knowledge helped me "survive" (understand) the following important parts of the text:

CATAPULT INTO LITERATURE PRACTICE

Covers (front and back): What do the covers (words and pictures) show us about what we might visualize in the story? What does the back cover tell us about the story (the words, pictures, or both)?

Author: What is the author's background? Has he or she written any other stories that might be like this? What were they about? Are the same characters in this story as in the others?

Title: What does the title lead us to predict about the story? What questions do you have about the title?

Audience: For whom was this story written? Old, young; male, female; city-dwelling, country-dwelling; past, present, or future readers?

Page 1: Read page 1 and think about what the story might be about.

Underlying message or purpose: With what you have thought about so far, what message or purpose might the author have for the readers? What might be the deeper meaning? How might it connect to your life?

Look at any visuals, maps, and sketches in the text. As we look through the story, what do the pictures, sketches, diagrams, or maps tell us?

Time, Place, Characters: From clues so far, what can we say about when the story takes place, where it takes place, and the characters? What can we guess might happen to the characters?

CATAPULT INTO LITERATURE PRACTICE

Covers (front and back): What do the covers (words and pictures) show us about what we might visualize in the story? What does the back cover tell us about the story (the words, pictures, or both)?

Author: What is the author's background? Has he or she written any other stories that might be like this? What were they about? Are the same characters in this story as in the others?

Title: What does the title lead us to predict about the story? What questions do you have about the title?

Audience: For whom was this story written? Old, young; male, female; city-dwelling, country-dwelling; past, present, or future readers?

Page 1: Read page 1 and think about what the story might be about.

Underlying message or purpose: With what you have thought about so far, what message or purpose might the author have for the readers? What might be the deeper meaning? How might it connect to your life?

Look at any visuals, maps, and sketches in the text. As we look through the story, what do the pictures, sketches, diagrams, or maps tell us?

Time, Place, Characters: From clues so far, what can we say about when the story takes place, where it takes place, and the characters? What can we guess might happen to the characters?

THIEVES BOOKMARK

T   **Title**—Read the title of the chapter and predict what the chapter is about.

H   **Headings**—Look at all headings and the table of contents. Turn them into questions that the text will probably answer.

I   **Introduction**—Read the introduction and any questions or summaries at the beginning. Predict the main idea.

E   **Everything I Know About It**— Think of everything I have seen, read, or done that may relate to this text.

V   **Visuals**—Look at pictures, graphs, diagrams, or maps, and read their captions. Notice lists with letters or numbers that point out important information. Read all the notes in the margins and notice **bold** and *italicized* words. Make notes (or a web) of what I plan to learn.

E   **End-of-Chapter Material**—Read end-of-chapter material, such as summaries or questions that I will try to answer by reading.

S   **So What?**—Why did the author write this? Why am I reading this? Knowing the purpose helps me comprehend. (S can also stand for text structure.)

THIEVES BOOKMARK

T   **Title**—Read the title of the chapter and predict what the chapter is about.

H   **Headings**—Look at all headings and the table of contents. Turn them into questions that the text will probably answer.

I   **Introduction**—Read the introduction and any questions or summaries at the beginning. Predict the main idea.

E   **Everything I Know About It**— Think of everything I have seen, read, or done that may relate to this text.

V   **Visuals**—Look at pictures, graphs, diagrams, or maps, and read their captions. Notice lists with letters or numbers that point out important information. Read all the notes in the margins and notice **bold** and *italicized* words. Make notes (or a web) of what I plan to learn.

E   **End-of-Chapter Material**—Read end-of-chapter material, such as summaries or questions that I will try to answer by reading.

S   **So What?**—Why did the author write this? Why am I reading this? Knowing the purpose helps me comprehend. (S can also stand for text structure.)

THIEVES PRACTICE

T From the title, predict what the text is about.

H Look at all headings (and the table of contents) and then turn two of them into important questions that you think the text will answer (Why...? How...?).

I Use the introduction and first paragraph to predict the main idea (or to create a big question you think the text will answer).

E Write down everything you know about the topic. Use the back of this paper, if necessary. Circle any of your notes you would like to know more about, or write a question about them.

V List three important visuals found in the text and predict how they will help you understand the text.

E Guess the answers for the end-of-chapter questions, read any summaries, and write down every boldface or italicized word.

S So what? Why do you think the author wrote this text? What does its structure tell you?

THIEVES PRACTICE

T From the title, predict what the text is about.

H Look at all headings (and the table of contents) and then turn two of them into important questions that you think the text will answer (Why...? How...?).

I Use the introduction and first paragraph to predict the main idea (or to create a big question you think the text will answer).

E Write down everything you know about the topic. Use the back of this paper, if necessary. Circle any of your notes you would like to know more about, or write a question about them.

V List three important visuals found in the text and predict how they will help you understand the text.

E Guess the answers for the end-of-chapter questions, read any summaries, and write down every boldface or italicized word.

S So what? Why do you think the author wrote this text? What does its structure tell you?

VISUALIZATION STATIONS

CHAPTER 5

Making Inferences and Predictions

* * *

The more you infer and predict,
the more chances you have
of being right.

Humans are wired to infer and predict. We watch people around us and look at their facial expressions to see how they feel. We make inferences about motives when we listen to politicians. We predict a book's appeal by the picture on the cover. We infer that a restaurant is expensive because it has valet parking.

Making an inference in reading is the process of combining the current text information with one's own experience in order to create meaning that is not directly stated in the text (Dole, Duffy, Roehler, & Pearson, 1991). It means creating connections and making educated guesses that go beyond the author's exact words or images. Inference might be seen as taking little "thinking steps" off the safe path of the literal and seeing if they lead to where the author intends. It means making educated guesses and filling in the blanks that are not in the text. If the inference is correct, then we have learned something new and will have that learning better anchored in our brains. If it is wrong, then we *still* learn something new—to make a different inference in a similar situation in future texts.

An inference about future information in a text is a prediction. We use the text clues and our background knowledge to predict what will happen next in a story or what we will learn later in a text. We then go through the text to confirm, discard, change, or make new predictions, based on new evidence that comes up. Prediction provides us with motivation and purpose for reading. It also helps the mind prepare itself to understand the upcoming ideas in the text. As we predict, we need to reflect on the main idea in order to make a logical prediction. This necessitates a certain amount of focus on text details and an ongoing handle on the main idea.

We must teach students to effectively and automatically mix the text and their background knowledge to make good inferences and predictions. If students rely too heavily on the text, they will miss a large amount of deeper meaning; if they rely too heavily on background knowledge, they will lose the direction of the text.

Types of Inferences

Text-to-Text Inferences

These inferences allow us to connect one part of a text to another. For a particular section of text, comprehension depends, in large part, on text information that preceded it. Proficient readers remember what was read earlier in a text and then connect it to what they are currently reading (Keene & Zimmermann, 2007). For example, readers need to remember characters, their traits, and their relationships; the order of events; the setting; causes and effects; foreshadowing; and key vocabulary terms within a text as they read. Authors usually expect the reader to make these text-to-text inferences within the specific text being read. They also may assume that the reader has read certain other texts, but authors have much less control over these text-to-other-texts connections.

Text-to-Self and Text-to-World Inferences

When we make inferences, we connect the text information to our own experience and knowledge of the world. For example, I may think of the tree as a symbol of growth in a story, or the dry lake as a metaphor for death. As I read on, these inferences might be confirmed, perhaps in a class discussion, or we may conclude that they were nothing more than a tree and a dry lake. I may infer that, because I know ice floats, all other solid versions of a liquid will float, and I would be wrong. Many authors expect readers to make text-to-self and text-to-world inferences—they want us to apply what we read and learn to past or present situations, problems, and settings in the world.

Teachers must create environments in which students feel safe about making many and varied inferences. Students should be encouraged to discuss, interpret, define, argue, and write down their inferences about the text and how it relates to their lives and the world around them. Inference, because it extends past the known, is one of the main ingredients of creative thought and expanded learning.

The following questions can be powerful igniters of text-to-text and text-to-self and text-to-world inferences. Ideally, we can figure out ways to make such inference-generating questions automatic for students.

Who is doing the action? Why?

How does a part fit into the overall text?

What are the effects of an event, both psychological and physical?

What feelings does a person experience?

What is the author's purpose?

What if I had been in that situation?

How does this apply to my life or the world around me?

What does this word mean?

Teachers have used this type of "during-reading" prompting for both instruction and assessment. It is an effective way to get students to (a) stop and think while they are reading, and (b) show us what they are thinking as they read. If their predictions (inferences, questions, summaries, and so forth) seem to distract or hinder comprehension, then we can take steps to build such habits in our lessons and activities. Figure 15 demonstrates inference and prediction practice with a short story that has readers guessing (inferring and predicting) right away, starting with the title.

Figure 15. Inference and Prediction Practice

Any predictions at this point? Why?

_____

_____

_____

_____

Any inferences or predictions at this point? Why?

_____

_____

_____

_____

A Mosaic of Memories

"Put your boots on. We'll find it this time," my dad said as he set his spy novel on the table. He was talking about the lost whiskey factory that supplied the surrounding area with illegal moonshine during the prohibition. Neighbors said the factory was hidden several miles up the creek that flowed near our house. The prohibition police never found it. I doubted we would ever find it either—that is, if it ever existed. But the search wasn't the only reason to journey up there.

The other reason was the patio. The back patio was a collection of the big flat rocks we (I) had lugged down from the headwaters of the creek. The patio was only half-done. I wondered if we would ever complete it.

"Who's gonna carry the rocks?" I asked.

"Does it really matter? Come on, let's go," he said with a grin. I knew what that meant.

We crossed the road and meandered through the bushes to start yet another journey up the creek. The creek was big enough for salmon to swim up each fall and spawn in the little pools.

"These two began their lives here, swam hundreds of miles through the ocean, and now have returned to the same crik, just as their parents did--without even a single map or gas station along the way to ask directions! I hope this cycle never ends. It's one of the wonders of life that these noble ocean fish begin and end their lives in the forest. A thousand years ago it would have been just like this. Hopefully it'll be like this a thousand years from now."

Further up the creek, the walls of the tiny valley closed in and everything got steeper. The rocks got bigger...and flatter. I thought he might forget, but he never forgot. He had begun his search for that clever and elusive quarry—large patio rocks.

Then in a flash I saw him spring in for the kill. "Look at this one! It's perfect!" he exclaimed. A "perfect" 40-pound rectangular rock was snatched up before it could get away and deposited into my backpack. "Good exercise, eh?" he said. We were still going up...and still looking for rocks. Two more smaller rocks were soon caught and added to the ancient green army pack that was digging into my lower back.

Then I fell into a hole. As I pulled myself out, I looked down and found the proof. There at my feet was a large ceramic moonshine jug, looking as if it had been left there after the shooting of an old movie. To my dad, it was like finding the El Dorado treasure.

"We found it! Wait'll your mother sees this!" he continued. I didn't think mom would be particularly excited about the dirty jug, or her filthy son and husband, but she would be happy to see that we were now three rocks closer to finishing the patio. She had often mentioned that these rocks could be purchased at a nearby garden store with free delivery. But my dad wouldn't think of it. Why wouldn't he just buy the rocks?

(continued)

Figure 15. Inference and Prediction Practice (*continued*)

| Any inferences (about meaning) or predictions (beyond the text) at this point? Why?

 _____
 _____
 _____
 _____ | I was exhausted by the time we reached the cabin. "Now let's warm up your feet. " Dad said, as he began to build a fire.

 Today, the dusty moonshine jug now rests in the corner of the attic. My father barely remembers our quest for that unholy grail, 22 years ago. He sits in his chair, looking out the window and nodding off to sleep. I build a fire and he puts his feet up on the hearth to warm them.

 I walk outside and look down at the almost-finished patio of flat rocks, among them the famous 40-pounder, caught on Jugday. I finally begin to see why he didn't want to buy the rocks. Perhaps it wasn't frugality. Perhaps he had planned all along that some day our patio of rocks would be a collection of memories.

 "Put your boots on. We'll find it this time," I say to my son, as he watches a salmon splash its way up the creek |

Modeling

Teaching students how to make helpful inferences and predictions while reading requires lots of modeling. Repeated exposure and teacher scaffolding (e.g., asking the questions that lead to good predictions and inferences) are the best ways for students to cultivate comprehension-enhancing habits. The danger of modeling can be too much teacher talk. Ensure that students have frequent opportunities to do what you are modeling or they will tune out. Encourage risk taking but always emphasize how important it is to build overall meaning of the text—and not to stray too far away from it. Students can get overly distracted from the text's meaning when they haphazardly construct predictions and inferences that are too disconnected from textual evidence.

Tools Chart for Inferring and Predicting

Table 13 shows the usefulness of this chapter's activities for various content areas. On the left side of the table, a √ in a column indicates that the activity is useful in that stage of reading. On the right side of the table, a √ in a column indicates that the activity is helpful for comprehension of common texts used in that content area. A √√ on the right side of the table means that the activity is especially helpful for that type of text and that you should try it as soon as possible.

Table 13. When and Where to Use the Activities in Chapter 5							
Before Reading	During Reading	After Reading	Activity	Social Studies	Science	English/ EL
	✓	✓	Cause and Effect Timeline	✓✓	✓	✓
	✓	✓	Character Report Card	✓✓		✓✓
✓	✓		Dialogue Comic Strip	✓✓	✓✓	✓
✓	✓		Image Inferences and Predictions	✓	✓	✓✓
✓			Inference Advertisements	✓✓	✓	✓
✓	✓		Prediction Basketball	✓✓	✓	✓
✓	✓		Prediction Chart	✓	✓	✓✓
✓			Prediction Path	✓	✓	✓✓
	✓		Prediction Signals	✓	✓	✓✓
✓			Quotation Café	✓	✓	✓✓
✓	✓		Sticky Symbols and Drawings	✓✓	✓	✓
	✓	✓	T+B=I Inference Machines	✓✓	✓	✓✓

Activities for Inferring and Predicting

CAUSE AND EFFECT TIMELINE

The Cause and Effect Timeline can be used for narrative and expository texts. The graphic organizer asks students not only to determine the sequence of events in a story or historical account but also to establish or infer the causes of those events. Students can, if you so desire, be asked to draw lines to connect the events from the upper part of the graphic organizer to the causes in the lower part. You can use this activity for stories, novels, history texts, biographies, science observations, and more.

Procedure

1. Make a copy of the Cause and Effect Timeline reproducible at the end of this chapter on page 117. Cut out the two halves lengthwise, and fasten them together side by side to make one long timeline as follows:

2. Above the thick line, write events with or without year dates. Each event should go above one of the lower arrows.

3. Put the causes of the events below the line, inside the arrows. Causes can be inferred. Each cause should be directly under its corresponding event. Make sure you can support each cause with evidence.

4. Draw additional lines, if applicable, to connect upper events to additional causes below; that is, some causes also will contribute to other events in addition to the ones written directly above them, or some events will, in turn, cause new events. Therefore, these new lines you draw will be diagonal. Students should be able to explain why they draw each additional line.

5. Have students share their timelines with partners and describe their inferred causes and effects. Use language such as "One possible cause might have been…because…"

6. Connect more timeline halves, if necessary.

Variations

• Have students use the timeline to write a summary of a text that the timeline describes. Students should describe their inferences and their reasons for them.

- Fill in an empty timeline to show students how to create a logical story or account using the timeline's event and cause categories. Explain how different events usually will have different paragraphs in the story.
- Have students take notes on the timeline about the sequence of events in a video or science experiment and then write a report on the experience.

CHARACTER REPORT CARD

This is an engaging activity in which students get to "grade" the characters in a book or history chapter on certain traits or qualities. The students must use evaluation thinking skills and must find evidence for their choices.

Procedure

1. Choose a story and decide which characters you would like to evaluate. Students can help you decide.

2. Brainstorm a list of up to four possible traits that the characters have in varying degrees. Traits can be positive or negative. (Have some traits in mind before generating a list with the students.)

3. List the character names on the left side of a sheet of paper and write the traits across the top, alternating with columns for grades, as shown:

Character	Courage Grade	Comments (Evidence)	Tenacity Grade	Comments (Evidence)
Jen	A	Because she faced up to Ron	B	She kept saving $
Octavio	B–	Lied about necklace	C	Quit school to work
Mirko	C	Let his brother…		

Following are some possible traits you may want to use:

Self-assured	Mischievous	Caring
Secretive	Creative	Naïve
Persevering	Patriotic	
Greedy	Patient	

4. Generate a grading system such as the classic A-B-C-D-F system; a system of points; designations of "Approaching Standard," "Meeting Standard," and "Exceeding Standard"; or some other system.

5. Show students how to start with the trait columns before entering the grades. Find evidence in the text for each character's traits and then discuss the grades with students. For example, you can model phrases such as, "I think she deserves an A in courage because she...."

6. Model for students how to respectfully disagree with another opinion and how to quote evidence. Instruct them to give more weight to evidence in the second half of the narrative than in the beginning, given that people change during stories.

7. Have students do this activity with partners or in groups. Have students brainstorm the language they can use to describe their thinking, such as "As the story progressed she became more...because...."

DIALOGUE COMIC STRIP

This activity helps students to summarize and infer conversations that are important to the text. The Dialogue Comic Strip can be used with narrative or expository text. With expository text, the students must infer and empathize with the relationship between two objects, people, animals, or concepts, and must generate a possible dialogue that shows that the students understand the key ideas in the text.

For example, in science class, a snake might say to a mouse, "I have adapted teeth that contain poison to kill you." The mouse replies, "I have adapted my ears to hear you slithering 10 feet away. Bye!" Or a geologist may say to a volcano, "Are you about to erupt?" It might reply, "No, I'm just venting a little steam." In social studies, a colonist may say, "King George, we really need to talk about this problem of taxation without representation. Our rights are...." In math, one side of an equation may say to the other, "If you get to be divided by 42, then my side gets to be divided by 42, too!"

Procedure

1. Model this process with several different texts if students have not done this activity often.

2. Give each student a copy of the Dialogue Comic Strip reproducible sheet located at the end of this chapter on page 118. You can also use Comic Life software to create templates or products on the computer. Tell students to modify or create three of the most important conversations from the text and fit them in the dialogue bubbles. Students should not copy any actual dialogue from the text. Encourage them to synthesize and infer dialogues that might have happened, but point out that they should have evidence to support their inferred dialogues.

3. Have students put the speakers' names in the parentheses. They also can add quick drawings of the speakers, if desired.

4. Have the students write an explanation in each lower box for why each conversation was important. They should relate it to the main idea of the text.

5. Have students share their responses with a partner or group.

6. Share one or two student examples on the board or overhead projector.

Variation

Have students infer conversations that happened before or after the events of the text.

IMAGE INFERENCES AND PREDICTIONS

Images can be used to teach students to infer and predict. Images including video can build the habit of using clues to build meaning. This is a visual way to train students' brains to use evidence in order to make logical inferences. This habit then transfers over to reading as students use evidence from the text (and pictures) and combine it with background knowledge.

Procedure

1. Bring into the classroom images or video clips such as paintings, photos, pictures of sculptures, news events, and so forth.

2. Cover the image and display it for students. One part at a time, uncover the image (I use sticky notes) and, at each point, have students think to themselves about what they infer the image is or means and why. If it is a video clip, play a short piece and keep playing it in pieces. Students can use a sentence starter such as: "I infer that...because in the past I have seen that....."

3. Have students share their ideas in pairs and, finally, share as a whole class.

4. Using a two-column chart, keep track of students' guesses on one side and their reasons for each guess on the other. Students can also keep such a chart in their binders.

5. Have students use each new clue to make another guess about the meaning of the image or clip.

6. When finished, discuss the different inferences and predictions, or discuss different interpretations (i.e., if you use an abstract painting or obscure video clip).

7. Discuss how this habit can help during reading.

INFERENCE ADVERTISEMENTS

This activity uses a series of magazine advertisements to show how authors expect readers to make inferences in order to influence us. This activity grabs students' attention because they see such advertisements on a daily basis, and they do not like to be unknowingly influenced into buying or doing anything. This activity is motivating and effective at garnering class participation. Remember to model the questions that generate the inferences, then to have students notice these questions. For example, ask, How does this saying influence potential buyers?

Procedure

1. Choose an advertisement to use with the class. Find a magazine with ads that put a clever line or two of text combined with odd and eye-catching pictures. Show only the clever saying from the advertisement on an overhead projector, without the picture. Ask students what they think it means.

2. Show the full advertisement with the picture and ask students its meaning.

3. Ask students what the reader has to know to understand the advertisement or to think it is clever.

4. Ask students why the advertisement's writers thought they could sell the product in this way. This can foster very fruitful discussion about people's motivations.

5. Make a chart with space for a description of the picture, the saying, and the background knowledge that all feed into one space for the inference, as shown:

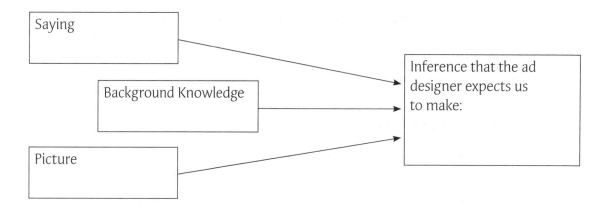

6. Ask students to bring in advertisements and have them lead the class in this same activity.

Variations

• Show the picture with the text covered and ask students to guess what the advertisement is for and what the slogan might be.

• Cover parts of the picture and unveil them, one part at a time, as students guess the advertisement's meaning.

• Bring in advertisements for the same type of product from different magazines and analyze how and why they are different.

PREDICTION BASKETBALL

This is a kinesthetic and cooperative activity that puts a little more fun into making predictions. It also can be used for other comprehension habits as a way of mixing up answers and creating random participation.

Procedure

1. Have students read a text and stop at a point you designate. Have each student write one major prediction on a half sheet of paper, along with his or her evidence for the prediction.

2. Put a makeshift basketball hoop (wastebasket, box, or coffee can) somewhere in the class. You can take it down and move it around to help students who are further away and to avoid having students get out of their seats.

3. Have students crumple up their predictions and try to throw them into the "basket."

4. Open and read the predictions that make it into the basket. Quickly discuss the prediction and agree if there is enough evidence to support it.

5. Have students randomly pick up the rest of the predictions that did not go into the basket, one prediction per student, and have each student read a prediction to a partner. Some students will not have one—they can just listen and ask for evidence or share a new prediction. Have the pairs discuss the quality of the predictions and the reasons each predictor had for his or her prediction.

PREDICTION CHART

This activity is helpful for teaching students to use good evidence for making predictions. It breaks down the process and shows students how prediction should naturally happen in the brain while reading. The Prediction Chart is most helpful for narratives, but I have seen science and social studies teachers use it successfully as well.

Procedure

1. Discuss with students why it is important to predict while reading. Create a list of reasons on the board. Discuss predictions about television shows, movies, and stories. Remind students that they are to be detectives who look for clues and put them together to solve a case (which equates to understanding a story, in this instance).

2. Make a transparency from the reproducible Prediction Chart at the end of this chapter on page 119 and put it on an overhead projector. Start with the title of the movie (when you start with a movie, write *watch* or *look at* over the book icon to avoid confusion with the

word *read*) and have students predict what the movie is about as you fill in the first box of the top row.

3. Ask students why they predicted what they did. Put the answers in the second box in the top row.

4. Now show the first five minutes of the movie or video. Stop it and ask students if any of the title-based predictions came true. If so, note them in the third column of the top row.

5. Have students help you fill in the second row by making new predictions in the first column and providing evidence in the second column.

6. Continue with another short portion of the video and then repeat the above steps to fill in the third row.

7. Recommended: To avoid photocopying, have students create their own three-column prediction charts on their own sheets of paper.

Variation

Picture Predictions: For this variation, cover a text or picture. In front of the class, uncover successive parts of the picture and have students generate hypotheses based on prior experience about what they think the picture is or what they think the text says *and why*.

Write the predictions in the first column of the Prediction Chart and students' reasons for the predictions in the second column. Have them notice how many of their reasons come from background knowledge. As the text is uncovered and predictions are shared, model the process of discarding (pruning) conflicting predictions by crossing them out on the Prediction Chart. Emphasize the process of creating new hypotheses based on new or revised background knowledge and schemata.

PREDICTION PATH

This activity, adapted from the work of Wood (1988), helps students build the vital habit of focusing on initial text clues in order to predict a working main idea (as well as theme and purpose) for reading. In this activity, a reader taps into background knowledge to create a possible "map" for progressing through a text, predicting, and gathering important information along the way to "reach the destination" of effective comprehension.

Procedure

1. Remind students that the author wrote the text for a reason. Model for students how to look at the title and other initial clues to predict this purpose. Ask, Why do we think the author wrote this?

2. Predict the purpose and write it (in pencil) in the oval at the top of the reproducible Prediction Path form at the end of this chapter on page 120. (You can fill in yours on an overhead transparency and students can be given blank photocopies for their own future work.) Students should use pencils so that they can make changes during reading. Remind students that the purpose can change. Around the oval, you can put the clues and evidence for the purpose you generated.

3. In the signs along the road on the form, put major clues, headings, and ideas that help you make your way to the destination (purpose). Around the signs, you can put supporting details and paraphrases that describe the importance of the sign's heading. The signs can be filled in at any reading stage: before, during, or after.

4. Revise the purpose while reading as the text changes your initial ideas for it.

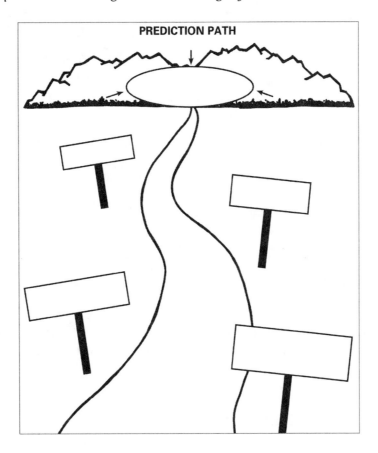

PREDICTION SIGNALS

Proficient readers have become accustomed over many years and pages to automatically recognize key signals in a text. These signals, some of which are in the left column in Table 14, are academic words and phrases that help the reader predict the content and type of text coming up. They trigger the reader's brain to receive certain types of information that will help

Table 14. Prediction Signals	
If the Text Contains	**You Might Predict That You Will Find...**
A question	An answer
A subheading	Details that describe it
Therefore	A conclusion or outcome of previous text
For example Such as For instance In fact To illustrate this point	One or more examples that illustrate the main point of the paragraph or text
In other words That is Consists of Means	A definition or simpler explanation
However But Whereas On the other hand In contrast In comparison Yet	A difference or unexpected outcome
Just as Likewise Also Just like Similarly In the same way Moreover Furthermore	A continuation or comparison that shows similarities

to form the main idea. The activity gives needed practice for readers in the recognition and use of text signals so that eventually their use becomes unconscious and automatic.

Procedure

1. Teach signal words to students during a minilesson or over the course of studying a long text that contains them.

2. Model how to make a quick note in the margin or on a sticky note when you encounter a signal word. Then, model how to make a prediction from what you read.

3. Have students practice making predictions and have them share their predictions with partners.

4. You may want to make a poster from Table 14 to display in the classroom for students.

5. Optional: For some of the signals, try creating hand gestures to use during read-alouds. (For example, for the word *however*, I move my arm to the left and then quickly reverse it to the right.)

QUOTATION CAFÉ

This activity emulates a café setting where intellectuals share thoughts and opinions about the nature of life, literature, and the world. (Some teachers even have little tables and serve soft drinks.) It is an effective and fun prereading activity that works well for building students' oral language, prediction, and inference skills.

Procedure

1. Select important headings, quotations, or visuals (clues) from the text that students will read. Put them on small strips of paper or on note cards. If they are not all different clues, you can color code the same ones so that students don't talk to others with the same clue.

2. Tell students the title of the text to be read. You can also show an image, but don't give too much away.

3. Hand out one clue to each student and allow each student time to read and think about his or her particular clue in order to predict how it might fit into the overall meaning and main idea of the text.

4. Have students circulate around the classroom to get other opinions by reading their clues to other students. In pairs, students continue to guess the meaning and main idea of the text by using the clues.

5. Tell students to notice how their predictions improve as they hear more and more clues and predictions from other students.

6. Optional: Ask students to guess the sequence of their pieces in the text. They can line up in physical order according to their clues.

7. Lead a brief discussion on what the students predict the text is about.

8. Have students read the text. Stop them at times and have them check to see if their predictions about the main idea are correct.

STICKY SYMBOLS AND DRAWINGS

For this activity, students create symbols and drawings on sticky notes that become visual reminders of texts. Mental images help students to visualize text concepts and make them more likely to remain in long-term memory (Hyerle, 2008). In this activity, students use inference to create symbols and to fill in parts of drawings that are not explicitly mentioned in the text. Even the initial process of creating symbols as a class or in small groups is valuable.

Procedure

1. Explain concepts and ideas that might arise (e.g., character, metaphor, climax, compare and contrast, cause and effect) during comprehension of a difficult text. You may want to develop symbols for your class: For example, social studies classes may use symbols for greed, war, technology, art, religion, literature, disease, revolution, democracy, and lust for power.

2. Model how to create a symbol or drawing for a concept, and have students practice doing so in pairs. The symbols should not be too elaborate because they may be drawn many times.

3. Encourage students to identify ongoing concepts and themes in texts and to create corresponding symbols or drawings. Students can then draw symbols on sticky notes as they read a text.

4. You could even develop symbols for the comprehension habits in this book. When students catch themselves stopping to predict or summarize, they can quickly attach a sticky note with the corresponding symbol to the spot on the text. You can predraw the symbols in order to avoid having students stop too long when reading a text.

5. Encourage students to develop their own symbols and drawings because ownership is a large part of being able to independently use a skill or concept in lasting ways. Each time students finish a whole story's worth of drawings, they can organize the sticky notes on sheets of paper and keep all the drawings in their notebooks.

T+B=I INFERENCE MACHINES

Inference machines are visual organizers that show what the brain is doing when it makes an inference. The brain looks at the text, thinks about how the text relates to something similar in the reader's background, and then makes an assumption or guess that is connected to the main idea of the text in some way. The process is somewhat like an assembly line: The brain puts two things together—text information (T) and background knowledge (B)—to create a novel product of thinking—an inference (I). Hence, the title of the activity: T+B = I Inference Machines.

Procedure

1. Begin by modeling this activity for students on the board or screen. (See the reproducible form provided at the end of this chapter on page 121.) Pick an important (inference-worthy) part of the text and note it in the "text" box.

2. Although it seems logical (i.e., mathematical) to fill in the "Background" box next, readers tend to generate the inference next. To create this inference, use the text to make a

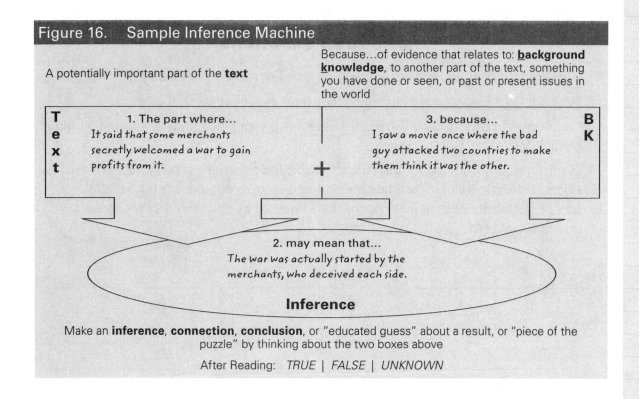

Figure 16. Sample Inference Machine

A potentially important part of the **text**

Because...of evidence that relates to: **background knowledge**, to another part of the text, something you have done or seen, or past or present issues in the world

T **e** **x** **t**

1. The part where...
It said that some merchants secretly welcomed a war to gain profits from it.

+

3. because...
I saw a movie once where the bad guy attacked two countries to make them think it was the other.

B **K**

2. may mean that...
The war was actually started by the merchants, who deceived each side.

Inference

Make an **inference**, **connection**, **conclusion**, or "educated guess" about a result, or "piece of the puzzle" by thinking about the two boxes above

After Reading: *TRUE | FALSE | UNKNOWN*

connection, conclusion, or educated guess about a result, prediction, or piece of the puzzle. Think of causes and effects, author's purposes, clues provided by the author, and vocabulary with new or multiple meanings.

3. Think about the reason for your inference based on background knowledge, another part of the same text, something you have done or seen, or past or present issues in the world. Put this in the "Because..." box. Figure 16 shows a filled-in inference machine.

Variation

Venn Diagram: This activity is a simplified version of the T+B=I Inference Machines activity. It works because many students already are familiar with Venn diagrams. You simply "mix" text information with background knowledge to create the inference in the middle section of a Venn diagram, as shown here:

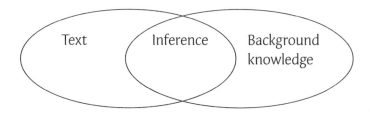

Text   Inference   Background knowledge

Reflection Questions

1. Why are predicting and making inferences important for comprehension?

2. Why is it OK if readers make incorrect predictions and inferences?

3. Choose a short text that you will teach. Write down your predictions before and during reading. Were they helpful? How?

4. Write an inquiry question for this chapter's habit and a teaching activity. Gather evidence over time and make adjustments based on student work (e.g., How can I best help students develop inference habits, evidenced by journal responses and test questions, using the .... activity?).

NOTES: _____

_____

_____

_____

_____

_____

_____

_____

_____

_____

_____

CAUSE AND EFFECT TIMELINE

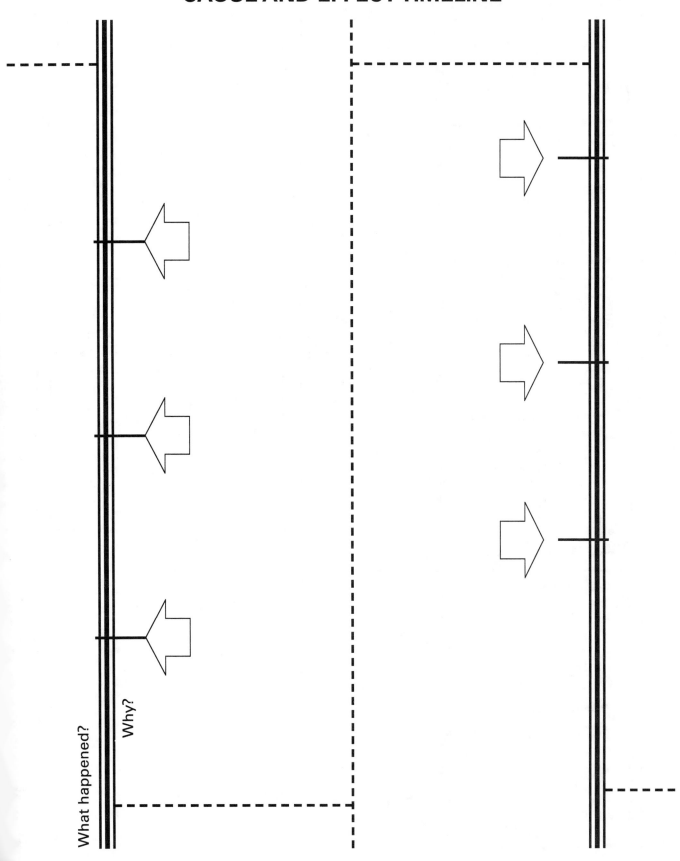

What happened?

Why?

DIALOGUE COMIC STRIP

Building Reading Comprehension in Grades 6–12: A Toolkit of Classroom Activities (second edition) by Jeff Zwiers © 2010. Newark, DE: International Reading Association. May be copied

PREDICTION CHART

Student Name _____

Text Title _____

Pg.	What do you think the next part is about? (Be specific)	Why? (Use evidence from text, pictures, and/or your prior knowledge)	READ	Was your prediction confirmed or not? How do you know?	Pg.
	Revised or New Prediction		READ		
	Revised or New Prediction		READ		

PREDICTION PATH

T+B = I INFERENCE MACHINES

A potentially important part of the **text**

Because...of evidence that relates to: **background knowledge**, to another part of the text, something you have done or seen, or past or present issues in the world

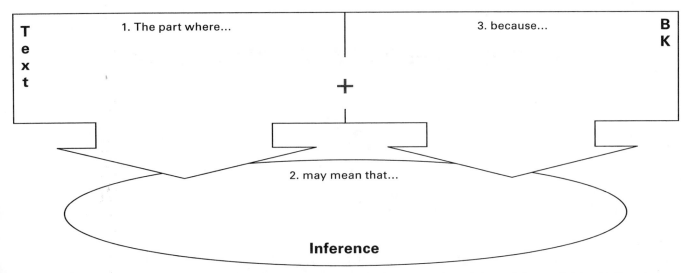

Make an **inference, connection, conclusion**, or "educated guess" about a result, or "piece of the puzzle" by thinking about the two boxes above

After Reading: *TRUE | FALSE | UNKNOWN*

A potentially important part of the **text**

Because...of evidence that relates to: **background knowledge**, to another part of the text, something you have done or seen, or past or present issues in the world

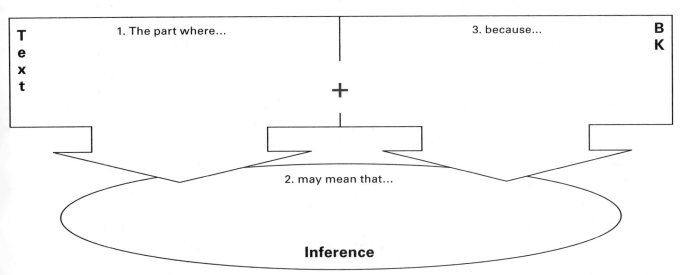

Make an **inference, connection, conclusion**, or "educated guess" about a result, or "piece of the puzzle" by thinking about the two boxes above

After Reading: *TRUE | FALSE | UNKNOWN*

CHAPTER

Generating and Answering Questions

* * *

A question is much more motivating

when it's your own.

Students are tired of answering questions. For years, they have sat in classes where a teacher or a text presents a long list of questions that they must answer promptly. Weeks of standardized tests, mostly composed of more questions, make matters worse. Students typically get praise or points for the right answers and sad looks or points off for the wrong answers. If boredom from these question sessions doesn't set in, frustration does. Rather than continue this stimulus–response game that covers standards on a cursory level at best, we need to prepare students to generate and answer their own questions. This habit gives students a much more personal investment into what they will think about and what they will look for as they read.

Why is questioning by the reader so important? Questions give us purpose for reading, and their answers help us actively shape the text's meaning (Ciardiello, 1998). Questions help us focus on the most important parts of text, and they help us to fill in the key information. Authors tend to write with several questions in mind that they intend to answer with their text. When we ask similar questions during reading, they will lead us to where the author wants us to go. The question–answer combination (in concert with inferences and predictions) becomes a set of "bearings" that we take in order to find our position in a text, analogous to the use of stars for navigation by sailors. We hold a question in our minds, such as How can I help students build the habit of questioning? (our question for this chapter), and this question becomes a post upon which we later attach the information in the text.

Our students already ask a myriad of questions about life: Why did she say that? What was the movie about? Who cares? How does this have anything to do with my life? What did you do last night? How can I make more friends? Where is my homework? How come I have to do this? Like the other comprehension habits, we need to shape and develop the questioning that students *already do* and transfer it into the arena of academic reading comprehension.

What are good questions? is a good question. Good questions ask about connections between two parts of the same text, between the text and other texts or life experiences of the reader, and between the text and more general world events or situations. Good questions

Table 15. Asking Good Questions	
We Need to Train Students to Ask About...	**Sample Questions**
The ways in which the text relates to real life	How does this compare to the 2003 war in Iraq? How could this affect the air in my community?
Character motives, ethics, symbolism, and metaphors	Why did she leave her family? Was that acceptable at that time? How can the river symbolize friendship?
Deeper concepts and more information than what the text offers (inferences)	I wonder why water floats in its solid state? What if it sank like most other precipitates? Why didn't they give up some land?
The text's main idea and theme	What is the author saying about animal adaptations? What was the gist of this story?
Varying perspectives	If I were the boy, what would I have done? I wonder what the enemy thought as he pulled the trigger?
Author's style, format, and purpose	I wonder why the author used first person? Why did the author use this strange dialogue? Why did she write this letter to the president?
Why certain parts were included or excluded by the author	Why did that character need to die at the end? Why is there an extra section on artificial diamonds in this chapter?
The meaning of keywords and phrases	What does *numinous* mean? I wonder if *sidereal* means something to do with stars?
Cause and effect	Why did Napoleon start the war? How does a light bulb give off light? What were the long-term results of dropping the atom bombs in Japan?
Comparison and contrast	How is this novel similar to the last one? How is this president unlike the others?

help a reader stay focused and moving toward the overall purpose of the text. Table 15 shows some good types of questions, with samples of each.

Levels of Questions

The first thing that usually happens when we tell students to make up questions is that we hear a lot of trivial and superficial questions. That is, students tend to avoid thinking about what they want to know, and they just blurt out the first thing that resembles a question. A good question helps the reader to understand the various layers of information that an author is trying to communicate to readers. Good questions come in three layers: On-the-surface questions, also known as "right there" questions, are the concrete and practical questions that help a reader keep track of explicit information. Under-the-surface questions, also called inferential questions, help a reader to understand implied or "read between the lines" information. They also require a reader to fill in needed concepts from background knowledge. Even deeper are the life application questions, sometimes called "text and me" questions, which help a reader connect the text to his or her own life or to the world. Good questions at all three levels do not occur without modeling and practice. Teachers need to model and scaffold them on a daily basis in a variety of ways.

This book contains a reproducible poster of the different levels of questions that all readers should ask (see page 136). Feel free to copy, enlarge, or modify this poster and put it up for students to see and appreciate.

Good Questions for Before, During, and After Reading

Each stage of comprehension includes questioning: We must ask good questions *before* we read to prepare us to find and store the information. *During* reading, we must ask questions to make sure we are sculpting the main idea and achieving the purpose we established for reading. *After* reading, we must ask questions to further organize what we have read and to fit it into the lesson we are learning. The following is a list of sample questions that facilitate comprehension in different stages of reading. Feel free to make your own list and to create a poster collaboratively with students for them to refer to daily.

Before

- Why am I reading this text?
- What do I already know about this topic?
- How can the text structure help me to read?
- What will this text be about?

During

- Is this text making sense?
- What just happened?
- What will happen next?
- Did I miss anything?
- What makes this text difficult to understand?
- How does _____ relate to _____?
- What does this _____ remind me of?
- What caused _____?
- What does _____ mean? Why do I think so?
- What would happen if _____?
- How does _____ affect _____?

- What information is important enough to remember as I read the rest of the text?

- What am I supposed to be learning by reading this text?

- Why is _____ important?

After

- So what?

- Did the reading end the way I predicted?

- What do I want to remember?

- How could I communicate what I read to someone else?

- Why did the author write this?

- In what ways is this text like anything else I have read?

- What was I supposed to learn by reading this text?

Tools Chart for Generating and Answering Questions

Table 16 shows the usefulness of this chapter's activities for various content areas. On the left side of the table, a √ in a column indicates that the activity is useful in that stage of reading. On the right side of the table, a √ in a column indicates that the activity is helpful for comprehension of common texts used in that content area. A √√ on the right side of the table means that the activity is especially helpful for that type of text and that you should try it as soon as possible.

Before Reading	During Reading	After Reading	Tool Name	Social Studies	Science	English/ EL
✓	✓	✓	Big Questions	√√	√√	√√
✓	✓	✓	Central Question Diagram	√√	√	√
✓	✓	✓	Hot Seat	√√	√	√√
✓	✓	✓	It Says, I Say, and So	√√	√	√
		✓	Question Starters	√√	√	√√
✓	✓		Question the Author	√√	√	√√
✓	✓	✓	Question Tree and Sea	√√	√	√
✓	✓	✓	Socratic Sessions	√√	√	√√
✓		✓	Student-Created Quizzes and Tests	√√	√√	√√
			Talk Show	√√	√	√√

Table 16. When and Where to Use the Activities in Chapter 6

Activities for Generating and Answering Questions

BIG QUESTIONS

Big questions, like the ones in the list below, are mostly controversial and philosophical questions that challenge students to continually reconstruct and reevaluate their thinking about important issues in texts (Zwiers, 2004). Examples of questions and discussions based on them will help students ask their own big questions as they read. Start a list of questions similar to the one in Table 17 that relates to the texts in your curricula. Most questions have direct connections to literature, science, and social studies. They can also be used with other activities in this and other chapters.

Procedure

1. Model out loud the questions you generate when starting, reading, and finishing a text. For example, Are humans basically good or evil? Should we drastically limit the emission of greenhouse gases? Should we have waged war in Iraq?

2. Model your thoughts and describe how you look at all sides objectively and generate evidence for each from the text and from life. You can even stand in different sections of the room to show different stances or solutions. Bring up the limitations of each side, as well.

3. Give student groups different texts and have them generate possible big questions for it before, during, and after reading it. Have students do a Think-Write-Pair-Share in which they think, then write, then share with a partner, and finally share with the class.

4. Share questions and discuss how big, or important, they are (or not) for us as students, humans, and so on.

5. Record the questions on a poster for use over time.

6. Encourage students to bring in big questions that come up in other classes, when watching television, reading the paper, or in discussions with others.

Table 17.   Examples of Big Questions

- Are humans progressing or digressing?
- What person from the past or present do you admire, and why?
- What animal(s) has characteristics that you think more humans should have?
- Are media messages about women harmful?
- If there were to be a nuclear war in two weeks, what would you do and why?
- Should parents be able to refuse medical treatment for their children because of religious reasons?
- Should tobacco advertising be banned?
- Is television viewing harmful?
- Is it ethical to clone animals? Humans?
- Does mass media influence a society's values?
- Should some illegal drugs be legalized?
- Is technology the answer for improving education?
- Is it right to use animals for research purposes?
- Did the early American colonists commit genocide?

CENTRAL QUESTION DIAGRAM

This activity teaches students to connect to evidence in their background knowledge in order to answer complex questions posed about a text. It teaches students to compare their opinions and reasons with those mentioned in the text. It also requires students to see both sides of an issue and to modify their background knowledge when necessary. This activity is based on work by Alvermann (1991) and Wiggins and McTighe (2005) on asking essential questions.

Procedure

1. Give each student a copy of the Central Question Diagram at the end of this chapter on page 137. Work with students to generate a central question from the text and have them write it in the center box. You might already have a central question in mind. Refer to your curriculum standards for the unit, if needed.

2. Before reading, have students individually generate their reasons for choosing "Yes" or their reasons for choosing "No" in response to the central question. (They can choose both, if they want.)

3. Optional: Have students discuss their reasons with a partner before reading the text.

4. Have students read the text, jotting down reasons for both positions on the appropriate sides of the diagram as they read.

5. Ask students to come to a conclusion and decide which answer is better, if either. Have them write their conclusions in the box at the bottom of the diagram.

6. Conduct a discussion on the conclusions and come to a consensus as a class. Emphasize the evidence used to support both sides of the issue.

HOT SEAT

The Hot Seat provides motivation to thoroughly understand a text, often by taking on different points of view. For example, when a student assumes the role of a character in a narrative or acts as a historical figure, the student can infer reasons for the character's actions by referring to evidence from the text or other sources.

Procedure

1. Model the process of assuming the role of the author, a historical figure, a scientific subject (e.g., raindrop, moon, molecule, octopus, tectonic plate, etc.), an expert on the text's subject, or a character from the text.

2. Give students sample questions or question starters on 3" × 5" cards to ask you as you model what to do. Sit in a specially designated seat at the front of the room (the hot seat). Say something such as, "I am Huck Finn. What would you like to know?" or "I am

General Lee. Shoot your questions at me," or "I am a carbon molecule. Fire away," or "I am Stephen Hawking. Do you have any questions about the universe?" Let the students ask you questions, and answer them as the character you are playing.

3. Then, have students practice the activity themselves in pairs or in groups of four to six members. One student should assume the hot seat role and take the questions.

4. Other students ask questions about purpose, motivations, feelings, actions, or other content. They can use questions such as the following:

- Why did you do this?
- How did you feel about the other characters?
- How did you change? Why?
- What will you do now?
- How did your invention change the world?
- If you had..., how would the event or story have changed?
- Why are you important for my life?

5. Play Whole-Class Hot Seat: Groups can nominate a student who did well in the small groups to go to the front of the classroom. Allow some time for students to prepare good questions. Optionally, you may want to chart questions into the three levels—on-the-surface, under-the-surface, and life application—and even evaluate the questions generated in terms of their helpfulness in understanding the text.

IT SAYS, I SAY, AND SO

This activity (adapted from Beers, 1998) helps students to look critically at the text and generate questions that call for inference and interpretation. The chart is useful for under-the-surface and life application questions.

It Says, I Say, and So provides a succinct method for building two habits at once: implicit questioning and inference. It shows students that it is OK—even helpful—to question a text and then guess the answers to those questions. Yet the activity also stresses the importance of basing one's questions and guessed answers on hard evidence found in the text. Also, the activity helps students to visualize connections (i.e., inferences) between the text and their own thinking processes. Finally, this is a simple activity that can be done many times across many different types of texts, both narrative and expository. If used enough, the process will become a key habit that will last throughout students' lives whenever they read.

Procedure

1. Give students some background on the topic to be studied and have them generate questions. Have students create a table on their own sheets of paper similar to the sample shown at the end of this activity; they should write their questions in the first column.

(You also may put questions into this column in order to directly model certain types of questions.) Remember, asking good (implicit) questions requires *a lot* of modeling and scaffolding before students can do it on their own.

2. Optional: One helpful preparation activity is to brainstorm good questions and then choose the best ones. Then, go on to analyze *why* the best ones are good. See previous sections of this chapter for ideas on what makes a good question.

3. Have students look for text sections that could answer the question and copy them into the "It Says" column.

4. Have students use their inference skills to create their own interpretations of the text in the "I Say" column.

5. Have students use the first two columns as a foundation upon which they construct an answer in the "and So" column, as in this sample It Says, I Say, and So chart for a study of the ozone.

Question	It Says	I Say	And So
Why is the ozone layer depletion dangerous?	The layer prevents certain types of sunlight from reaching the planet's surface.	The more sun we get, the warmer it is, and ice may start to melt. Too much sun is also bad for skin.	If the ice melts, then the ocean level rises, and many places just above sea level may flood.

QUESTION STARTERS

Sometimes students need a little help to ask good questions. Starters such as these can help students form a variety of questions so that eventually they are automatic.

- Why did the man...?
- Who...?
- Why did they continue to...?
- If you had..., what would you have done?
- Should she have...? Why?
- Would you have...? Why?

- Why did the author include...?
- Why is the picture of...?
- What do you think happened after...?
- How might this chemical react with...?
- How would you solve this...?
- Why would you use a picture of...?

Procedure

1. Create the beginnings of questions (question stems) for the given text. Refer to the previous list for some ideas.

2. Have students use the question stems to create their own questions (they can work in pairs or individually). Emphasize that the students are to act like teachers and are to ask good questions that make us think (but that can be answered).

3. Have students first answer the questions verbally (if they are working in pairs) and then in writing, if there is time. If they cannot answer a question, they should describe why they cannot answer it.

4. Have students read aloud their questions and answers to a partner and then to the class.

QUESTION THE AUTHOR

This activity (adapted from Beck et al., 1997) allows students to think about the techniques that authors use—or should use—to clearly communicate their ideas to readers. This type of critical reading empowers students to take a metacognitive look at texts and understand what makes them effective or ineffective. When students realize that their lack of comprehension may in part be due to the poor quality of writing, they feel more empowered to analyze the text and pick it apart. A desired side effect, of course, is that they understand the text better when they have to criticize and question it. This can, of course, ultimately translate not only into better comprehension but also into better writing and oral skills.

Procedure

1. Explain to students that some texts are not well written and that understanding what authors do and don't do can help comprehension. Point out that we can question the author's use of features and vocabulary, which gives us a better overall picture of text meaning.

2. Similar to a think-aloud, model the process of reading aloud and then asking a question directed to the author. For example, you may ask, Why would you include this paragraph in this text? Does it connect to a future part? Why didn't she add another line to elaborate on how...?

3. Model other questions to the imaginary author, such as the following:

- Why did you write this?
- What are you trying to tell me?
- Why are you telling me this?
- What's missing here?
- What do I have to know or figure out?
- How could you have stated this more clearly?
- What did you mean by this phrase?
- How does this connect with what you already wrote?
- Why did you use a _____ as the main character?

- Why did you use the analogy of a _____?
- What did you expect us to know already?

4. After showing students how to question the author about a variety of texts, have students practice the activity in pairs. Guide students and encourage them as they ask questions and use evidence from the text to support answers. One student plays the part of the author and the other asks the questions. Keep in mind that when students answer questions such as How can this be more clearly stated? they also will build essential summarizing habits.

5. Students can write down their questions (e.g., on sticky notes) if they think it will be helpful. Remind them that eventually they will be asking these questions automatically as they read.

QUESTION TREE AND SEA

Good questioning is a vital habit for the comprehension of difficult material (Harvey & Goudvis, 2007). The Question Tree and Question Sea diagrams (both at the end of this chapter on pages 138 and 139) give students the scaffolding needed to develop the habit of asking explicit (on-the-surface) and, more important, implicit (under-the-surface and life application) questions. You can rename the question levels if you like. For example, some educators call them *right there*, *author and you*, and *on your own* questions (Buehl, 2009; Helfeldt & Henk, 1990). Whatever names you give them, the Question Tree and Question Sea help you to show and model these various levels of questions. The Tree and Sea diagrams can be used with multiple types of images.

Procedure

1. Start with pictures, videos, pantomimes, and simple texts to generate questions, and use the Different Levels of Questions sheet located at the end of this chapter on page 136 to brainstorm different questions.

2. Explain the different levels of questions and then have students help you place your questions in the correct levels of the Question Tree or Question Sea diagram. The goal is to have questions in all three categories that help you to better understand the text. For each question generated, have students think about whether the author would want his or her readers to ask that question.

3. Guide students through a written text and have them generate questions that relate to the text. Fill in questions where they belong on the diagram. Do this with both narrative and expository texts.

4. Remind students that under-the-surface and life application questions usually

- require extra thinking
- have more than one answer
- require more research

131

- are not directly found in the text
- involve opinions and educated guessing
- refer to the author's message
- teach lessons about life, love, hope, meaning, truth, and so forth

5. Have students share their best questions and discuss how such questions help with comprehension. Discuss what makes some questions relevant to the text and others irrelevant.

SOCRATIC SESSIONS

Inform students that Socrates—one of the greatest thinkers of all time—spent much of his time asking questions. In Socratic Sessions (adapted from Moeller & Moeller, 2002), students have the chance to discuss important questions inspired by the text. They also have a chance to "Socratize" (i.e., keep asking deeper and deeper questions).

Procedure

1. Generate an initial implicit (under-the-surface) question that relates to the purpose of the text. The question will likely contain some type of opinion, interpretation, or controversy.

2. Model how to ask further questions that bring up important points and counterpoints. That is, model how to dig deeper into the issues. For example, on the topic of drug legalization, deeper questions might be, Why do people want to legalize drugs? What does *addiction* really mean? Why do people use drugs?

3. Remind students that they may be accustomed to having teachers come up with these deeper questions most of the time, but now it is their turn. With enough practice, students' reading and thinking will improve drastically. Let students practice being Socrates—who, by the way, challenged many people with his many radical questions.

4. Encourage students to engage in the following appropriate behaviors for discussion:

- Using the text to defend your position
- Listening well to others before responding to them
- Seeing multiple sides of an issue
- Using phrases such as "I agree with...and would like to add...," "I disagree with ...because...," or "Could you clarify the point about...?"
- Paraphrasing other students' responses (e.g., "So you are essentially saying that...," So your point is....")

5. Have students summarize the session orally or in writing. If they are new to the summarizing process, you will need to model creating the summary, which includes the following:

- Thoughts about the initial question

- The influence of additional questions
- The comments of others
- What the text had to say or not say
- A final conclusion and how it may have changed over time

STUDENT-CREATED QUIZZES AND TESTS

This activity is powerful for a variety of reasons. First, it causes students to think of interesting questions. It also forces them to think of the answers. Students tend to remember questions and answers better when they are involved in the process of creating them. Also, it gives students more ownership of their learning and classroom processes. When I have done this, students have come up with most of the questions I would have asked anyway. And many of their questions sparked great discussion.

Procedure

1. Model how you read a paragraph and come up with a question that might be used on a quiz.
2. Have students read a text and jot down questions they have about it. These questions might be used later or might be discarded.
3. Give students some guidelines, if you wish, such as "generate three *why* questions, two *how* questions, two *what* questions, and one *if* question."
4. Have students meet in pairs to finalize their quizzes. Have them look at the questions with teacher eyes, to see if answering the question will show them that the quiz taker truly understood the text.
5. Share the questions with the class, or gather them and create a quiz or test to give to students. The better the questions the students create, the more likely you will use them and the better they will do on the quiz because they should know the answers!

TALK SHOW

Many students are familiar with talk shows on television and radio. In a talk show, the host usually asks a range of questions that are meant to prompt some interesting responses and discussion.

Procedure

1. Model good and bad examples of questions that are based on a text. Emphasize to students that the richer the questions, the more interesting the answers to those questions will be.

2. As a class or in pairs, pick a character, author, or person from the text, and decide on the type of expert who will answer the questions.

3. Working in pairs, students read a text and prepare questions that they think will generate interesting answers for an audience.

4. The pairs practice one on one—with one student acting as the host and the other acting as the interviewee—then in front of another pair. They do not memorize answers but can keep improving the responses by helping each other.

5. Pairs volunteer to present their talk show in front of the class. Discussion can ensue if the topic evolves into one. The host can also engage the audience with questions.

Reflection Questions

1. Why is questioning by the reader so important? What kinds of questions are most helpful?

2. Choose a short text that you will teach. Write down your questions before, during, and after reading. What level questions were they (surface, below, life application)? Were they helpful? How?

3. What are big (essential, overarching) questions in your content area(s)? What are medium-size questions that support the big questions?

4. Write an inquiry question for this chapter's habit and a teaching activity. Gather evidence over time and make adjustments based on student work (e.g., How can I best help students develop questioning habits, evidenced by classroom discussions and essays, using the .... activity?).

NOTES: _____

_____

_____

_____

_____

_____

_____

_____

_____

_____

_____

DIFFERENT LEVELS OF QUESTIONS

On-the-Surface Questions

- Usually have one correct answer found in the text (you can point to it)
- Involve summarizing, paraphrasing, and literal retelling
- Inquire about facts, details, and events
- Often begin with *Who, What, Where,* or *When* (some on-the-surface questions may begin with *Why, How, Should, Could,* or *Would*)

Under-the-Surface Questions

- Can have more than one correct answer
- Are not explicitly stated in the text
- Often begin with the words *Why, How, Should, Could,* or *Would* (some under-the-surface questions may begin with *Who, What, Where,* or *When*—often followed by "do you think..." and then often followed by another *Why?* question)
- Usually require one or more of the following:
  - Filling in gaps, making inferences, "reading between the lines"
  - Predicting, speculating, asking what the text means
  - Hypothesizing and evaluating
  - Challenging the text
  - Experimenting, solving problems, thinking divergently
  - Reflecting, expressing major understanding

Life Application Questions

- Connect the text to self or knowledge of the world
- Ask about author's purpose, message, moral, or symbolism
- Explore cultural or psychological ideas
- Extend beyond the text into the reader's own experience
- Include opinions
- May include "How does this part relate to my past, present, or future?" "What is my opinion about what the text says?" or "How does this text help me learn what I need to learn?"

Building Reading Comprehension in Grades 6–12: A Toolkit of Classroom Activities (second edition) by Jeff Zwiers © 2010. Newark, DE: International Reading Association. May be copied for classroom use.

CENTRAL QUESTION DIAGRAM

Question with Should..., Could..., Would..., or Do you think that....

YES, because...

My reasons *before* reading:

Reasons from the text *after* reading:

Central Question

Conclusion

NO, because...

My reasons *before* reading:

Reasons from the text *after* reading:

Source: Adapted from Alvermann, D.E. (1991). The discussion web: A graphic aid for learning across the curriculum. *The Reading Teacher, 45,* 92–99. *Building Reading Comprehension in Grades 6–12: A Toolkit of Classroom Activities* (second edition) by Jeff Zwiers © 2010. Newark, DE: International Reading Association. May be copied for classroom use.

QUESTION SEA

On-the-Surface Questions

Who...?   Where...?   When...?   What...?

Under-the-Surface Questions

Why...?   Would...?

How...?   What if...?

Life Application Questions

If I were..., how...?

How does this text relate to real life?

QUESTION TREE

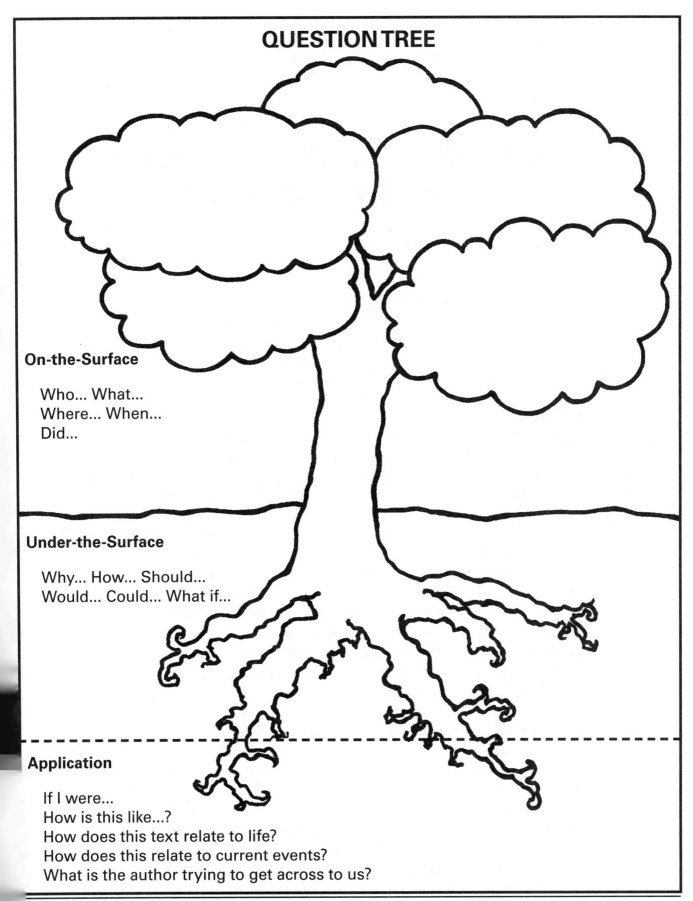

On-the-Surface

Who... What...
Where... When...
Did...

Under-the-Surface

Why... How... Should...
Would... Could... What if...

Application

If I were...
How is this like...?
How does this text relate to life?
How does this relate to current events?
What is the author trying to get across to us?

CHAPTER 7

Understanding and Remembering
Word Meanings

* * *

The dictionary never seems

to get it right.

Many teachers consider a lack of vocabulary knowledge to be the primary reason for students' poor comprehension, especially in science and social studies classes. These teachers then proceed to look for ways to fill students' brains with as many word meanings as possible. Unfortunately, a large number of vocabulary-teaching methods are limited to either the infamous "look it up, use it in a sentence, take a quiz on Friday" strategy or the "just read it" strategy. Rather than overwhelm students with random word meanings, we need to teach students to teach themselves about words and their meanings. That is, we must teach students to be constructivist detectives of meaning. They need to be able to quickly and automatically notice the clues inside and outside the new words and phrases they encounter in texts.

Teaching word meanings, especially before reading, has been found to be effective for word learning and text comprehension (Marzano et al., 2001). However, because the purpose of this book is to develop habits of comprehension, this chapter emphasizes ways for developing the habit of figuring out words as students read. For those teachers who also want some guidelines for good instruction of vocabulary words, I do provide a "quality control" checklist to help you assess whether your arsenal of vocabulary teaching techniques aligns with vocabulary research.

Vocabulary instruction that is associated with extensive dictionary time and the creation of random sentences that contain the new words is not effective enough to warrant the time used for it (Beck, McKeown, & Kucan, 2002; Nagy, 1988). At the same time, however, just plain independent reading also is not sufficient for our below-grade-level readers. Many of these students have not developed the habit of figuring out words, hypothesizing their meanings, retaining them, and using them to understand complex texts—particularly science and social studies texts. Remember that students, on the average, acquire approximately 3,000 words per year (Nagy, 1988; Sedita, 2005). That would be about 100–150 words per week—which is one long vocabulary quiz. Where do most of the 3,000 words come from? The answer is from lots of real reading and the automatic habits of using context and word parts.

Therefore, the activities in this chapter are included to help you support and scaffold the development of the following word meaning habits: (a) using semantic and syntactic context clues; and (b) using the meanings of common roots, prefixes, suffixes, and similar words.

Using Context: Scoping Out the Word Neighborhood

Most of what we have learned has not been explicitly taught to us. We have observed, inferred, and built our background knowledge to form patterns of the way the world works. For this reason, all the cues that we recognize from past experience become clues that we use to create meaning in the present. These current clues trigger our background knowledge (i.e., schemata) to tell us the meaning that was associated with similar clues in the past. Then, we make an educated guess about the current meaning(s) of the clues.

We do this with words all the time. We use context clues to help us to create and sculpt meanings of unknown or multiple-meaning words (Allen, 1999). In a sense, we "scope out the neighborhood" around the word (or phrase) to guess the meaning that fits the best in those surroundings. For example, you probably automatically used context to extend the meaning of *sculpt* in the beginning of this paragraph. You did not even begin to think that I was referring to the more common meaning: "to form a piece of art out of clay or marble." We start with the common or concrete and then extend and guess, depending on the context of the sentence or paragraph. Upon reading a recent article on drinking alcohol, a student once described to me how she used context clues help her figure out the meaning of the word *deleterious* when she saw it in front of the word *effects*. Her background knowledge told her that the effects of drinking alcohol (liver damage, nausea, etc.) were bad, and, therefore, she guessed that the word meant *harmful* or *negative*. Most of the words we know came from context—not just one or two experiences and exposures, but perhaps 7, 10, even 50 or more. Each exposure to a word provides further conscious and unconscious clues that help us to better sculpt or solidify its meaning.

Yet even before we expend energy on the figuring-out process, we need to judge whether the unknown words we encounter are important. Some less important words may actually take up too much brain time and should be skipped. Be careful with expository texts, however, as many of their unknown words tend to be the most important for overall meaning and, therefore, should not be skipped. A simple way to check is to notice if the meaning of more than one paragraph hinges on the meaning of an unknown word. If so, we need to take the time to figure out the word.

Using Context Clues With Text Signals

We can point out the following context clues and have students watch for them. These are usually clues that the author purposely gives to help the reader.

- **Explanation or definition:** The author explains or defines the word in the same sentence in which it is introduced. Following are some signal words and punctuation for this type of clue and some sample sentences in which they are used.

Signal Words and Punctuation	Sample Sentences
is, are, has	A proton is a positively charged particle in the nucleus of an atom.
	Carnivores are animals and plants that eat meat.
	A person who is afraid of crowds has agoraphobia.
means	A democracy means that the government is formed by all the people.
defined as	The denouement is defined as the climax of a story.

- **Synonym or restatement:** The author uses more familiar terms to explain the new word. Following are some signal words and punctuation for this type of clue and some sample sentences in which they are used.

Signal Words and Punctuation	Sample Sentences
likewise	Jan looked at him with disdain. Likewise, he despised her.
especially	The war decimated the population. The South was especially short on labor in the years that followed.
or	The antediluvian, or ancient, carvings told us nothing.
in that	She was adroit at her job in that she could finish it in half the time of her coworkers.
similarly	Peregrine falcons migrate from pole to pole each year. Similarly, humpback whales make a long journey south each winter to breed.
in other words	His aphasia did not hinder him. In other words, his inability to speak didn't keep him from effectively communicating.
that is	His simple glance was a harbinger of danger. That is, his eyes were signs foretelling rough waters in their relationship.
a phrase set apart between commas	She used a metronome, a small machine that ticked out the timing of the music, as she practiced her violin.

- **Antonym or contrast:** The author offers the opposite meaning of the unknown word. Following are some signal words for antonym clues and some sample sentences in which they are used.

Signal Words	Sample Sentences
Some..., but others....	Some believed that the man was altruistic until the end, but others say that he gave only for selfish reasons.
On the other hand	She was audacious. On the other hand, he was timid and meek.
not	Francine was not blithe at all. She was sad and serious.
despite	Now they were confident, despite their usual diffidence.
although	He acts as if he agrees with the government, although I know about his iconoclastic beliefs.
yet	Its power seemed immutable, yet one day, it ended.
but	The gray kitten was lethargic in the morning, but at night he was quite lively and awake.
by contrast	She was quite efficacious in her job. By contrast, her brother wasn't able to do his work.
then again	Some liked his laconic speeches. Then again, others preferred longer and more detailed orations.
and then	We were getting along fine, and then we had our first altercation.

- **Cause and effect:** With a cause-and-effect clue, we automatically attempt to make the connections shown below. This process helps us guess word meanings.

Cause	Effect	Sample Sentences
Phrase or sentence with unknown word	Phrase or sentence with known words	The horse was so *fatigued* that he collapsed before he finished. Given the *paucity* of resources, the people were forced to move on.
Phrase or sentence with known words	Phrase or sentence with unknown word	The existence of a rattler in the Alaskan woods presented quite a *conundrum*. The drought lasted many years. Never had the land been so *desiccated*.

We predict the word's meaning as we think about how the causes relate to the effects, and then we read on to see if the prediction is confirmed. Some signal words from this clue type are as follows.

Signal Words	Sample Sentences
therefore	It occluded my vision; therefore, I crashed.
for this reason	She was a neophyte. For this reason, she had much to learn.
in this way	The shell was petrified. In this way, it was preserved in stone for millions of years.
consequently	They were a bellicose race. Consequently, their wars with neighboring nations depleted their resources.
given	Given the paucity of resources, she couldn't find enough information for her report.
resulting in	He had a proclivity for getting into trouble, resulting in frequent detentions.
such that	The insects were rapacious such that nothing in their path was left uneaten.
this is due to	He has a saturnine outlook on life. This is due to the death of his friend.

- **Examples of the word:** Some signal words for this type of clue are as follows.

Signal Words	Sample Sentences
such as	Many animals have mottled coats, such as the leopard, the ocelot, and the giraffe.
for example	He often was tenacious. For example, one time he climbed a mountain in a brutal storm, even after losing his food.
for instance	Some animals are omnivores. Bears, for instance, eat whatever meat or plants they can find.
once	He was zealous. Once, he sat on the courthouse steps for a week to get the city to change a law.
in one case	Many are xenophobes. In one case, a woman avoided people for two years.
one time	His loquacious speeches were famous. One time, he talked for three hours.

Using Context Without Signals

Semantic Context. The preceding section presented ways in which the author provides some extra contextual support in the text by using signal words or punctuation. But students also must be able to figure out a word that is not so obviously supported. In these cases, the reader must think beyond the sentence in which the word appears and use the bigger semantic picture to figure out the word's meaning. This process, according to many teachers, is a big challenge for their below-grade-level readers. It requires extra thinking (storing the word's possible meanings in the brain) because the clues are not as obvious or "local." The clues may be found several paragraphs or even many pages away. Consider the following example:

> He was quite *prolific* in his later years. During this time, he painted scenes from his hometown and neighboring villages. He painted streets, bridges, haystacks, cathedrals, and houses. He believed that almost every scene deserved to be put onto canvas. For this reason, he created so many paintings that his apartment could no longer hold them. He began to sell them for several dollars apiece. Now, long after his death, each painting is worth even less.

After reading the whole paragraph and looking for clues for the word *prolific*, such as "his many works of art," a reader might finally guess the meaning as "making many." (The reader may also associate the *pro-* in *prolific* with similar words: *produce, procure, proceed,* etc.) Then again, the reader may think *prolific* has another meaning, such as *poor* or *senile*. The reader would need to hold this "probable meaning" in the brain somewhere and recall it the next time the word *prolific* was seen in context, at which time he or she would compare it to the new context and then confirm or change it.

Pictorial Context. You might be surprised to know how many students do not even look at the pictures in the texts they read. Even fewer take the time to think about how the pictures support the text and its unknown words. This is unfortunate because sometimes the entire purpose of a picture is to explain a key word or concept. With think-aloud activities, you can show how important it is to consider the pictures and how they help us comprehend new words and concepts (Farr, 2001). Remind students that, as the saying goes, a picture is worth a thousand words—and maybe more.

Syntactic Context. Syntactic context means using the location of the word in a sentence to figure out its grammar role, which then helps us figure out its meaning. If we know the unknown word is a noun, verb, adjective, or adverb, we can (a) get a better idea of what is missing or what we need to figure out (e.g., "I know this is an action"), and (b) decide if figuring out the word is important. Verbs and nouns tend to be more important than adjectives and adverbs in most texts.

Multiple Meanings Rule!

Most words have more meanings than we realize. Yet we often do not realize this because we use context so quickly and automatically that the alternative meanings do not even pass through our minds. I realized this one day when an English learner said to me, "But I thought the word *cool* meant cold." I answered, "Hmmm, you're right, but in this context it means unexcited or unemotional." Even this definition differs somewhat from a third definition of being likeable and popular. Another example of multiple meanings is the word *revolution*:

- The people took up arms and started a revolution. (war and violence)
- The wheel made 54 revolutions before stopping. (physical turns)
- A revolution was happening inside of him. (inner change—psychological)
- His ideas revolutionized the film industry. (change in the way things are done)

I first thought of a revolution only as a military overthrow of a government. Gradually, as I saw the word in new contexts, I created more meanings based on my original definition (thereby building words upon words, year after year). I gradually built up a flexible meaning into something similar to "a radical and significant change" to make *revolution* fit each text's situation. This is what we do as we learn new words and new meanings for familiar words.

There are two steps for using context to figure out multiple meanings. For example, here are the two steps for the sentence "His *bland* lectures put her to sleep more than once."

1. I first notice whether I already know at least one meaning of the target word (in this case, *bland*). My one known (concrete) meaning for the word is "without taste," such as food without salt or spice.

2. I start from this known meaning and try to connect it with how it is used in the current text I am reading. In this case, my concrete meaning does not work; lectures aren't eaten. I must add a more abstract meaning for the word so that it makes sense in this text. Therefore, I extend my original definition to mean "not interesting" or "boring."

This extension from a single meaning to multiple meanings, from the concrete to the abstract, and from the literal to the figurative presents one of the most challenging habits that students must develop. It also is one of the most empowering for academic success. Therefore, we must help readers develop the habit of using their existing knowledge of a word and extending it to fit into the present context (Stahl, 1999). For example, consider the sentence "The first astronauts blazed the way to new frontiers in space." *Blaze* to a student may just mean "a fire." The reader needs to have the habit of thinking about the common qualities of *blaze* and relating them to what the text is trying to say. The reader might think, "Perhaps *blaze* has to do with using fire to clear away the land and make it easier to do something with it. So maybe it means that astronauts made the way easier for future travelers." In later texts, that reader may see the word *blaze* in similar contexts, such as "blazing a trail," and further confirm this guess.

To teach the habit of figuring out multiple meanings, you should model the process often for your students with think-alouds. That is, describe how you connect words to previous knowledge and how you then tweak your existing definitions to make a logical prediction for this new context. Verbalize how you visualize word meanings and connect certain features, or submeanings, to make the new meaning fit with the sentence. While reading aloud, pause at times to let students think about a word and its meaning. Then give students various levels of scaffolded practice in paired think-alouds that emphasize vocabulary. (Many practice activities are included in this chapter; see Appendix A for a starter list of multiple-meaning words.)

Use the following types of tools for teaching students about multiple meanings:

• Vocabulary graphic organizers, such as charts, that sort and define the variations of a word or term

• Brainstorms that generate long lists of related words

• Pictures, diagrams, and drawings that explain and show the meanings of difficult words

Word Surgery: Using Word Parts and Similar Words

Context (especially when used only one or two times) is not always enough to help us figure out a word. If we also employ the meanings of word parts and similar words, we can get even closer to the meaning the author intends. For example, if I have no clue of the meaning of *amorphous* from context, I might examine the prefix *a-* (which I know means "not") with the root *morph-*, which I know means "shape," to get a meaning such as "without shape or form; hard to grasp." Using knowledge of word parts, because it can be applied to many words, is an important subhabit of figuring out word meanings (Allen, 1999). We should teach students how to remember and use prefixes, suffixes, and root words in order to figure out unfamiliar words. (See Appendix B for common prefixes, suffixes, and roots.) This can become a habit that extends to other classes and texts for life. One way to model the use of word parts is by thinking aloud (see Read-Aloud Think-Aloud [RATA] activity in Chapter 8) when you reach an unknown word. Stop and "cut up" the unknown word on the board, then compare the parts to known words. Students help to predict what the word means.

Using similar words and cognates from other languages is another important vocabulary skill. Similar words often have similar word parts with similar meanings. For example, if a reader sees the word *antediluvian*, he or she may relate it to *antechamber* and *dilute* or *deluge*. This could lead to a rough guess of "before a flood," and in context would probably lead to the meaning of "ancient."

For English learners, depending on what their native language is, many "big" content words look similar to a word in their native language and often mean the same thing. These are called cognates. Students should be taught to watch for these similarities as they read. They also should hear the word pronounced in English because it may sound very different from how it is pronounced in the native tongue. Examples from Spanish include *revolución*, *popular*, *diligente*, *pronunciar*, and *actividad*. The Word Meaning Checklist located at the end of this chapter on page 172 synthesizes the previous sections to help students build skills for figuring out unknown words while they read. The checklist offers questions that proficient readers often ask as they encounter new words in challenging texts.

"Mores" and "Lesses" of Vocabulary Instruction

Following are some general guidelines for teaching students how to build vocabulary. The lists are provided to remind you of the best practices and best uses of time for teaching vocabulary. Some instructional guidelines for doing more and less (or "mores" and "lesses" as I refer to them) might surprise you because they have been used for a long time in traditional instruction and assessment. Review each list and consider if and how much the mores and lesses fit your vocabulary instruction.

Do More

+ Use varied and interesting texts.

+ Teach vocabulary in the context of real reading.

+ Model vocabulary strategies all the way through grade 12.

+ Connect vocabulary to core concepts and related words.

+ Increase opportunities for students to use new words in and out of class.

+ Create opportunities for students to make inferences about words and talk about them.

+ Teach common prefixes, suffixes, and roots.

+ Provide minilessons on how to extend meanings of words from concrete to abstract.

+ Connect new words to students' background knowledge.

+ Provide narrative and expository reading options that relate to the curriculum and match the reading levels of the students.

+ Provide multimodal/multiple intelligences approaches for understanding and remembering words (drawings, symbols, movement, music, cooperation).

+ Provide time for a lot of reading.

Do Less

- Teach isolated vocabulary out of context.

- Use word lists that are unconnected to a text.

- Encourage rote memorization of definitions.

- Teach students to rely solely on context—or solely on decoding—to figure out words.

- Teach that all words must be figured out to understand a text.

- Encourage looking up definitions as the primary way of figuring out word meanings.

- Use vocabulary assessments that are not connected to real reading.

- Ask students to write original sentences using new words and concepts that they are just beginning to learn.

Research abounds on the vast quantity of words that students learn from real reading, as compared to vocabulary tests and quizzes that "teach" vocabulary out of context (Nagy, 1988; Texas Reading Initiative, 2002). Similar to the way in which we learn first and second languages, our brains grab onto unknown words as building blocks of understanding, generate possible word meanings, and retain the words for later testing and eventual solidification of their meaning. Therefore, we as teachers need to provide ample time for reading actual texts at the appropriate reading levels.

Tools Chart for Understanding and Remembering Word Meanings

Table 18 shows the usefulness of this chapter's activities for various content areas. On the left side of the table, a √ in a column indicates that the activity is useful in that stage of reading. On the right side of the table, a √ in a column indicates that the activity is helpful for comprehension of common texts used in that content area. A √√ on the right side of the table means that the activity is especially helpful for that type of text and that you should try it as soon as possible.

Table 18.		When and Where to Use the Activities in Chapter 7				
Before Reading	During Reading	After Reading	Activity	Social Studies	Science	English/ EL
✓	✓	✓	Connect the Words	✓✓	✓✓	✓
✓	✓	✓	Example Webs	✓✓	✓✓	✓
✓	✓		FigFigs	✓	✓	✓
✓	✓	✓	Guess and Adjust	✓	✓	✓
	✓	✓	Keywords Web	✓✓	✓✓	✓
	✓	✓	List-Group-Label Plus	✓✓	✓✓	✓
	✓		Multiple Meanings Table	✓✓	✓✓	✓
	✓		New Words in Context Chart	✓✓	✓✓	✓
	✓		SCUBA Diving Into Word Meanings	✓✓	✓	✓
	✓	✓	Self-Selected Vocab Quizzes	✓✓	✓	✓✓
✓	✓	✓	Two-Word Sentence Stickies	✓✓	✓✓	✓✓
	✓	✓	Vocabulary Bank Notes	✓✓	✓✓	✓
	✓	✓	Word Bank	✓✓	✓✓	✓✓
	✓		Word Remembering	✓	✓	✓

Activities for Understanding and Remembering Word Meanings

The activities in this chapter were chosen for the following reasons: They do not require large amounts of class time on just a few isolated words; they emphasize the use of context and word parts during reading of content texts; they require minimal dictionary use; and they challenge students to think about, process, and remember words in the construction of meaning.

CONNECT THE WORDS

This activity encourages students to see connections and relations between important vocabulary terms. It becomes a visual way to make connections and remember the words—even after the test.

Procedure

1. Use the Connect the Words reproducible at the end of this chapter on page 164. Make a transparency of it to use for modeling this activity with the students. Identify the most important theme, word, or phrase in a lesson or section of text, and write it in the central diamond.

2. Find two or three other important words (or have the students find them, if you feel they are ready for this) and write them in the ovals at the outer corners of the sheet.

3. Think aloud (model) and describe the connections between the words in the ovals and the word in the center diamond. These connections should be written in the rectangles.

4. Have students work in pairs to generate one or two other important words to fill the remaining empty ovals. (Students can supply more words if you want to add ovals to the graphic.) Have students also fill in the remaining connection boxes. (See Figure 17 for a filled-in sample.) Pairs can ask one another, "How does this word relate to that word?"

5. Have pairs of students share their connections with one another.

6. Information from the boxes can later be used in writing compositions.

EXAMPLE WEBS

In this activity, which is very similar to using a semantic map, students find and generate examples of abstract and complex terms from the text. Generating examples helps the terms become more concrete and memorable for students. Thus, this activity serves two purposes: It helps students to better remember key terms as they read and it helps students build the

Figure 17.   Sample Connect the Words Activity

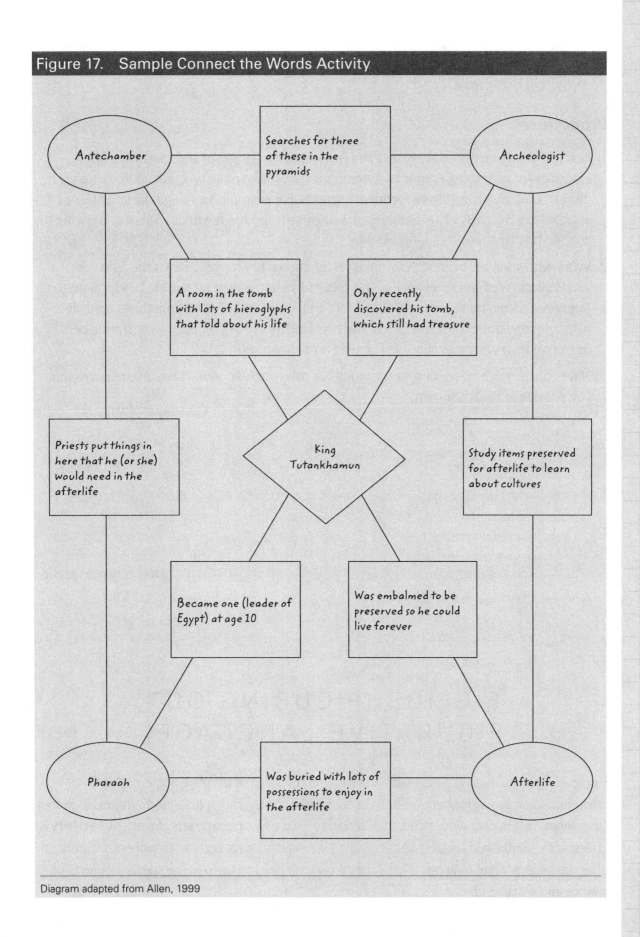

Diagram adapted from Allen, 1999

habit of thinking of examples, a skill that will serve them in the future when they want to communicate challenging concepts to others.

Procedure

1. Pick several key terms from the text and model how you look for and think of helpful examples for each term. One or two examples are usually in the text, but it also helps to think of examples from life and from other texts. For example, you might pick the term *antagonistic*. You then write examples of antagonistic around it with a symbol or drawing to provide further support as shown below.

2. Work with students to create examples for additional key terms. Discuss the features and limitations of certain examples and come to an agreement on the most helpful ones. Remind students that no example is perfect and, often, knowing its limitations actually helps you remember the term better. Instruct students to ask for examples (from a person or from a text) whenever they hear or read an abstract term.

3. Have students generate examples in groups or pairs on their own. They can use terms that you provide or find their own.

FIGFIGS (FIGURING OUT FIGURATIVE LANGUAGE)

FigFigs is a powerful way to help students develop the habit of thinking about multiple meanings, idioms, and figurative language such as analogies, metaphors, and symbols (adapted from Bean, Singer, & Cowan, 1985). In addition to its use in language arts classes, this activity is effective in science and social studies classes. These classes have texts with words that students often know at a literal level but whose meanings they need to learn in the special contexts of science and social studies.

Procedure

1. Use the FigFigs reproducible at the end of this chapter on page 165. Make a transparency to use on an overhead projector to model the activity for students. In the left-hand column, put the unknown word or expression from the text. This word may be figurative, such as an idiom, symbol, or metaphor, or it may be an additional meaning of a known word (e.g., a mouse for a computer).

2. In the right-hand column, write down what the word is actually describing in the text.

3. In the middle space, write an explanation of the word's meaning. Note how the two meanings are similar, what the author was trying to emphasize, or why you think the author used this particular word (or why people, in general, use it). Figure 18 shows a sample form filled in.

4. Have students determine whether any language in the middle or right-hand columns "came up figurative." That is, did the explanations also contain figurative terms? If so, place those terms down the left-hand column and keep filling in the rows. For example, in Figure 18 the word *trapped* was used in the figurative column. It was then put in the next figurative row and the word *escape* could even be put below it.

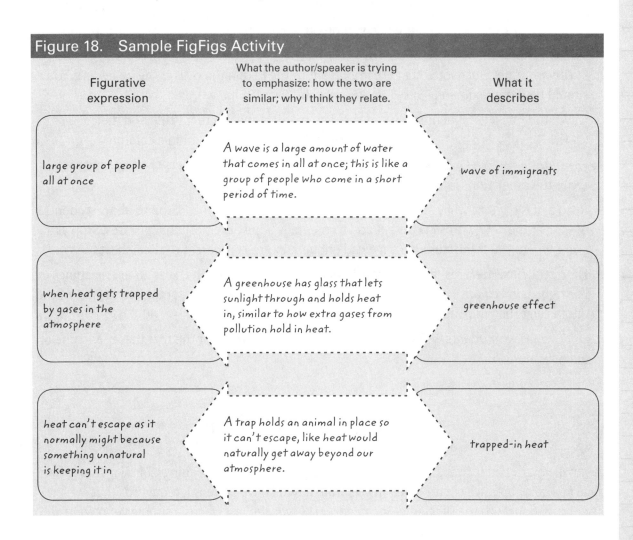

Figure 18. Sample FigFigs Activity

Figurative expression	What the author/speaker is trying to emphasize: how the two are similar; why I think they relate.	What it describes
large group of people all at once	A wave is a large amount of water that comes in all at once; this is like a group of people who come in a short period of time.	wave of immigrants
when heat gets trapped by gases in the atmosphere	A greenhouse has glass that lets sunlight through and holds heat in, similar to how extra gases from pollution hold in heat.	greenhouse effect
heat can't escape as it normally might because something unnatural is keeping it in	A trap holds an animal in place so it can't escape, like heat would naturally get away beyond our atmosphere.	trapped-in heat

5. You may scaffold the activity by filling in certain boxes or columns beforehand and creating handouts from that, then letting the students fill in the rest.

6. Students can build up a large set of FigFigs throughout the year. Instead of the box-and-arrow graphic, you could have students use a simple grid with three columns that they can easily draw in their notebooks. Keep a large FigsFigs chart on the wall, if desired.

GUESS AND ADJUST

This quick and easy activity (adapted from Poindexter, 1994) serves three important purposes: (1) building background knowledge for reading, (2) using word parts to predict word meaning, and (3) figuring out words using context related to the title and author's purpose.

Procedure

1. Write the title of a text to be studied on the board or, preferably, in a graphic organizer such as the Guest and Adjust form at the end of this chapter on page 166. Also, give a copy to each student to fill out while you fill out your copy. You can make your copy into a transparency, if you choose.

2. Write any other clue words that are important to the text in the oval at the lower left. You should have approximately 3 to 5 new words and 6 to 10 clue words.

3. Have students guess the meanings of the new words using the text's title and their knowledge of word parts. They should write their guesses in the middle column.

4. Have students do a Quickwrite (see activity in Chapter 4) that predicts the text content; write the predictions in the triangle.

5. Read aloud the text while students follow along in their own books. Stop to allow students to look at the new words in context and to mentally adjust their original guesses. Stop at a point where you think students have had enough text to compare it to their sheets.

6. Have students finish reading the text on their own, and then fill in the adjusted meanings in the right-hand column of the graphic organizer. See Figure 19 for a completed sample of the organizer. (The prediction is a little off.)

7. Optional: Have students write a final three-sentence summary of the text that uses some of the new words.

KEYWORDS WEB

We make many connections when we figure out and store word meanings. Similar to creating files on a computer, we create "files" in the brain in which we store related words that somehow connect to the file name or category. This vocabulary web is a simple yet powerful

Figure 19. Sample Guess and Adjust Activity

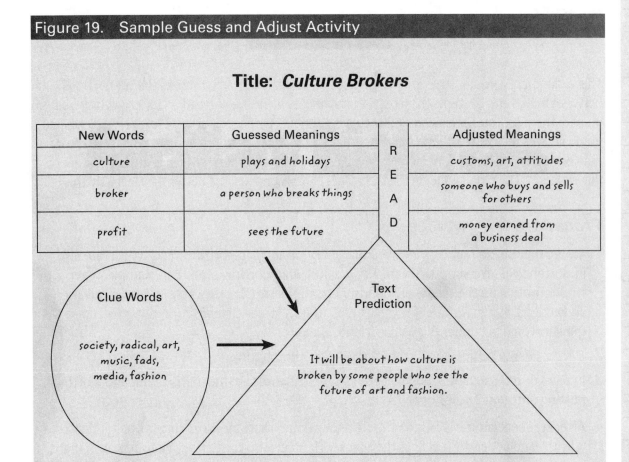

Title: *Culture Brokers*

New Words	Guessed Meanings	R E A D	Adjusted Meanings
culture	plays and holidays		customs, art, attitudes
broker	a person who breaks things		someone who buys and sells for others
profit	sees the future		money earned from a business deal

Clue Words

society, radical, art, music, fads, media, fashion

Text Prediction

It will be about how culture is broken by some people who see the future of art and fashion.

way to develop the habit of creating connections between new words and the concepts that need to be learned.

Procedure

1. Use the Keywords Web reproducible at the end of this chapter on page 167. Write a central theme or concept in the center oval. Give a photocopy of the web to each student and make a transparency of it as well.

2. Place the web on an overhead projector and fill in two or three keys with important words to emphasize in the lesson or text the students are working on.

3. Have students copy the words onto their own papers and pick one or two more words from the lesson to write in the remaining keys. Have students write descriptive words around each key on the branches provided.

4. As a multimodal option, students can put a symbol next to each word. Have them choose symbols that will help them remember the meanings of the words and have them draw their symbols on the branches with each word.

LIST-GROUP-LABEL PLUS

This variation of a vocabulary strategy developed by Taba (1967) emphasizes the connections between words and concepts from texts that students have already read on a topic, which help to prepare them for future texts on similar topics. Students gather important words from texts and gradually sort them into coherent groups. They can change up groups and put words into more than one category, but they must negotiate the process with others—which is the key feature of this variation. The more students use the words in oral contexts, the better they learn them.

Procedure

1. Model the thinking process involved in classifying and categorizing ideas (which are also important skills for summarizing). Think aloud while sorting items. For example, when students bring up the theme of friendship from the text, I ask for categories for qualities and actions. When a student says, "listen," I think aloud, "Listen is something you do so I think it would fall under the 'What friends do' category."

2. Have students gather words from texts on a common topic.

3. In pairs or groups, have students agree on which words are most important and worthy of putting onto small strips of paper.

4. After students put the words on the strips, have them sort the strips into groups and discuss why they go under the headings they chose. They can also cluster them into semantic maps.

5. Students share a category and justify why they put the words into that category. You can make a sort chart with columns or create a semantic map for this. The category names go at the top of the columns in a chart or in the ovals of a semantic map. Figure 20 shows a sample sort chart.

6. If you sort the information with a semantic map or web, you can use it to give a minilesson on going from maps to outlines, which can be useful later if the students are asked to

Figure 20.   Sample Sort Chart for List-Group-Label Plus

outline the text. Once the web is created, students can use the form as a note-taking sheet while reading.

7. Optionally, students can write a paragraph that uses most of the words in the category. You can model this early on in the year.

MULTIPLE MEANINGS TABLE

This is a quick activity that can benefit students who need to develop the habit of understanding multiple meanings and using word parts. Remind students that people often use one word for several different purposes. There usually is a reason that we use a particular word. For example, we say *mouse* for the computer accessory rather than *dog*, because the item looks like a mouse. This activity also can be done with the help of a dictionary, using it to provide extra meanings in the meaning boxes.

Procedure

1. Provide students with several important multiple-meaning words to discuss and look up, some of which may only have two meanings. Give each student a copy of the Multiple Meanings Table located at the end of this chapter on page 168 (you can model the activity with a transparency of it), and have students write a multiple-meaning word in the first space in the left column.

2. Have students notice the parts of the word and write the parts and their meanings in the next column.

3. Have students create a short list of similar words that could have related meanings in the next column.

4. Have students look up the word in the dictionary and summarize (not copy) the meanings and definitions in the Multiple Meanings column. Optionally, you can have students discuss and mark whether the meanings are more abstract or concrete, literal or figurative.

5. In the far right column, have students write what the definitions have in common. (This is the higher order thinking step that will help the students apply the word in different settings in the future.)

NEW WORDS IN CONTEXT CHART

The matrix in this activity helps students to systematically think about word meanings and then remember them. It also is a good record of the words that students are encountering and attempting to learn. The matrix builds the habit of using both context and word parts to figure out word meanings.

Procedure

1. Create a matrix similar to the one shown (or have students create their own) and model how it is used with a sample text.

2. Put a sentence from the text with a new word or phrase in column 1 and circle the new word.

3. Put word parts and related words in column 2.

4. Use columns 1 and 2 to predict the word's meaning.

5. Read further in the text and see if the text helps form the word's meaning, and then discuss the word in class or use a dictionary to find the word's meaning.

6. Use or generate a sentence, rhyme, or picture that helps the students to remember the word's meaning.

1. Word or Phrase in Context	2. Word Parts, Related Words	3. Prediction of Meaning From Columns 1 and 2	4. Meaning From Discussion or Dictionary	5. Sentence, Rhyme, or Image That Helps Me Remember Its Meaning
She circumvented the fire by diving under it.	Circum-	Went around	Avoided	Circumference is round = go around

SCUBA DIVING INTO WORD MEANINGS

SCUBA (adapted from Salembier & Cheng, 1997) is a catchy acronym students can use to remember the important steps of figuring out an unfamiliar word: Sounding it out, Checking the clues, Using the main idea, Breaking the word into parts, and Asking for help.

Procedure

1. Create a poster similar to SCUBA Diving Into Word Meanings at the end of this chapter on page 169, or enlarge the reproducible version and display the poster in your classroom.

2. Model the SCUBA process for students by thinking aloud while you use it with a sample text.

3. Have students work in pairs to practice the SCUBA process. You can create SCUBA cards (four to a page) and have students write on the back, using the SCUBA process for several words during reading.

4. After reading, hold a class discussion about the effectiveness of the SCUBA process.

SELF-SELECTED VOCAB QUIZZES

If we must give quizzes, let's let students learn words that (a) they don't already know, and (b) are useful. This brief activity, which should take less than 10 minutes, is powerful because it gives students some choice in what they will learn. They take ownership of the words, which creates better retention.

Procedure

1. Let students choose five to seven words from their reading and have them write the words in their notebooks in two different spots: one spot for words and meanings, and the other spot for the words only. Students could even write the words on the left side of a sheet of paper and the definitions on the right side and then fold the paper in half to hide the definitions. Some words may be "strongly suggested" or made obligatory by the teacher.

2. At quiz time, have students copy the words from their "words only" section and write them on a card or half-sheet of paper (which will be less intimidating than a full sheet of paper). They should then write the word meanings or a sentence with each word in it. They then grade themselves by using the definition sheets they created in their notebooks. You can circulate during this activity to observe and assess students' work.

3. Students can share a couple of words with a partner or the whole class for extra credit, if there is time.

TWO-WORD SENTENCE STICKIES

The task of putting two keywords into one sentence is more challenging and memorable than just creating sentences with one new word. As students read a text, they choose two words they should learn from a section or page. Then they construct a new sentence that uses both words. The sentence should relate to the text.

Procedure

1. Give students several 2" × 2" sticky notes.

2. Students read the text and note the two new words they want or need to learn on the back of the sticky note for the appropriate page.

3. They then construct, individually or in pairs, a coherent and logical sentence that uses both words. The sentences will often be in the following formats: cause and effect, subordination/classification, relationship, compare/contrast, and so forth. Discourage students from simply writing two definitions, unless the definition of one word includes the second word. Sentences should show that students understand the word meanings.

4. Have students share the sentences with each other and then with the entire class. Write or synthesize a few sentences to put on the wall.

5. Optionally, after reading, have students write a six-sentence paragraph, using new sentences with six of the words. The paragraph should be coherent and the words do not have to be limited to one per sentence.

VOCABULARY BANK NOTES

This activity is similar to many word map activities that abound in literature on teaching vocabulary (see Nagy, 1988). It also is very similar to using vocabulary study cards but with a slightly more interesting twist that makes the words more valuable. You can, of course, guide students toward the more "valuable" words if they are choosing words that are too easy or not the target concept words you need to teach. The activity is geared more for middle school, but many high school teachers with whom I have worked have modified it with success.

Procedure

1. You or the students should choose words and terms that have "value" in your class and in other content areas.

2. Photocopy the Vocabulary Bank Notes reproducibles at the end of this chapter on pages 170 and 171 (note the front and back sides), and cut the copied pages to make one bank note per student. Have students fill in one or both sides of each bank note.

3. Have students create a list of the bank note words and put the list in their notebooks for later reference.

4. Have students show their bank notes to you or turn them in for you to assign values to the notes. Each note should be valued between $5 and $20. You should orally check to see if each student knows his or her word and why it is important. If not, do not give value to that particular bank note until the student knows it. Choose certain days of the week to have students take five minutes to share and discuss their words with a partner. They share the notes they have been making that week during reading, homework, or other learning activities.

5. Optional: At the end of the quarter, semester, or marking period, students can buy prize items for large sums of bank note money (e.g., a candy bar for $450). Remind them that they must still know all the words they "spend" in order to get their items.

WORD BANK

The best use of space on your wall could be an area you will call the Word Bank. Word banks are sections of the classroom wall that are devoted to the display and study of important words (Cunningham, 1995). New and important words in the bank can serve as a constant and quick reference for reinforcing content and academic concepts. The bank concept is a way to give different values to various words, which can be combined with the previous activity in this chapter, Vocabulary Bank Notes.

Procedure

1. Along with students, think about which categories to use for the words you will put in the bank. (I usually make two or three categories.) Use different colors for different categories. The headings might include ones such as these:

- Words From Chapter 5
- Words With Familiar Word Parts
- Culture Words
- Academic Language Words
- Idioms and Multiple-Meaning Words

- Long Words
- Algebra Words
- Words Borrowed From Other Languages
- Adjectives
- Favorite Long Words

2. Cut some pieces of paper (e.g., 8½" × 14" sheets cut the long way to become 4¼" × 14") on which to write the words, and then "prime the pump" by putting a couple of sample words up as you explain the categories. Each word should be written as large as possible, and its meaning should be written in small letters below it.

3. Have students read a text and choose words that they want to put on the wall, including choosing a category for each word. Have them justify why each chosen word is important to the current lesson or unit and why it goes into the particular category they say it does.

4. Use the words and have students use the bank's words as much as possible in as many ways as possible, in writing and speaking.

Variation

You can assign monetary values (as in the Vocabulary Bank Notes activity) to the relative importance of words. Students can argue for more value for certain words and less value for others. An example of the language they might use is, "This is an important word because...."

WORD REMEMBERING

Even if students are figuring out new words, they still need to remember what the words mean for future texts. Here is a quick way to help students get in the habit of remembering important words.

Procedure

1. Pronounce the word several times.
2. Relate it to other similar words that you know (e.g., *paramount* → *mountain*).

3. Create a visual image or connection in your mind for the word, using the text when possible. (Use mnemonic strategies.) I often remember the word *pedantic* by picturing an ant with glasses reading a large book.

4. Draw or cut out a picture that illustrates the word's meaning.

5. Make up a sentence or rhyme that uses the word and helps you to remember the meaning. For example, for the word *forge*, you could say, "The blacksmith has to forge five swords for King George."

6. Have students practice and follow these steps on their own. They can also invent their own remembering strategies.

Reflection Questions

1. Why aren't the typical "look up a word, write the definition, and use it in a sentence" methods of vocabulary very helpful?

2. Choose a short text that you will teach. Write down the words and terms with which your struggling readers will struggle. How will you teach students to figure out the words in the text (or at least guess their meanings)?

3. Why does reading a lot help increase a person's vocabulary so much?

4. Write an inquiry question for this chapter's habit and a teaching activity. Gather evidence over time and make adjustments based on student work (e.g., How can I best help students develop vocabulary habits, evidenced by classroom quizzes and essays, using the .... activity?).

NOTES: _____

_____

_____

_____

_____

_____

_____

_____

_____

_____

_____

_____

CONNECT THE WORDS

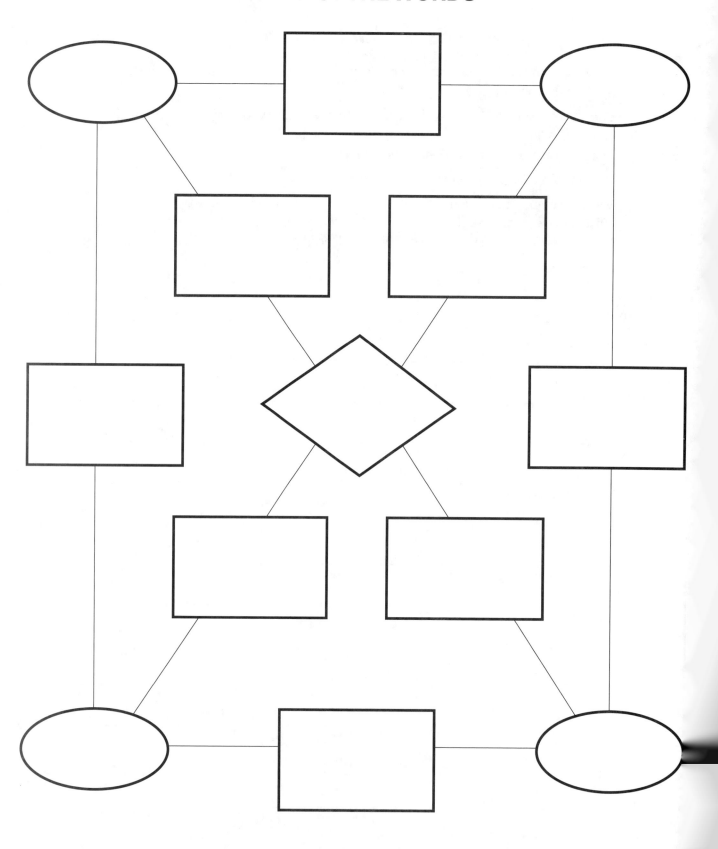

FIGFIGS
(e.g., metaphors, analogies, idioms, symbols)

On the left, write down the figurative expression from the text/talk, such as idioms, symbols, metaphors, and so forth. On the right, write down what it is describing. In the middle arrow, write down why you think the author chose this description, how the two are similar, and/or the reasons why you think the two relate. Examples: It all boils down to, obstacles on a journey (used in a business meeting), like a chess game (to describe a relationship), the branches of tree (choices in life), the slings and arrows of outrageous sorrows, the Trickle Down Theory, let's shift gears for a moment, etc.

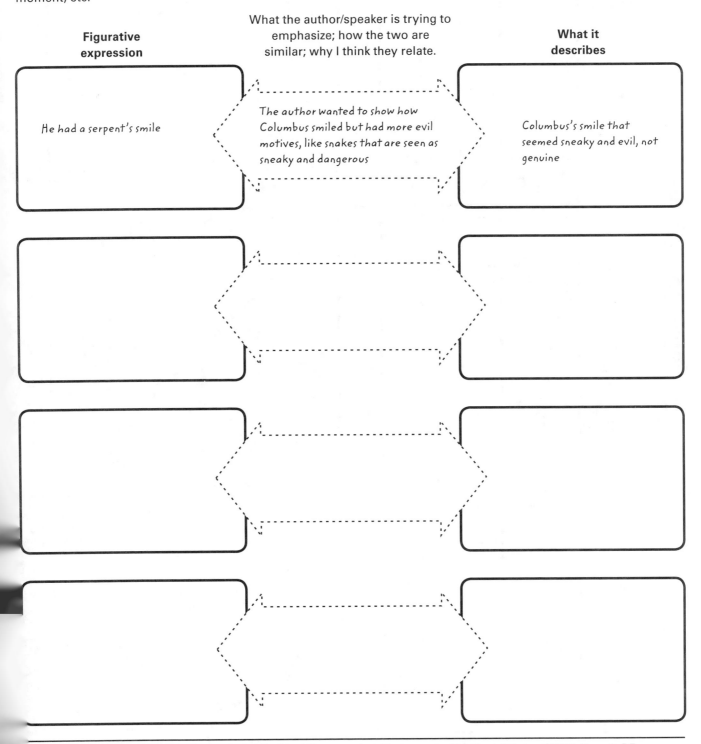

Figurative expression

What the author/speaker is trying to emphasize; how the two are similar; why I think they relate.

What it describes

He had a serpent's smile

The author wanted to show how Columbus smiled but had more evil motives, like snakes that are seen as sneaky and dangerous

Columbus's smile that seemed sneaky and evil, not genuine

GUESS AND ADJUST

Title:

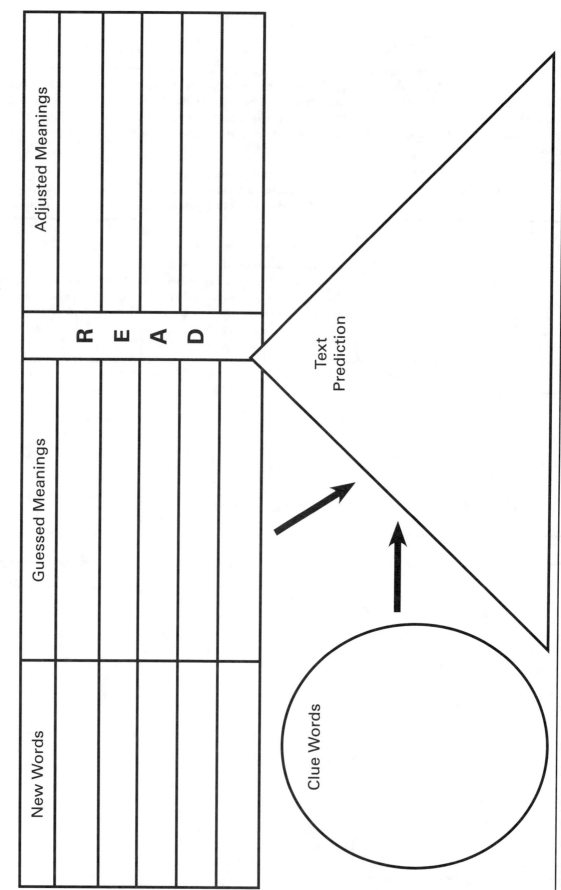

New Words	Guessed Meanings		Adjusted Meanings
		R	
		E	
		A	
		D	

Text Prediction

Clue Words

KEYWORDS WEB

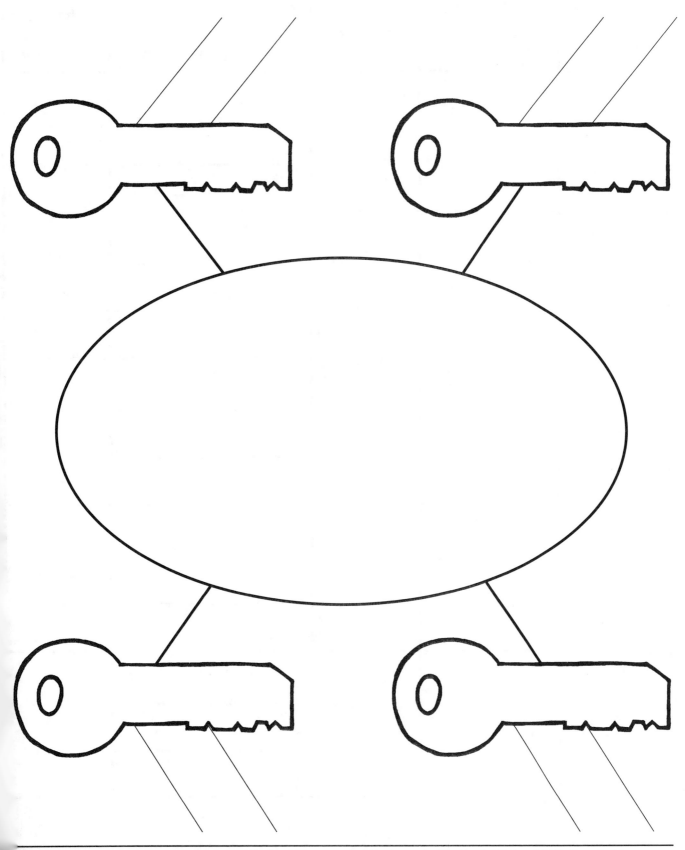

MULTIPLE MEANINGS TABLE

Word	Word Parts and Meanings	Similar Words	Summaries of Multiple Meanings	What They Have in Common
			1. 2. 3.	
			1. 2. 3.	
			1. 2. 3.	
			1. 2. 3.	
			1. 2. 3.	

SCUBA DIVING INTO WORD MEANINGS

S **Sound** it out. Say the whole word to yourself a couple of times.

C **Check** the clues in the sentence and paragraph and think about what word would fit best in place of the unknown word.

U **Use** the text's main idea and the pictures to make a good guess for the word's meaning.

B **Break** the word into parts that have meanings that you recognize, and/or think of similar words.

A **Ask** for help from a peer or teacher, or use a glossary or dictionary.

Source: Adapted from Salembier, G.B., & Cheng, L.C. (1997). SCUBA-dive into reading. *Teaching Exceptional Children, 29*(6), 68–71.

Building Reading Comprehension in Grades 6–12: A Toolkit of Classroom Activities (second edition) by Jeff Zwiers © 2010. Newark, DE: International Reading Association. May be copied for classroom use.

WORD MEANING CHECKLIST

IMPORTANCE

☐ Is the word important enough to figure out? Do I need to know it to understand the text?

CONTEXT

☐ How do the sentence, paragraph, and nearby pictures give me clues to the word's meaning?

☐ Which known word or phrase could I use to replace the unknown word?

☐ Does my replacement make sense grammatically?

☐ Does my replacement fit into the overall text meaning?

WORD PARTS

☐ Which parts of this word have meanings that I recognize?

☐ What are some words I know that are similar or have similar parts?

PREDICTED MEANING

☐ When I combine the previous two steps, what is the best meaning that I can store in my mind for now?

☐ How can I best remember the meaning?

CHAPTER

Monitoring One's Own Comprehension

* * *

You want me to retell
what I just read?
But I wasn't listening!

Comprehension monitoring means being aware of our level of understanding as we read and then using this awareness to guide us (Keene & Zimmermann, 2007). Comprehension monitoring is an unseen "higher level" of reading, similar to the unseen director of a play, who keeps the show running smoothly and fixes the problems as they arise. This director is behind the scenes, managing the actors (comprehension habits) to produce the play (text meaning).

Teaching students to monitor their comprehension is difficult. As teachers, it helps to reflect on how we monitor our own comprehension when we read and then to figure out how to model this habit for our students. We must work hard and be creative to make our thinking processes visible to students. At the same time, we must also create opportunities for students to practice comprehension monitoring enough so that they gradually own the habit.

Basic elements of comprehension monitoring include the following:

- Establishing a purpose for reading, and keeping in mind whether or not the purpose is being met by checking to see whether each new piece of text fits, or changes, that purpose for reading.

- Combining new information with previously stored information in your brain.

- Realizing when a current part of the reading clashes with your evolving main idea or expectations.

- Controlling your attention, commitment, attitudes, and motivation during learning. Questions that help with this step include the following:

    Can I keep other things out of my mind long enough to concentrate on this text?

    Am I committed enough to read it all and go back over it, if necessary?

    Do I believe I have the ability to understand this?

    Am I motivated enough to expend the energy to understand this?

- Using "fix-up" strategies when comprehension breaks down. These are called strategies because they are more conscious and noticeable techniques (i.e., one can better remember using them) for overcoming comprehension problems than the automatic habits in other chapters. Fix-up strategies include the following:

  - Rereading the text
  - Reading further to see if things clear up
  - Sounding out words
  - Adjusting reading rate (slowing down or speeding up)
  - Noticing extra clues such as text structure, pictures, introductions, back cover, questions, and so on
  - Asking for help and using additional resources

Good readers do not just zoom in on the details at the expense of losing sight of the big picture that the author is trying to convey. Rather, good readers have the habit of frequently "zooming out" to think about the big picture—the main idea—in order to avoid getting lost. For example, as you read this book, you may focus on specific strategies that interest you while staying aware of the overall purpose—that of building good reading habits in all students in all content areas.

Effective comprehension monitoring involves making a split-second decision about whether the reader has comprehended the current sentence well enough to proceed to the next sentence. (You just did that if you are now reading this sentence.) We are constantly asking, Did the sentence fit well enough into my main idea for this text? If so, then we proceed. If not, we modify our comprehension. Many teachers, however, tell me that their students tend to vary—often drastically—in their criteria for attaining a satisfactory level of comprehension in order to continue forward in a reading. That is, students might not know when they are comprehending—or, even worse—when they are not. Some students, for example, may think that just saying all the words correctly is enough and that by doing so the text will magically sink in by the time they finish it. Others might get through an entire text without establishing any purpose for reading it.

Students need to acquire the habit of establishing an overall purpose for reading (e.g., plot, description, persuasion, etc.) and then must learn to frequently zoom out to see if that purpose is being met, or if it needs to be modified in some way as indicated by the text's details. The following checklist helps students to notice when they are not comprehending.

Six signs that you are stuck in the mud of not comprehending:

- The pictures inside your mind stop forming or moving.
- Your questions, predictions, and inferences are not getting answered.
- Your mind wanders from the text; you read it but are thinking about something else.
- The current page has nothing to do with what you thought the big picture or author's purpose was for the text.
- You cannot summarize the last few paragraphs or pages.
- Characters appear and you cannot remember who they are.

One subtle way to reduce these comprehension problems is to have students use bookmarks with reading and thinking reminders. For example, you can use or adapt the bookmarks found in this book: Comprehension Bookmark (this chapter, page 198), Reading Habits Bookmark (this chapter, page 199), and THIEVES Bookmark (Chapter 4, page 96). Nudge students to use the bookmarks by announcing a "bookmark moment," in which students stop what they are doing to reflect on which bookmark items they are doing and not doing.

Motivation

Comprehension monitoring takes a considerable amount of mental energy. Much of this energy comes from motivation, both internal and external (Alvermann & Phelps, 2001). If a student is motivated to genuinely understand something in a text, he or she often will expend the energy to monitor comprehension in the reading process and work through problems. However, if he or she is not motivated, a reader will monitor comprehension just enough to get by. Just getting by provides a poor workout for the "mental muscles" of comprehension monitoring. Over time, obviously, lack of motivation contributes to "metacognitive atrophy" in reading.

The following are some motivation suggestions to use with students:

- Create interesting and fun learning tasks (not just "answer-10-questions" exercises).
- Provide texts that are interesting and relevant.
- Provide plenty of "frontloading," prereading, and background knowledge building.
- Provide enough time for the reading to be done.
- Provide opportunities for students to examine and share their thinking processes.
- Provide practice with practical and functional texts, including applications, articles, rules, directions, manuals, warranties, contracts, bills, letters, the "fine print," and so on. Very few classes ever teach how to comprehend and use these texts, yet much of real life requires knowing how to read them.
- Provide opportunities to practice with less and less teacher support over time. This allows students' comprehension monitoring to become second nature and eventually automatic.

Metacognition allows students to take the reins of their thinking. And as they do begin to do so, ideally long before sixth grade, they make our jobs easier and increase their chances of success in all that they do. As Baker and Beall (2009) argue, "Indeed, the momentum is shifting such that students may eventually have the opportunity to contribute as much to their own learning as do their teachers. The development of metacognition is a critical component of that process" (p. 378).

Tools Chart for Monitoring Comprehension

Table 19 shows the usefulness of this chapter's activities for various content areas. On the left side of the table, a √ in a column indicates that the activity is useful in that stage of

Table 19.		When and Where to Use the Activities in Chapter 8				
Before Reading	During Reading	After Reading	Activity	Social Studies	Science	English/ EL
✓	✓	✓	Academic Conversations	✓✓	✓✓	✓✓
✓	✓	✓	Comprehension Target Talk	✓✓	✓✓	✓✓
✓	✓		Discussion Starters	✓✓	✓	✓✓
	✓		Genre Transformation	✓✓	✓✓	✓✓
✓	✓	✓	Habit Stations	✓✓	✓✓	✓✓
✓	✓		Mental Multitasking Practice	✓✓	✓✓	✓✓
	✓		Multiple Intelligences Corners	✓✓	✓	✓✓
✓	✓	✓	Observation and Feedback Record	✓✓	✓✓	✓✓
	✓		Read Aloud Everything	✓✓	✓✓	✓✓
✓	✓		Read-Aloud Think-Aloud (RATA)	✓✓	✓✓	✓✓
	✓		Think-Aloud Checklist	✓✓	✓	✓✓
	✓	✓	Think-Aloud Hand Signals	✓✓	✓	✓✓
	✓		Think-Aloud Note Grids	✓✓	✓✓	✓✓
✓	✓	✓	Think-Notes	✓✓	✓	✓
✓	✓	✓	Why, Why, Why Chart	✓✓	✓✓	✓

reading. On the right side of the table, a √ in a column indicates that the activity is helpful for comprehension of common texts used in that content area. A √√ on the right side of the table means that the activity is especially helpful for that type of text and that you should try it as soon as possible.

Activities for Monitoring Comprehension

ACADEMIC CONVERSATIONS

The quality of student conversations in class can make significant positive differences in overall learning and comprehension. Academic Conversations (Zwiers & Crawford, 2009), similar to literature circles (Daniels & Bizar, 2005), allow students to hold extended conversations about texts. To build students' academic conversation skills, you develop five core "moves" that keep text-based conversations from ending or from heading off into "tangentland" (see Table 20).

Table 20.   Academic Conversation Moves and Prompts

Features/Moves/Skills of Conversations (with symbols and hand motions)	Stems for Prompting the Feature	Stems for Responding
Elaborate and clarify (Pull hands apart)	Can you elaborate? What do you mean by…? Can you tell me more about…? What makes you think that? Can you justify that? Can you be more specific?	I think it means that… In other words,…
Support ideas with examples from this text, other texts, the world, and one's own life (Index finger on pinky of other hand, palm up)	Can you give an example from the text? Can you show me where it says that? What are examples from other texts? What is a real-world example? What is an example from your life? Are there any cases of that?	For example,… In the text it said that… One case showed that… An example from my life is…
Build on or challenge another's idea (Layer hands on each other and build up)	What do you think about my point that…? Can you add to this idea? Do you agree? What might be other points of view?	I would add that… I want to expand on your point about… Then again, I think that… I see it another way… Yet I wonder also if…
Paraphrase (Put thumb and index finger together)	Is that clear? Do you see what I'm saying?	So, what you are saying is that… Let me see if I understand you…is that right?
Synthesize whole conversation (Cup both hands into a ball)	What have we discussed so far? How should we synthesize what we talked about? How can we bring this all together?	We can say that… The main theme/point of the text seems to be… As a result of talking, we think that we should…

These are most effective in pairs to maximize the amount of talking and attentive listening in a short period of time. Here is a brief overview of the activity and its procedures (Zwiers & Crawford, 2009).

Procedure

1. Give minilessons in which you model the prompting and use of each conversation move along with its hand motions and symbols. You can also have pairs of students model their conversations in front or in the middle of the class as the rest of the class observes and takes notes. The models should emphasize the minilesson skill to be learned that day.

2. After reading a text or engaging in a reciprocal teaching session, have students get into pairs and use the conversation moves to deepen and extend their conversations. Have them come up with different perspectives and support their ideas with information from the text.

3. After students summarize their conversations in pairs, have them share a synthesis of their ideas with the entire class. You can chart their ideas and invite others to add to the ideas in a whole-class discussion.

COMPREHENSION TARGET TALK

When students discuss texts (narrative and expository) in groups, they develop academic thinking and language habits. One of the glitches that I and other teachers have noticed during many group discussions of text is the lack of evaluation of ideas. That is, students can be overly content with any idea that somewhat fits into a reading habit category. They don't filter out the unhelpful ideas.

Teachers often ask for a way to get students to (a) assess the value of their idea for comprehending, and (b) as a group, discuss, filter, prune, evaluate, and build on ideas to make them more useful for comprehension. A popular version of cooperative group work for text discussion is reciprocal teaching (Palincsar & Brown, 1984), which focuses on four comprehension habits: questioning, clarifying, summarizing, and predicting. I have worked for several years with teachers who have since grouped clarifying and questioning together, while adding a fourth skill, connecting and visualizing. I put the skills into a target visual with comprehension in the center. You can have students simply fill in the quadrants or, even better, have them evaluate the usefulness and relevance of the thought. The more useful the thought, the closer it goes to the center. If there is disagreement, great! This allows students to discuss and support their ideas with logical reasoning and evidence from the text. Of course, model this several times and show how not all ideas are equal, and how some even waste time in the group, and in your head.

COMPREHENSION TARGET TALK

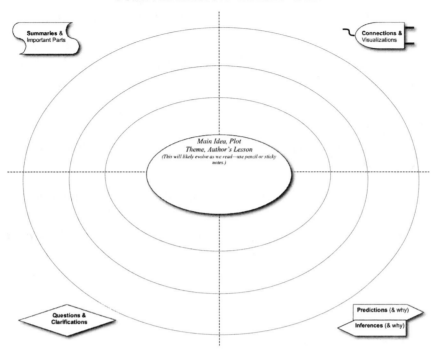

Procedure

1. Model how to consider the value of various ideas and fill in the Comprehension Target Talk form located at the end of the chapter on page 197. For example, create a wild tangent about your uncle's pet iguana and show it being off the paper. Then come up with a valuable connection, draw the shape, and note it.

2. Assign students to groups of two to four and have each group decide on the order of facilitation and on who will start as facilitator. The facilitator or the person to the left or right can take notes on the target visual.

3. Before reading, build students' interest in the text and engage the prior knowledge of the students by using anticipation guides (Chapter 4), semantic webbing (Chapter 3), brainstorming, THIEVES (Chapter 4), visual prompts, Quickwrites (Chapter 4), text scanning, minidramas, videos, and so on.

4. Summaries/Important Parts: The facilitator summarizes the key points of the just-read text, and the other students add to (or subtract from) the summary. The group members discuss the usefulness of the summary to the overall text meaning and place it in the summary shape, evaluating where it goes on the diagram (close to or far from the bull's eye).

5. Questions & Clarifications: Each group's facilitator decides on a stopping point in the text, and the students silently read as a group. When all members finish (early finishers can jot down extra notes), the facilitator prompts for on-the-surface and under-the-surface questions (see Chapter 6) from the group or puts a question out to the group. Questions might also be used to clarify concepts or vocabulary. Students discuss possible answers to each question. The group members discuss how important the question might be to the text's overall meaning and the recorder puts a shape on the diagram with the question in it.

6. Connections & Visualizations: The facilitator asks members to make connections to other texts, the world, or their own lives. They also share what they visualized as they read. They discuss the usefulness of the connections and visualizations and write them inside the shapes on the diagram.

7. Predictions/Inferences: Each group's facilitator predicts what happens next in the text, based on prior evidence: "I predict that...," and "My evidence is...." Other students can agree or disagree and give their evidence for doing so.

8. Continue the process with other members of the groups facilitating the process.

Work with students to develop norms for group interaction (you can put these on a poster to hang in the classroom), such as the following:

- Everybody helps.

- Give reasons for your suggestions.

- No one is finished until everyone is finished.

- You have the right to ask for help.

- You have the duty to offer help.

- You have the duty to play your role.

DISCUSSION STARTERS

This activity should be used the whole year. It helps students to broaden their types of thinking about reading through discussion with you and with other students. As students hear and use these discussion techniques, they acquire the habits of complex thinking on which these techniques depend. That is, if we provide academic language for students to process text information, they will be better able to comprehend the text. We are giving them linguistic tools to explore new ways of thinking.

Procedure

1. Make laminated signs or posters of some discussion starters to put on the wall. Some sample ideas are shown in Table 21.

2. Explain each discussion starter and model how it can be used. For example, you can act out a concept and have students say, "I infer from your actions that you are frustrated." Or you might prompt students to ask you for evidence or examples when you say, "Babies who listen to Mozart end up smarter than those who listen to rock music."

Table 21.   Sample Discussion Starters

Predictions, Inferences, Questions

Prompts and Questions	*Sample Response Starters*
• Why do you think...?	• From the part about..., I infer that...because....
• What do you predict will happen?	• I have a question about....
• What can you infer from...? Why?	• I predict that...because....
• Any questions about...?	• I think it means that....
• Why did the author...?	• I wonder why....

Reactions, Opinions, Feelings

Prompts and Questions	*Sample Response Starters*
• What is your opinion about...?	• In my opinion...because....
• How do you feel the author...?	• I agree with (student's name) because....
• What would you have done in...?	• I disagree with (student's name) because....
• Does anyone disagree? Why?	• I was surprised when....
• If you were (character), how would you have...?	• When..., I felt....
	• I think (person) should have....
	• I was confused when....
	• I was disappointed when....
	• I would have...because....

Evidence, Connections

Prompts and Questions	*Sample Response Starters*
• What evidence from the text supports what you say?	• I think it means that...because....
• Could you give an example of...?	• I would like to add to what (student name) said about....
	• This relates to when I....

3. Throughout the school year, continually refer students' attention to these discussion starters in order to expand and cultivate these ways of thinking about text. You also should push students to supply text-based evidence for their classroom comments and opinions.

GENRE TRANSFORMATION

In Genre Transformation (Zwiers, 2004), students transform a given text into a different type of text or genre. The new form should retain and clarify the important ideas that the student understands from the original. This requires a large amount of inference, synthesis, and comprehension of the important parts of the text.

Examples include the following:

- Turning a story into a poem, letter, commercial, diary, play, song, comic book, or book jacket

- Turning a textbook chapter into a newspaper article, poster, biography, interview, letter, narrative, poem, or news program with video
- Turning a biography into a letter, interview, poem, short story, comic strip, or poster

Procedure

1. Model for students how to transform a variety of texts. In the beginning of the year, you will probably concentrate on only a few types of transformations such as a story into a poem or a history text into a letter.

2. Model the types of thinking skills that you want students to practice such as making the distinction between cause and effect, fact and opinion, being able to sequence events, using persuasion, and so forth. Tell students that you want to see evidence of this thinking in their text transformations.

3. Emphasize that readers must concentrate on the most important information in the text in order to effectively carry it over to a different text. Think about what the author of the original text wouldn't want you to forget when creating a new version of his or her text.

Variation

If needed, you can use an intermediary scaffold, such as a graphic organizer for main idea, to capture the elements needed for the new version of the text.

HABIT STATIONS

Once students have seen and practiced many of the habit-building activities in this book, they can practice them in stations. Stations allow students to work on habits that need to be strengthened, and they help make students aware of the different habits that are needed in the same text. They allow for both individual and group constructivist work, with a choice of activities.

Procedure

1. For each of the six comprehension habits (organizing text information by sculpting the main idea and summarizing, connecting to background knowledge, making inferences and predictions, generating and answering questions, understanding and remembering word meanings, and monitoring one's own comprehension), prepare stations throughout the classroom with posters of habit-building practice activities, along with copies of graphic organizers and activity ideas (many of which can be found in this book). It is a good idea to color-code the activities for each habit by using colored paper or by having students use different colors of pens for the activities at each station.

2. Have students form groups and bring their text (group or individual) to a designated station.

3. Students work on one habit during a specified time. This can consist of taking notes on sticky notes, creating and filling in graphic organizers, responding to questions in a journal, drawing, and so on. Students can put their work into notebooks.

4. Have students bring their texts to another table after 5–15 minutes to use with the new station's habit.

5. Have students rotate two or three times and then have them share with their group some examples of habit use and the ways in which the habits help to comprehend the text.

MENTAL MULTITASKING PRACTICE

Remember Figure 1, Attention in the Reading Process (Chapter 1, page 5)? Here is an engaging practice activity for developing more brain storage capacity in students as they read. During reading, we need to keep track of loads of facts, feelings, inferences, questions, predictions, and so on. All students can use more practice at storing and organizing information. This activity is a "quantity" exercise to address that need. This activity is just for quantity, though, so you will need to use other tools to help improve the quality of the thoughts (such as the Comprehension Target Talk, this chapter, page 197).

Procedure

1. Give each student five 3" × 5" cards. Create an overhead with five sections, which you will use to model the note cards. Model steps 2 through 7 below, then put students in pairs.

2. Choose five of the following categories: inferences, predictions, facts, questions, word guesses, feelings, summaries, character traits, or causes and effects. Have students write each chosen category on one of their cards, with the name of the category in large letters on one side of the card.

3. Have students read a text and jot down notes on the appropriate cards, beneath the category headings.

4. Have students cross off items that are no longer helpful or have been contradicted or answered as they get further into the text.

5. When a student reaches three or four items on a card, he or she should quickly hand it to his or her partner.

6. The partner asks the student to recall the items.

7. Partners should help each other if they cannot remember all the items. They can give one another clues instead of giving the outright answer.

8. If desired, you can allow "surprise checks" in which a partner spontaneously asks for a card or two and checks to see how much the other student remembers.

9. Later, you can gather the cards and assess how much and how well students are using the various comprehension habits.

MULTIPLE INTELLIGENCES CORNERS

Multiple Intelligences Corners allows students to understand a text through activities that emphasize different intelligences. The activity gives them a chance to use their stronger academic abilities (intelligences) while developing their weaker ones. You do not need to have students move around to various corners of the classroom, but it does add some engagement to the lesson. See Armstrong (2003) for some great ideas on using multiple intelligences to improve literacy.

Procedure

1. Observe and discuss with students which four intelligences would be good to use for the four corners. Ask students what they would like to work on and which intelligences help them to understand when they read. (I have chosen visual, verbal, musical, and kinesthetic for this example; some other intelligences that you might want to try are math and logic, interpersonal, intrapersonal, and naturalistic.) Create a station in the classroom for each of the four chosen intelligences.

2. Gather some practice activities that go with each intelligence and place them at the appropriate corner station. For example, there are many ideas you can use from this toolkit. For the visual corner, you can use graphic organizers, drawings, art projects, and posters. The music corner might include writing chants and songs in response to a text or video, listening to classical music while reading, or responding to songs or poems in a journal. The kinesthetic corner might include the creation of hand motions, drama, manipulatives, and tableaux. The verbal corner might have ideas for transposing genres, categorizing vocabulary cards, brainstorming ideas, prewriting, analyzing good writing samples, and creating newspapers, short stories, and magazines.

3. Have students start with one type of intelligence and then cycle through the intelligence corners, working in each corner for a set amount of time. Students can keep a notebook or a checklist for the varying types of work in each corner and can check these off each time to avoid repeating the same activity.

OBSERVATION
AND FEEDBACK RECORD

Teacher observation is the best assessment of student reading habits. Feedback is a key component of student learning (Barron & Darling-Hammond, 2008; Marzano et al., 2001). You can observe and interpret your students' comments as indicators of their comprehension habits. Table 22 shows some sample student comments.

Table 22. Student Comments and Comprehension Habits	
Comprehension Habit	**Student Comments**
Summarizing	This section tells about the caste system in India and how it can prevent people from choosing what jobs they want to do.
Connecting to Background Knowledge	When he gave her the money, it reminded me of when I gave my brother money for his bicycle.
	I have a picture in my mind of a cluster of round protons and neutrons with tiny electrons buzzing around it.
Inferring and Predicting	I think the whales find warm and protected waters because their newborns are safer.
	I predict that the next section will explain how the magnets make the motor run.
Questioning	How did humans first discover how to make iron tools? Why did she kiss that frog?
Figuring Out Word Meanings	"His clandestine acts were eventually discovered." Clandestine must be something like hidden or secret.
Monitoring Comprehension	"The lion stacked the antelope?" That couldn't be right. I need to reread it.

Procedure

1. Make a table like the one in Table 22 and use it to quickly jot down key phrases or sentences that students say during class discussions or readings. (You may only manage to write down a few comments a day, but this is fine.)

2. Later, go back and categorize the student comments you wrote and use this information to provide specific and helpful feedback to students about their thinking during reading. For example, you could say, "Great, Silvia, you connected to your background knowledge to help you understand this science concept!"

3. Optional: Place your filled-in table on an overhead projector and discuss the comments with a class.

READ ALOUD EVERYTHING

Too many teachers think that they should not read aloud because students aren't doing "the work." Actually, not reading aloud to students is much more harmful to many struggling readers who have not experienced good models of reading. Hearing the text read aloud allows students to see how the text should be read. Teachers in all content areas and classes should read aloud (Alvermann & Phelps, 2001).

Why read aloud? Because reading aloud does the following:

- Creates a community of learners
- Helps students develop interests for self-selection of reading material
- Models the joy of reading and learning from text
- Shows students how to use punctuation, intonation, and pauses to comprehend text
- Models to students the complexity of thinking involved in reading
- Builds...

  - Language fluency
  - Prior knowledge and practice connecting to prior knowledge
  - Students' understanding of story development and characterization
  - Listening skills and attention span abilities
  - Memory and summarizing abilities
  - Abilities to compare and contrast themes and characters
  - Habits of predicting, questioning, and visualizing
  - Abilities to interpret figurative language

- Provides...

  - Extensive practice in thinking about extended text
  - A common forum for discussing the text
  - Exposure to text and concepts that are above students' current independent reading levels

When should you read aloud? You should read aloud when you want to do the following:

- Emphasize the language in poetry, dialogues, or plays
- Introduce challenging texts and new concepts
- Grab students' attention at the beginning of a lesson
- Get students hooked into a long text
- Expose students to the text when the photocopier breaks or you do not have time to make photocopies

Procedure

1. Read aloud a large variety of materials—directions, novels, poems, articles, editorials, children's books, newspapers, textbook chapters, math story problems—to show students how they can read and think about these texts. And find interesting materials! The more interesting the texts are, even if they are challenging, the more students will read and practice all the habits in this book.

2. Read the first section, or up to half, of the text to get students hooked into the reading. As you read aloud, have students read along, take notes, or fill in graphic organizers that highlight the teaching point/focus habit. Stop at crucial points to emphasize the focus habit, such as summarizing, questioning, or predicting, and then let students continue reading on their own and practicing the focus habit.

In general, don't force students to read aloud, especially in front of the entire class. Create a safe environment where students can occasionally read aloud, but where students who choose not to read aloud will not feel left out.

READ-ALOUD THINK-ALOUD (RATA)

Many struggling readers have never seen what constitutes good, active thinking during reading. Think-alouds (Davey, 1983; Farr, 2001; Robb, 2003), which are found in most reading strategies books, make the invisible more visible. If you use think-alouds on a regular basis, students can gradually acquire any comprehension habit. Think-alouds are times when you stop to describe aloud your thinking process while you are doing something. In our case, we are interested in making visible the fleeting habits of reading comprehension. Read-Aloud Think-Aloud (RATA) is a special combination of reading aloud and modeling aloud one's thoughts for others to hear. RATA is good for times when you do the following:

- Realize you have come to confusing parts in a text and then clarify them with fix-up strategies
- Ask yourself questions
- Make predictions and inferences and see if they are answered or confirmed
- Continue to guess and sculpt the main idea and summarize chunks of text
- Visualize what is happening in the reading and modify mental images, as the text dictates
- Connect to prior knowledge or experience and then prune away or discard connections that are not helpful
- Make analogies and modify them, as the text dictates
- Monitor your understanding of the author's purpose

Procedure

1. Use a wide variety of materials (stories, textbooks, essays, articles, graphs, pictures, etc.) to model. You also can bring in a text that is difficult for you (e.g., a college biology book) to give students a genuine sense of your thinking struggles and how you approach challenging texts.

2. Have a teaching focus. Consider which habit or skill you want students to learn and emphasize it during reading. It is tempting to do too many things during even the simplest texts. Stick to the point. Focus on the focus.

3. Place the text you are reading on an overhead projector or computer screen so students can follow along. Uncover the text as you read aloud and then pause to make comments about what you are thinking in order to comprehend the text. (Do not do this too often, though, or the activity gets slow and tedious.)

4. Verbalize your thoughts about the teaching focus: predictions, pictures, confusing parts, connections to background knowledge, summaries, and so on. I relate the habit to the evolving purpose or main idea along the way. Emphasize how you monitor your comprehension, including modifying the main idea, using fix-up strategies (looking back, reading on), and connecting pieces of text. Table 23 shows a sample think-aloud session, with the reading habits used for each step listed in parentheses after the step. For summary/main idea, an example might start with, "So far, I think this is about...."

5. After reading a portion of the text in this manner (or whenever you feel it is appropriate), you can stop reading from time to time and ask students to think aloud to the class. Later,

Table 23. Sample Think-Alouds	
Fiction: *To Kill a Mockingbird* by Harper Lee	Nonfiction: Article on the duck-billed platypus
- To Kill a Mockingbird? I think this is a metaphor, and it must be important because it is the title but I have no idea what it means. I will keep it in mind if any killing happens in the book. (understand word meanings; monitor comprehension) - Why does the story begin with the story of Jem's broken arm? What will this novel teach me about life back then? About life now? Is Boo Radley a good or bad person? (ask questions) - In this part where the town in described as slow and sleepy, I am picturing a few people walking through a dusty small town, people sitting on porches. (visualize and use background knowledge) - Based on Scout's attitude about school and people and her propensity to say whatever is on her mind, I predict that she will get in trouble a lot throughout the book. I also think that someone will be killed because of the title. And I hope/predict that a mockingbird explanation comes up at some point. (predict) - This chapter basically described the small and slow-paced setting and how Scout, the narrator, was very opinionated and defiant. It also talked about the mystery of Boo Radley and his past. (summarize) - I'm still not sure what the main plot is, though. Usually in the first two chapters I get a sense of the overall problem. Maybe it is about Scout's attitude. Perhaps it will mainly be about Boo Radley. It could be about not going to school, like the Ewells. I will keep these in mind and read on. (sculpt main idea; monitor comprehension)	- This first section talked about how difficult it is to study platypuses (is it platypi?) because they spend so much time in the water and underground. (summarize) - The next section looks like it will cover how they are dying because of pollution. (predict) - Interesting. They use electric responses in their bills to find food in murky water. That sounds like bat radar. (use background knowledge) - This part describes the strange trait of laying eggs despite being a mammal. I wonder if any other mammals lay eggs? (summarize and ask question) - This photo shows the amazing adaptations of the platypus that have allowed it to survive since the time of the dinosaurs. (sculpt main idea)

have students practice this activity on their own in pairs, reading aloud and stopping to think aloud to their partners.

6. Keep track of student think-aloud comments because such observations are excellent indicators of the students' strengths and weaknesses in reading. Use checklists, anecdotes, handheld computers, or another convenient method for recording your notes.

7. Remind students that questions are good, confusion is OK if you fix it, and reading comprehension is proportional to the amount of hard thinking that you do.

Here are some effective think-aloud starters:

- I predict that the next section will be about...because....
- I would like to know more about....
- I wonder why....
- I have a picture in my mind of....
- I think that....
- This is like that time when I....
- This reminds me of....
- This is similar to how....
- I'm not sure what this word means. What word would make sense in this sentence? If I substitute the word _____, does it make sense enough to move on?
- I don't understand this section. I'll read ahead a few lines to see if it becomes clearer. If not, I guess I'll reread it.

Finally, be brief! Listening to the teacher's thoughts can get boring really fast. Have one teaching point to model and don't belabor the point.

Variations

- **RATA Pair Notes:** For this activity, one student in a pair reads aloud and thinks aloud, while the other listens and takes notes on a sticky note. The listener categorizes each thought as one of the six reading habits presented in Chapter 1. The reader then puts the notes at the spots in the text where he or she stopped to think aloud. Later the notes can be used to create written responses and collected (and categorized) on a page in the student's notebook.

- **30-30-30 RATA:** In this variation, the text is divided into thirds and reading and thinking are scaffolded. Each 30 roughly stands for a percentage of the total amount of text read by the teacher or the students. For the first 30% of the text, read and think aloud while students listen and (optionally) take notes. Emphasize a habit (e.g., summarizing, questioning, etc.) for students to practice with the teacher as a class (the next 30%) or independently (the last 30%). For the middle 30% of the text (or up to 50% for difficult texts), read aloud and stop occasionally to allow students to think aloud, either with partners or the whole class.

Students can take notes during this section if you like. For the last 30% of the text, have students read silently and take notes on sticky notes, paper, or graphic organizers to practice the think-aloud habits you want to emphasize. After reading, think aloud again to model the process of bringing text parts together and determining the author's purpose.

• Have students use the Comprehension Bookmark (page 198) or Reading Habits Bookmark (page 199) to spark think-aloud ideas. Use this approach for activities other than reading, such as making clay objects, drawing, writing a poem, organizing a presentation, creating a webpage, and so on. Think-alouds with these activities can be effective because they make the "model" thinker's thoughts visible to the learners in a variety of contexts. Try the activities in the following order, which is from concrete to abstract: Think aloud while making a clay figure, then think aloud while drawing, then think aloud with narrative and then with expository text.

THINK-ALOUD CHECKLIST

The Think-Aloud Checklist is a way to keep track of the comprehension habits and their roles in constructing meaning. You can use this activity with many of the other tools in this toolkit. You also can and should use it with other forms of information processing such as videos, songs, dialogues, art, and math problems.

Procedure

1. Give each student a copy of the Think-Aloud Checklist located at the end of this chapter on page 200 and explain each item on the list, using examples. Have students brainstorm examples of what a person would say for the different habits.

2. Encourage students to bring in samples of texts that you might be unfamiliar with or have trouble easily understanding, such as textbooks in subjects other than the one you teach or lyrics from songs that are popular with students. You can use warranties, research articles, or legal documents—anything you might struggle to understand.

3. Read aloud students' samples and stop at times to think aloud. Students should take notes on your thoughts. Let students discuss their notes with a partner, if desired.

4. Give students examples of helpful thoughts, which get a score of 2 on the checklist. These can include thoughts that relate to the main idea and author's purpose and thoughts that show comprehension the way the author probably intended. Then, also give examples of less helpful thoughts (score of 1), which are random or tangential thoughts that may actually hinder comprehension (e.g., "The greenhouse effect reminds me of my uncle's green house that we painted last year. I fell, and that hurt me.").

5. Put a blank checklist on the overhead projector and fill it in together as a class (using just a few examples) as students share how they interpret each of your think-aloud comments. You also could have a student fill in the checklist while you read and think aloud. The process of assessing you will help students notice the use or lack of habits in their own reading. In addition, assessing you familiarizes them with the habits and gives them the rare experience of being the assessor. (You can also have students use the Comprehension Target Talk visual on page 197 to evaluate thoughts.)

6. Once students are comfortable with the process, have them use the checklist in pairs: One student reads and stops to think aloud while the other uses the checklist. Pairs offer more practice and students are more likely to share their thoughts in smaller settings. As above, the partner uses the Think-Aloud Checklist to assess the reader's ability to construct meaning and monitor comprehension.

7. To assess a student, have the student read. The student then pauses at certain points to verbalize his or her thinking process to you. Pauses can be initiated by either the student or teacher. Simply record the types and quality of comments made by each student. You can create your own checklist, continuum, or visual (e.g., Target).

Variation

Have students do a self-assessment using the following prompts:

- My most common type of comment was _____ because _____.
- The type of comment I think I should make more often is _____ because _____.
- Thinking aloud helped me _____ with this text.

Complete the following prompts yourself about the students:

- Student strengths noted are _____.
- Areas for improvement are _____.
- The most common type of comment by this student is _____.
- A type of comment to include more often in the next think-aloud is _____.

THINK-ALOUD HAND SIGNALS

This activity is a kinesthetic way to involve students during read-alouds and think-alouds. Research abounds showing the success of using extra-verbal ways to reinforce concepts (Druyan, 1997; Marzano et al., 2001). And movement is more fun than simple desk work for most struggling students, especially when they have to learn challenging and abstract concepts.

Procedure

1. First, do a teacher-directed version of the activity: Read aloud to the students and think aloud as you read. Have the students listen to your think-aloud, mentally categorize each thought, and then respond with the corresponding hand signal from the list in Table 24.

Table 24.	Descriptions of Hand Signals for Comprehension Habits
Background Knowledge:	One hand waving behind you, pulling things out of an imaginary backpack
Summarizing:	Both hands up, thumbs and index fingers diagonally framing a big, imaginary picture and then reducing it
Questioning:	Both hands palms up, next to shoulders, eyebrows raised
Inferring:	One hand palm down, moving from high to low, as if diving into in water
Prediction:	Hand held horizontally above the eyes, as if looking far off into the distance
Word Meaning Using Parts:	Chopping motion with one hand
Word Meaning Using Context:	Each hand held out together in the shape of a C; then hands are moved further apart to form a semicircle
Monitoring Meaning:	Index finger on temple

This can show you which students do and do not understand the various reading habits, so that you can provide extra support to students who need it. It also is a quiet activity.

2. When students are ready for more responsibility, do a student-directed version of the activity. This can be later in the same text or with a new text. Read aloud to the students and stop at a certain point, telling the students to do the hand signal that corresponds to their current thought. You can call on a student or two. For example, you could say, "Ana, I noticed from your hand motion that you made an inference. What inference did you make? Why?" Then, you could ask the class, "Did anyone else make a similar inference?"

3. You also can stop at some points during the read-aloud and give a hand signal that prompts students to use the indicated habit. They can write down their results or thoughts or share their thoughts with the class.

4. When you feel that students are ready, have them do an independent version of this activity: Students can work in pairs, following the procedure outlined in step 1 above. One student can be the teacher while the other is the student and then the partners can switch roles.

Variation

You also can make up hand signals for other thinking skills such as compare and contrast, evaluate, persuade, fact versus opinion, cause and effect, and so on.

THINK-ALOUD NOTE GRIDS

Think-Aloud Note Grids are checklists for students to use while you are modeling a think-aloud or when they are thinking aloud in pairs. Students can use two types of grids, one for recording another's thoughts and one for recording their own thoughts. Feel free to change the right-hand columns of the grid as desired to include any type of habit or thinking skill that you wish to emphasize. By analyzing students' think-aloud notes, you can assess the quantity and quality of their thoughts during reading.

Procedure

1. Teach students how to categorize comprehension habits when they hear another person describe his or her thoughts during reading. Practice with the Think-Aloud Note Grid located at the end of this chapter on page 201 by making up think-aloud statements and having students discuss which column to check for each one. You can do this step on an overhead projector.

2. Give each student a copy of the Think-Aloud Note Grid. Start by modeling the think-aloud process with a high-interest activity such as interpreting a picture, watching a video, reading a cartoon, or reading an advertisement.

3. Present the video, picture, text, or other medium, and think aloud as you go through it. Have students take very quick and short notes on your think-aloud in the "Thoughts" column of the grid as you think aloud.

4. Have students categorize each of your think-aloud thoughts by placing one (or more) check marks in the right-hand columns.

5. Have students discuss their notes and your thoughts in pairs or groups to reach a consensus or to notice patterns. For example, you may want to have them tell you which habits you used frequently and which ones it appears you need to work on.

6. Have students take notes on their own thoughts as they read a text and have them notice which habits they used frequently or infrequently. This is a great chance for students to take metacognitive stock of their reading behaviors.

THINK-NOTES

This is a variation of thinking aloud in which the reader writes down thoughts on sticky notes next to the text (see Figure 21). This is effective for building the habit of comprehension monitoring because it is simple enough to do on a daily basis.

Procedure

1. For modeling, use a computer or an overhead projector with colored transparency squares that imitate sticky notes. Read aloud to the students, writing your thoughts on these notes to emphasize the overall gist of the text and any problematic points that you encounter. You can put different types of thoughts on different colors of notes. For example, summaries could go on yellow, inferences on pink, questions on blue, and vocabulary on green.

2. You also can have students cut different shapes of notes to use for different comprehension habits. An oval could be the evolving main idea, a diamond could be a question, and so on. Put an initial for the habit at the bottom of each note (e.g., B for background knowledge usage, M for main idea sculpting, S for summarizing, I for inferring, P for predicting, Q for questioning, W for word meaning interpretation, C for monitoring comprehension).

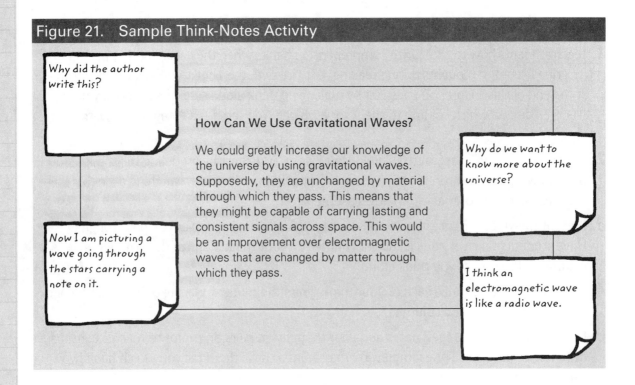

Figure 21. Sample Think-Notes Activity

Why did the author write this?

Now I am picturing a wave going through the stars carrying a note on it.

How Can We Use Gravitational Waves?

We could greatly increase our knowledge of the universe by using gravitational waves. Supposedly, they are unchanged by material through which they pass. This means that they might be capable of carrying lasting and consistent signals across space. This would be an improvement over electromagnetic waves that are changed by matter through which they pass.

Why do we want to know more about the universe?

I think an electromagnetic wave is like a radio wave.

3. For practice, have students go through the process with various types of text. You can require a minimum amount of certain colors or shapes of notes, if necessary. Help students who are having trouble by offering more examples.

4. When finished, students can collect the notes in a journal and organize them by type or by importance to the meaning of the text. Then, students can critique their notes and see if they can improve in certain areas.

WHY, WHY, WHY CHART

The Why, Why, Why Chart is a simple activity for building the vital habit of setting up a purpose for reading different types of text. It challenges students to think about various purposes for reading and to think about the topic of each text.

Procedure

1. Create a chart, such as the following sample, on a laminated poster or written on note cards, an overhead projector, or in students' notes. Feel free to modify the questions.

WHY might the author write this type of text (genre)?	WHY do people read this type of text?	WHY might the author have written this particular text?
WHY might I read this if I didn't (don't) have to?	WHY did the author give the text this title?	WHY might the teacher want us to read this?

2. Give a minilesson to the whole class on how these questions can help comprehension. Discuss how writing is communication and knowing why the author wrote it helps us see what he or she was trying to communicate. These "why" questions can help us focus on the main message of the text. Ask students, "Why is this 'why' question important?" for each of the six boxes in the chart.

3. Have students fill in the chart as they read a particular text.

4. Hold a class discussion after reading to see if any of the answers changed and to synthesize what was learned.

Reflection Questions

1. Why is comprehension monitoring a difficult habit to teach?

2. Choose a difficult text. Quickly read aloud the text to a partner. Stop when the listener indicates; the listener then describes his or her comprehension. The reader can take notes.

3. How does comprehension monitoring build student independence of thought and self-reliance?

4. Write an inquiry question for this chapter's habit and a teaching activity. Gather evidence over time and make adjustments based on student work (e.g., How can I best help students develop comprehension monitory habits, evidenced by discussions and journal entries, using the .... activity?).

NOTES: _____

_____

_____

_____

_____

_____

_____

_____

_____

_____

_____

_____

COMPREHENSION TARGET TALK

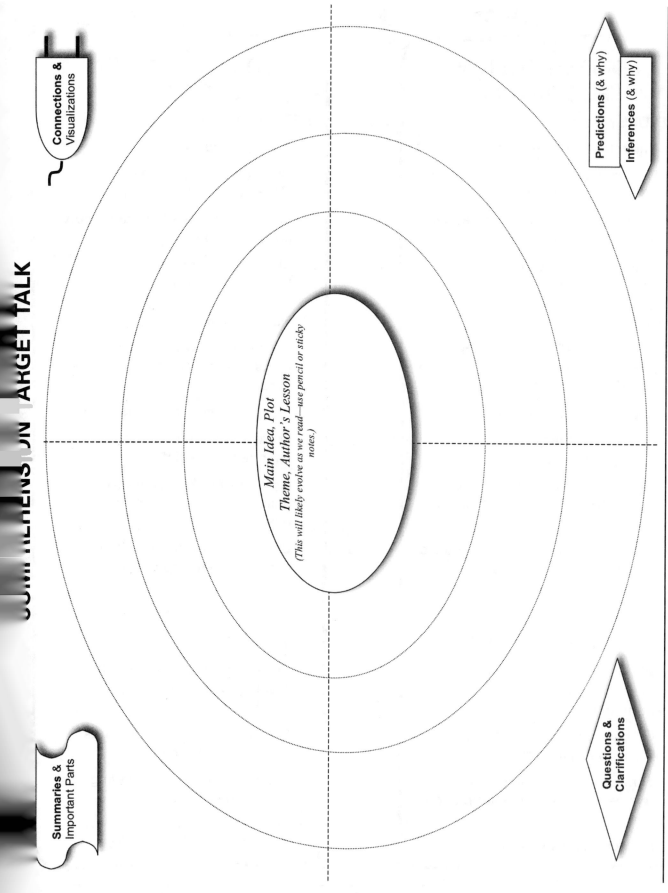

Connections & Visualizations

Predictions (& why)

Inferences (& why)

Main Idea, Plot
Theme, Author's Lesson
(This will likely evolve as we read—use pencil or sticky notes.)

Summaries & Important Parts

Questions & Clarifications

Building Reading Comprehension in Grades 6–12: A Toolkit of Classroom Activities (second edition) by Jeff Zwiers © 2010. Newark, DE: International Reading Association. May be copied for classroom use.

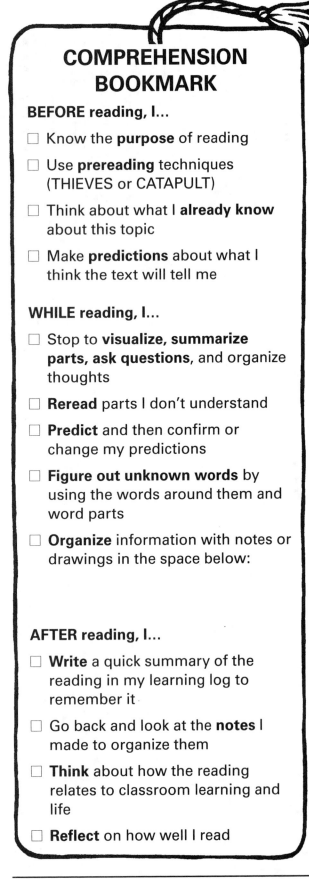

COMPREHENSION BOOKMARK

BEFORE reading, I...

☐ Know the **purpose** of reading

☐ Use **prereading** techniques
(THIEVES or CATAPULT)

☐ Think about what I **already know**
about this topic

☐ Make **predictions** about what I
think the text will tell me

WHILE reading, I...

☐ Stop to **visualize, summarize
parts, ask questions**, and organize
thoughts

☐ **Reread** parts I don't understand

☐ **Predict** and then confirm or
change my predictions

☐ **Figure out unknown words** by
using the words around them and
word parts

☐ **Organize** information with notes or
drawings in the space below:

AFTER reading, I...

☐ **Write** a quick summary of the
reading in my learning log to
remember it

☐ Go back and look at the **notes** I
made to organize them

☐ **Think** about how the reading
relates to classroom learning and
life

☐ **Reflect** on how well I read

COMPREHENSION BOOKMARK

BEFORE reading, I...

☐ Know the **purpose** of reading

☐ Use **prereading** techniques
(THIEVES or CATAPULT)

☐ Think about what I **already know**
about this topic

☐ Make **predictions** about what I
think the text will tell me

WHILE reading, I...

☐ Stop to **visualize, summarize
parts, ask questions**, and organize
thoughts

☐ **Reread** parts I don't understand

☐ **Predict** and then confirm or
change my predictions

☐ **Figure out unknown words** by
using the words around them and
word parts

☐ **Organize** information with notes or
drawings in the space below:

AFTER reading, I...

☐ **Write** a quick summary of the
reading in my learning log to
remember it

☐ Go back and look at the **notes** I
made to organize them

☐ **Think** about how the reading
relates to classroom learning and
life

☐ **Reflect** on how well I read

Building Reading Comprehension in Grades 6–12: A Toolkit of Classroom Activities (second edition) by Jeff Zwiers © 2010. Newark, DE: International Reading Association. May be copied for classroom use.

READING HABITS BOOKMARK

B **Background Knowledge** It will probably help that I already know.... This part connects to what I know about....

M **Main Idea and Author's Purpose** So far, this text is about.... The author wrote this in order to....

S **Summarizing** This section or paragraph was about....

Q **Questioning** I wonder why.... How....

I **Inferring** I bet that... because.... I think that.... Based on this part, I assume that....

P **Predicting** I predict that... because....

W **Word Meaning** This word means...because it has the word part.... The word means...because of its context....

C **Monitoring Comprehension** I don't get it; I will read it again.... I will read on to see if this part gets clearer to me....

READING HABITS BOOKMARK

B **Background Knowledge** It will probably help that I already know.... This part connects to what I know about....

M **Main Idea and Author's Purpose** So far, this text is about.... The author wrote this in order to....

S **Summarizing** This section or paragraph was about....

Q **Questioning** I wonder why.... How....

I **Inferring** I bet that... because.... I think that.... Based on this part, I assume that....

P **Predicting** I predict that... because....

W **Word Meaning** This word means...because it has the word part.... The word means...because of its context....

C **Monitoring Comprehension** I don't get it; I will read it again.... I will read on to see if this part gets clearer to me....

THINK-ALOUD CHECKLIST

I think... *I remember when...* *This boils down to...* *I predict that... because*

Comprehension Habits		2 = *Helpful* 1 = *Attempt*					
BKN: Connects to background knowledge (self/world)							
Connects to previous part of the text or to other texts							
Notices a conflict with background knowledge							
Background Knowledge Notes:							
SUM: Summarizes to reduce and remember information							
Connects summaries to **main idea and/or author's purpose**							
Summarizing Notes:							
INF: Makes logical **inferences** based on BK and text **evidence**							
Makes logical **predictions** based on BK and text **evidence**							
Confirms or **disconfirms** inferences and predictions							
Inference and Prediction Notes							
QUE: Generates good **questions** that provide direction or purpose							
Hypothesizes, seeks, and notices **answers** while reading							
Question Notes:							
WOR: Uses **context clues** to figure out words							
Uses knowledge of **word parts** to figure out words							
Word Meaning Notes:							
MON: Makes statements or questions indicating **confusion**							
Uses **fix-up strategies** (look back, read ahead)							
Uses **text structure**							
Challenges text; critiques style, format, clarity							
Comprehension Monitoring Notes:							

THINK-ALOUD NOTE GRID

#	Notes on _____'s thoughts	Use Background Knowledge	Fix Up and Monitor Comprehension	Predict or Infer	Question	Summarize	Figure Out Vocabulary (Context/Word Parts)	Main Idea/Author's Purpose

PART III

Ancillary Materials

APPENDIX

Multiple-Meaning Words

This appendix contains examples of words with more than one meaning. Use them to show students how words can have both concrete and abstract meanings and how a reader must use context to figure out which meaning is which. For example, consider the multiple meanings of *bank* in this sentence: "The man was on the bank until it fell into the river."

arms
- ☐ appendages with hands
- ☐ weapons for war

bank
- ☐ a depository for money
- ☐ land on the edge of a river

bit
- ☐ piece of metal that goes in a horse's mouth
- ☐ past tense of *bite*
- ☐ a small amount (e.g., just a little *bit*)

book
- ☐ to reserve a spot or flight
- ☐ a bound text with pages

can
- ☐ to be able (e.g., I *can* go)
- ☐ a metal container

case
- ☐ a situation or legal action (e.g., The *case* was unsolved)
- ☐ a receptacle for storage (e.g., guitar *case*)

date
- ☐ a social engagement
- ☐ a specific day on the calendar (e.g., Today's *date* is...)

fair
- ☐ legal and equitable
- ☐ a place with rides and cotton candy
- ☐ pleasant (e.g., The weather is *fair*)

fire
- [ ] to get rid of an employee
- [ ] flames and heat
- [ ] to shoot a weapon

game
- [ ] willing or interested (e.g., I'm *game* to try eating bugs)
- [ ] a sports contest (e.g., a baseball *game*)

get
- [ ] obtain (e.g., *Get* me a hamburger)
- [ ] become (e.g., I *get* angry when...)
- [ ] come (e.g., *Get* over here!)
- [ ] understand (e.g., I *get* it)
- [ ] receive (e.g., You'll *get* a cold out there)
- [ ] be allowed to (e.g., I *get* to go to the zoo today!)

grave
- [ ] a tomb or other burial place
- [ ] serious (e.g., The situation was *grave*)

jam
- [ ] a spread made from fruit
- [ ] to pack tightly (e.g., *Jam* another coat in the case)
- [ ] a clog (e.g., traffic *jam*)

kind
- [ ] gentle and benevolent
- [ ] type (e.g., What *kind* of animal is that?)

last
- [ ] to endure (e.g., It will *last* forever)
- [ ] final

light
- [ ] pale (e.g., a *light* color)
- [ ] visible energy used to illuminate an area (e.g., Turn on the *light*)
- [ ] to enliven (e.g., *light* up a room)
- [ ] not heavy

long
- [ ] extending for a great distance or time (e.g., a *long* rope)
- [ ] to want intensely (e.g., I *long* to see you)

mean
- [ ] nasty, unpleasant, or aggressive (e.g., The bully was *mean*)
- [ ] to intend (e.g., I *mean* what I say)
- [ ] a mathematical "middle" (e.g., The *mean* score was 43)

net
- ☐ remaining after all deductions (e.g., The *net* profit was $5.00)
- ☐ loosely woven fabric (e.g., The fish escaped from the *net*)

note
- ☐ written records (e.g., Take *notes* for me)
- ☐ a musical tone
- ☐ to be aware of (e.g., *Note* the differences)

over
- ☐ above, on top of
- ☐ done, finished

palm
- ☐ the inner part of the hand
- ☐ a type of tree
- ☐ a handheld computer

pass
- ☐ to go from one place to another
- ☐ to die (e.g., *pass* away)
- ☐ a ticket or permission slip (e.g., a hall *pass*)
- ☐ to throw a ball to another player in a game
- ☐ to hand something to someone (e.g., *Pass* me the peas, please)

play
- ☐ to sound an instrument or participate in a game
- ☐ a drama presented on a stage

present
- ☐ a gift
- ☐ here (e.g., She is not *present* today)
- ☐ to show or introduce (e.g., May I *present* to you...)

press
- ☐ to push down
- ☐ news media

race
- ☐ a group of people
- ☐ a speed contest for runners, cars, bicycles, and so on

rest
- ☐ to relax
- ☐ remainder (e.g., I'll eat the *rest*)

sole
- ☐ the bottom of a shoe
- ☐ a flat fish
- ☐ only (e.g., The *sole* reason is that I love you)

spell
- ☐ to write or say letters in the correct order (e.g., *Spell* your name)
- ☐ a period of time (e.g., Stay a *spell*)
- ☐ a magical incantation

spring
- ☐ the season after winter
- ☐ a bouncy wire
- ☐ a source of water
- ☐ an act of jumping, or fast growth

staff
- ☐ a stick or pole
- ☐ a group of workers

state
- ☐ condition (e.g., in a sad *state*)
- ☐ one of the divisions of a country (e.g., the *state* of Delaware)
- ☐ to say (e.g., Please *state* your name)

tire
- ☐ to become fatigued
- ☐ a rubber cushion around the wheel on a car

wake
- ☐ the churned waves behind a boat
- ☐ to come out of sleep
- ☐ a viewing before a funeral

wave
- ☐ a surge of an ocean or a sound
- ☐ to move the hand in greeting

well
- ☐ healthy (e.g., I feel *well*)
- ☐ a pit from which to draw water

will
- ☐ to intend (e.g., I *will* go)
- ☐ desire or preference (e.g., It is his *will* for you to go)
- ☐ a legal document for the disposition of property (e.g., He put it in his *will*)

yard
- ☐ three feet
- ☐ the land in front of or behind a house

APPENDIX

Prefixes, Suffixes, and Roots

Chapter 7 highlights the importance of learning how to figure out words by using their parts. The following is a convenient list that you can teach in creative ways to students so they can quickly figure out many words without having to consult a dictionary. One good way to teach them in general, of course, is for you to highlight word-part words that arise in context during the school year.

Word Part	Meaning	Sample Words
PREFIXES		
a-, an-, ab-	not, without	abnormal, amoral, apathy, atypical
ambi-	both	ambidextrous, ambiguous
ante-	before	antecedent, antechamber, anteroom
anti-	against	anticlimax, antidote
bene-, bon-	good, well	benediction, benefactor, benefit, bonanza
bi-	both, double	bicycle, bifocals, bilateral, biweekly
circum-, circ-	around	circumference, circumnavigate, circumspect
co-, col-, con-, com-	together, with	codependent, coexist, collect, collide, committee, congregation, conspire, convention, correlation, correspond
contra-, contro-, counter-	against	contradict, contraindication, controversy, counterpart
de-	from, down, away,	deceive, decline, deduct, defame, depart
	off, undo	depress, derail, derive
dia-	through, between	diagonal, dialogue, diameter, diatribe
dis-, dys-	apart, not, reverse,	disincentive, disinterested, dismiss, dissatisfied
	badly	distinct, distort, dysentery, dystrophy
ex-	out, from, former	exception, exclude, exhale, expose, extract
extra-	beyond	extracurricular, extraneous, extraordinary, extraterrestrial
fore-	before, in front	forecast, foregone, foreleg, foreshadow

Word Part	Meaning	Sample Words
homo-	man, one	homogenous, homophone
hyper-	over, above	hyperactive, hyperextension, hypersensitive, hyperthermia
hypo-	under	hypodermic, hypothermia, hypothesis
in-, im-, il-, ir-	1-in, into, within	illustrate, implicit, imply, import, income, inhabit, innate, involve, irrigate
	2-not	illegitimate, improbable, inactive, inane, incompatible, inept, irregular
inter-	between	interchange, interrupt, intervene
intra-, intro-	within, into	intramural, intravenous, introduce, introspection
macro-	large, excessive	macrocosm, macroeconomics
mal-	poor, badly	maladjusted, malady, malicious, malnourished
meta-	beyond, outside, change	metabolism, metacognition, metamorphosis metaphor
mis-	wrongly, incorrect	misfire, misfit, misguide, misinterpret, misquote, mistreat, mistrust, misunderstand, misuse
mono-	one	monochrome, monopoly, monotone
neo-	new	neoclassic, neophyte
non-	not	nonexistent, nonsense, nonviolent
paleo-	ancient	paleography, paleontology
para-	beside, almost	parachute, paramedic, paraphrase, parasite
peri-	around	pericardium, perimeter, peripheral, periscope
poly-	many	polygamy, polyglot, polygon
post-	after	posterity, posthumous, postpone, postwar
pre-	before in time, place, or order	precede, predict, prefer, prefix, preheat, preliminary, premature, premise, pre–Revolution
pro-	forward, for	procure, produce, prohibit, promote
quad-	four	quadrangle, quadrant, quadruplets
re-	back, again	reclaim, regain, reproduce, rescind, revise
retro-	backward	retroactive, retrospect
sub-	under	subdermal, subjugate, submerge, substandard, subterranean
syl-, sym-, syn-, sys-	with, together	syllogism, symbiosis, symbol, symphony, synchronization, system

Word Part	Meaning	Sample Words
trans-	across, through, beyond	transatlantic, transfusion, transit, transmigration, transmit
ultra-	beyond, excessive	ultraconservative, ultramodern, ultraviolet
un-	not, reverse	undo, unfair, unkind, unpretentious
uni-	one	uniform, unify, unilateral, united

SUFFIXES

Word Part	Meaning	Sample Words
-age	act of, collection of (v, n)	espionage, forage, passage, portage, salvage
-ance, -ancy	action, state, process (n)	allowance, persistence, resistance
-ar, -er, -or	one who, that which (n)	amplifier, collector, preacher, teacher, walker
-asis, -osis	process, condition (n)	hypnosis, osmosis, psychosis, stasis
-ate	make, cause (v)	congregate, cooperate, correlate, desegregate, meditate
-cide	kill (n)	genocide, homicide, pesticide, suicide
-dom	quality, office (n)	boredom, freedom, kingdom, wisdom
-ee	one who receives action (n)	employee, interviewee, nominee, trainee
-en	make (v), made of (adj)	darken, frozen, golden, wooden
-ese	language of, native person of (n), of a particular group (adj)	Balinese, Brooklynese, Chinese, Japanese Maltese
-fy	make (v)	amplify, calcify, certify, clarify, classify, simplify
-ice	condition, quality (n)	artifice, justice, malice

Word Part	Meaning	Sample Words
-ion, -sion, -tion	state of, act of, results of (n)	infection, inspection, opinion, reflection, rejection, suspension
-ism	system, condition (n)	activism, idealism, hedonism, plagiarism, racism
-ist	a person who, that which (n)	activist, artist, cyclist, racist
-ity, ty	quality, state of (n)	activity, creativity, frailty, sensitivity
-ive	having, making, causing (adj)	aggressive, conclusive, creative, exclusive
-ize	make, carry out (v)	criticize, hypothesize, realize, summarize, theorize
-less	without (adj)	careless, brainless, fruitless, heartless, useless
-ly	manner of (adv)	boldly, callously, carefully, haphazardly, mindlessly, surreptitiously
-ment	process, result of, act of (n)	amendment, endowment, experiment, government, sediment
-ness	state of, condition of (n)	darkness, duress, emptiness, helplessness, robustness
-ology, alogy	study of, theory (n)	astrology, biology, genealogy, ideology, neurology
-ous	having (adj)	malicious, pernicious, perspicacious, spacious, superfluous, unconscious
-tude	condition of (n)	altitude, amplitude, attitude, fortitude, vicissitude
-y	inclined to have (adj)	greedy, itchy, needy, seedy, shady

ROOTS

am, amor	love, like	amiable, amorous, enamored
anthro	humankind	anthropologist, anthropomorphic, philanthropy
arch	first, top, head	archaic, archangel, archetypical, monarch, matriarch, patriarchal
auc, aug	increase	auction, augment
aud	listen, hear	audience, audio, auditory, inaudible
aut, auto	self	autocracy, automation, autonomous, autopilot

Word Part	Meaning	Sample Words
belli	war, violent	bellicose, belligerent, rebellious
bio	life	autobiography, biome, bionic, biopsy, biosphere
card, cord, cour	heart, center	accord, cardiopulmonary, cordial, courage, discord
carn	flesh	carnivore, incarnation
cede, ced, ceed	surrender, yield, move	cede, concede, intercede, precede, proceed recede, succeed
chron	time	chronicle, chronological, synchronize
civ	citizen	civic, civil, civilian, civilization, civilize, civvies
claus, clud, clus	close, shut	claustrophobia, conclude, exclude, preclude, recluse
cogn, gnos	know	cognition, cognizant, diagnose, Gnostics, prognosis
corp	body	corporation, corporeal, corps
cosm	world, universe	cosmic, cosmos, microcosm
cour, cur, curs	run	concur, concurrent, courier, cursive, incur, occur
cred	believe	accredited, credentials, credit, creed, incredulous
crease, cresc, cru	grow, rise	accrue, crescendo, decrease
dem	people	democracy, demographics, epidemic
derm	skin	dermal, dermatologist, epidermis, taxidermy
dic, dict	speak, say	benediction, dedicate, dictate, dictator, edict, indicate, verdict
duc, duct	lead, guide	conduct, deduce, produce, viaduct
dur, dura	lasting, hard	durable, duration, endure
end, endo	within	endogenous, endoskeletal
erg	work	erg, ergometer, ergophobia
fac, fic, fect	make, do	faculty, fiction, infection, manufacture
fer	carry, bear	ferry, fertile, infer, refer
fid, feder	trust	confident, federal, fidelity, infidel
fin	end	confine, define, finale, finite, infinity
flu, fluc, fluv	flow	fluctuate, flue, fluent, flush, fluvial
forc, fort	strong	forceful, forte, fortify, fortitude
fract, frag	break	fractal, fraction, fragile, fragment, refract
gen	produce, birth, race	congenital, gender, genealogy, generate, genetic, genus, indigenous
geo	earth	geographic, geometry, geothermal
germ	essential, cause	germ, germane, germinate
grad, gress	go, step	aggressive, congress, degrade, digress, gradation, gradual, graduate
gram, graph	write	biography, geography, orthography, photography, sonogram, telegram

Word Part	Meaning	Sample Words
grat	pleasing	congratulation, grateful, gratitude, gratuity, ingrate
greg	crowd, gather, group	aggregate, congregate, gregarious, segregate
hab, habit	live, have	cohabitate, habitat, habitual, inhabit, rehabilitate
hetero	different	heterogeneous, heterosexual
hydr	water	dehydration, hydrogen, hydraulic, rehydrate
jud	lawyer, judge	judge, judiciary, prejudice
liber, liver	loosen, free	deliberate, deliver, liberal, liberation
loc, loco	place, near	allocate, collocate, local, locality, locomotive, relocate
locut, loqu	speak	circumlocution, loquacious, soliloquy
log, logy	word, study	analogy, apology, dialogue, illogical, prologue, theology
magn	great	magnanimous, magnification, magnificent, magnitude
man	hand	emancipation, manage, manicure, manifest, manipulate, manual
medi	half	median, mediate, medieval, mediocrity, medium
mem	remember	commemorate, memoir, memorial
migra	wander	immigrant, migration, migratory
mori, mors, mort	death, mortal	immortal, moribund, mortify, mortuary
morph	shape, form	amorphous, metamorphosis
nov	new	innovative, nova, novel, novice, renovate
omni	all	omnipotent, omnipresent, omniscient
ortho	straight, correct	orthodontist, orthodox, orthogonal, orthopedic
path	feeling, suffer	antipathy, empathy, pathetic, sympathy, telepath
pend, pens	weigh, hang	compendium, impending, pending, pendulum, pensive, suspend
phon	sound	cacophonous, euphonious, phonograph, symphony
photo	light	photoelectric, photogenic, photosynthesis, photon
pon, pos	put, place	deposit, disposition, exponent, oppose, postpone, postulate, posture, proponent, propose
port	carry	import, portable, report, support, transport
prim, proto	first	primal, primary, protagonist, prototype, protozoan
recti, reg	straighten	direct, incorrect, rectangular, regiment, regulate
rupt	break	corruptible, erupt, interrupt, rupture
scrib, script	write	describe, manuscript, prescription, scribble, scribe
secu, sequ	follow	consecutive, consequence, non sequitur, subsequent, sequential
sens, sent	feel	dissension, sensation, sensory, sentimental
solu, solv	loosen	absolve, resolute, resolve, solvent

Word Part	Meaning	Sample Words
spec, spic	look	aspect, conspicuous, despicable, expect, inspect, introspective, perspective, perspicacious, respect, retrospect, specimen, spectacle
spire	breath	aspire, inspire, perspire, respire, spirit
strict	make tight	constrict, restrict, strict, stricture
tele	far	teleconference, telepathy, telephone, telescope
tempo	time	contemporary, extemporaneous, temporal
terra	earth	extraterrestrial, terrain, territory
tox	poison	antitoxin, intoxicated, toxic
trib	bestow, pay	attribute, contribute, retribution, tributary
vac	empty	evacuate, vacant, vacation, vacuole, vacuous, vacuum
val	worth, strength	evaluation, valiant, valid, valor
vers, vert	turn	advertise, avert, divert, invert, revert
vict, vinc	conquer	convince, evict, invincible, victor, victory
vid, vis	see	invisible, supervision, video, vista
voc	call	advocate, invoke, provoke, vocabulary
vor, vour	eat	carnivore, devour, herbivore, omnivorous, voracious
zo	animal	protozoan, zodiac, zoology, zooplankton

REFERENCES

Allen, J. (1999). *Words, words, words: Teaching vocabulary in grades 4–12*. York, ME: Stenhouse.

Alvermann, D.E. (1991). The discussion web: A graphic aid for learning across the curriculum. *The Reading Teacher, 45*(2), 92–99.

Alvermann, D.E., & Phelps, S.F. (2001). *Content reading and literacy: Succeeding in today's diverse classrooms* (3rd ed.). Boston: Allyn & Bacon.

Armbruster, B.B., Anderson, T.H., & Meyer, J.L. (1992). Improving content-area reading using instructional graphics. *Reading Research Quarterly, 26*(4), 393–416.

Armstrong, T. (2003). *The multiple intelligences of reading and writing: Making the words come alive*. Alexandria, VA: Association for Supervision and Curriculum Development.

Aronson, E. (1978). *The jigsaw classroom*. Thousand Oaks, CA: Sage.

Baker, L., & Beall, L.C. (2009). Metacognitive processes and reading comprehension. In S.E. Israel & G.G. Duffy (Eds.), Handbook of research on reading comprehension (pp. 373–388). New York: Routledge.

Barron, B., & Darling-Hammond, L. (2008). How can we teach for meaningful learning? In L. Darling-Hammond, B. Barron, D. Pearson, A. Schoenfeld, E. Stage, T. Zimmerman, G. Cervetti, & J. Tilson (Eds.), *Powerful Learning: What We Know About Teaching for Understanding* (pp. 11–70). San Francisco: Jossey-Bass.

Baumann, J.F. (1986). *Teaching main idea comprehension*. Newark, DE: International Reading Association.

Bean, T.W., Singer, H., & Cowan, S. (1985). Analogical study guides: Improving comprehension in science. *Journal of Reading, 29*(3), 246–250.

Beck, I.L., McKeown, M.G., Hamilton, R.L., & Kucan, L. (1997). *Questioning the author: An approach for enhancing student engagement with text*. Newark, DE: International Reading Association.

Beck, I., McKeown, M., & Kucan, L. (2002). *Bringing words to life: Robust vocabulary instruction*. New York: Guilford.

Beers, K. (1998). *Reading strategies handbook for high school*. Austin, TX: Holt, Rinehart and Winston.

Bleich, D. (1975). *Reading and feelings: An introduction to subjective criticism*. Urbana, IL: National Council of Teachers of English.

Bourdieu, P. (1986). The forms of capital. In J.G. Richardson (Ed.), *Handbook for theory and research for the sociology of education* (pp. 241–258). New York: Greenwood.

Brown, J.E., & Stephens, E.C. (1999). *A handbook of content literacy strategies: 75 practical reading and writing ideas*. Norwood, MA: Christopher-Gordon.

Buehl, D. (2009). *Classroom strategies for interactive learning* (3rd ed.). Newark, DE: International Reading Association.

Carr, E.M., & Ogle, D. (1987). K-W-L Plus: A strategy for comprehension and summarization. *Journal of Reading, 30*(7), 626–631.

Ciardiello, A.V. (1998). Did you ask a good question today? Alternative cognitive and metacognitive strategies. *Journal of Adolescent & Adult Literacy, 42*(3), 210–219.

Cunningham, P.M. (1995). *Phonics they use: Words for reading and writing* (2nd ed.). New York: Addison-Wesley/Longman.

Daniels, H., & Bizar, M. (2005). *Teaching the best practice way: Methods that matter, K-12*. Portland, ME: Stenhouse.

Davey, B. (1983). Think aloud: Modeling the cognitive processes of reading comprehension. *Journal of Reading, 27*(1), 44–47.

Delpit, L. (1995). *Other people's children: Cultural conflict in the classroom*. New York: New Press.

Dole, J.A., Duffy, G.G., Roehler, L.R., & Pearson, P.D. (1991). Moving from the old to the new: Research on reading comprehension instruction. *Review of Educational Research, 61*(2), 239–264.

Druyan, S. (1997). Effect of the kinesthetic conflict on promoting scientific reasoning. *Journal of Research in Science Teaching, 34*(10), 1083–1099.

Duffala, J. (1987). *The teacher as artist*. Santa Rosa, CA: Author.

Duffelmeyer, F.A., Baum, D.D., & Merkley, D.J. (1987). Maximizing reader-text confrontation with an extended anticipation guide. *Journal of Reading, 31*(2), 146–150.

Farr, R. (2001). Think-along/think-alouds and comprehending lead to better comprehension. *The California Reader, 34*(2), 29–33.

Fletcher, C.R., & Bloom, C.P. (1988). Causal reasoning in the comprehension of simple narrative texts. *Journal of Memory and Language, 27*(3), 235–244.

Freire, P., & Macedo, D. (1987). *Literacy: Reading the word and the world.* Westport, CT: Bergin & Garvey.

Friend, R. (2001). Teaching summarization as a content area reading strategy. *Journal of Adolescent & Adult Literacy, 44*(4), 320–329.

Gambrell, L.B., & Bales, R.J. (1986). Mental imagery and the comprehension-monitoring performance of fourth- and fifth-grade poor readers. *Reading Research Quarterly, 21*(4), 454–464.

Gardner, H. (1999). *Frames of mind: The theory of multiple intelligences.* New York: Basic.

Gillet, J.W., & Temple, C. (2000). *Understanding reading problems: Assessment and instruction* (5th ed.). Boston: Allyn & Bacon.

Guthrie, J.T., & Wigfield, A. (2000). Engagement and motivation in reading. In M.L. Kamil, P.B. Mosenthal, P.D. Pearson, & R. Barr (Eds.), *Handbook of reading research* (Vol. 3, pp. 403–424). Mahwah, NJ: Erlbaum.

Harvey, S., & Goudvis, A. (2007). *Strategies that work: Teaching comprehension for understanding and engagement.* Portland, ME: Stenhouse.

Helfeldt, J.P., & Henk, W.A. (1990). Reciprocal question-answer relationships: An instructional technique for at-risk readers. *Journal of Reading, 33*(7), 509–514.

Hibbing, A.N., & Rankin-Erickson, J.L. (2003). A picture is worth a thousand words: Using visual images to improve comprehension for middle school struggling readers. *The Reading Teacher, 56*(8), 758–770.

Hyerle, D. (2008). *Visual tools for transforming information into knowledge* (2nd ed.). Alexandria, VA: Association for Supervision and Curriculum Development.

Irwin, J.W. (1991). *Teaching reading comprehension processes* (2nd ed.). Upper Saddle River, NJ: Pearson.

Jaworski, A., & Coupland, N. (Eds.). (1999). *The discourse reader.* London: Routledge.

Johns, J.L., & Berglund, R.L. (2001). *Strategies for content area learning: Vocabulary comprehension response.* Dubuque, IA: Kendall/Hunt.

Johnson, D., & Pearson, P.D. (1984). *Teaching reading vocabulary* (2nd ed.). Austin, TX: Holt, Rinehart and Winston.

Kagan, S. (1997). *Cooperative learning.* San Clemente, CA: Kagan Cooperative.

Keene, E.O., & Zimmermann, S. (2007). *Mosaic of thought: The power of comprehension strategy instruction.* Portsmouth, NH: Heinemann.

Lyons, C.A., & Pinnell, G.S. (2001). *Systems for change in literacy education: A guide to professional development.* Portsmouth, NH: Heinemann.

Manz, S.L. (2002). A strategy for previewing textbooks: Teaching readers to become THIEVES. *The Reading Teacher, 55*(5), 434–435.

Marzano, R.J., Pickering, D.J., & Pollock, J.E. (2001). *Classroom instruction that works: Research-based strategies for increasing student achievement.* Alexandria, VA: Association for Supervision and Curriculum Development.

McLaughlin, M., & Vogt, M. (2000). *Creativity and innovation in content area teaching.* Norwood, MA: Christopher-Gordon.

Merkley, D.M., & Jeffries, D. (2001). Guidelines for implementing a graphic organizer. *The Reading Teacher, 54*(4), 350–357.

Moeller, V.J., & Moeller, M.V. (2002). *Socratic seminars and literature circles for middle and high school English.* Larchmont, NY: Eye on Education.

Nagy, W.E. (1988). *Teaching vocabulary to improve reading comprehension.* Newark, DE: International Reading Association.

Ogle, D.M. (1986). K-W-L: A teaching model that develops active reading of expository text. *The Reading Teacher, 39*(6), 564–570.

Palincsar, A.S., & Brown, A.L. (1984). Reciprocal teaching of comprehension-fostering and comprehension-monitoring activities. *Cognition and Instruction, 1*(2), 117–175.

Pauk, W. (2001). *How to study in college* (7th ed.). Boston: Houghton Mifflin.

Peregoy, S.F., & Boyle, O.F. (2005). *Reading, writing, and learning in ESL: A resource book for K–12 teachers* (4th ed.). Reading, MA: Addison-Wesley.

Poindexter, C. (1994). Guessed meanings. *Journal of Reading, 37*(5), 420–421.

Pressley, M., Burkell, J., Cariglia-Bull, T., Lysynchuk, L., McGoldrick, J.A., Schneider, B., et al. (1990). *Cognitive strategy instruction.* Cambridge, MA: Brookline.

Readence, J.E., Bean, T.W., & Baldwin, R.S. (2001). *Content area literacy: An integrated approach* (7th ed.). Dubuque, IA: Kendall/Hunt.

Robb, L. (2003). *Teaching reading in social studies, science, and math.* New York: Scholastic.

Ryder, R.J., & Graves, M.F. (2002). *Reading and learning in content areas* (3rd ed.). Chichester, UK: John Wiley.

Salembier, G.B., & Cheng, L.C. (1997). SCUBA-dive into reading. *Teaching Exceptional Children, 29*(6), 68–71.

Sampson, M.B. (2002). Confirming a K-W-L: Considering the source. *The Reading Teacher, 55*(6), 528–532.

Sedita, J. (2005). Effective vocabulary instruction. *Insights on Learning Disabilities, 2*(1), 33–45.

Stahl, S.A. (1999). *Vocabulary development* (Vol. 2). Cambridge, MA: Brookline.

Stone, C.L. (1983). A meta-analysis of advanced organizer studies. *Journal of Experimental Education, 51*(4), 194–199.

Taba, H. (1967). *Teacher's handbook for elementary social studies.* Reading, MA: Addison-Wesley.

Taylor, B.M., Graves, M.F., & van den Broek, P.W. (2000). *Reading for meaning: Fostering comprehension in the middle grades.* New York: Teachers College Press; Newark, DE: International Reading Association.

Texas Reading Initiative. (2002). *Promoting vocabulary development: Components of effective vocabulary instruction* (Revised edition). Austin, TX: Texas Education Agency.

Tierney, R.J., & Readence, J.E. (2000). *Reading strategies and practices: A compendium* (5th ed.). Boston: Allyn & Bacon.

Urquhart, A.H., & Weir, C.J. (1998). *Reading in a second language: Process, product, and practice.* New York: Longman.

Villaume, S.K., & Brabham, E.G. (2002). Comprehension instruction: Beyond strategies. *The Reading Teacher, 55*(7), 672–675.

Vygotsky, L.S. (1978). *Mind in society: The development of higher psychological processes* (M. Cole, V. John-Steiner, S. Scribner, & E. Souberman, Eds. & Trans.). Cambridge, MA: Harvard University Press. (Original work published 1934)

Wiggins, G. (1998). *Educative assessment: Designing assessments to inform and improve student performance.* San Francisco: Jossey-Bass.

Wiggins, G., & McTighe, J. (2005). *Understanding by design* (2nd ed.). Englewood Cliffs, NJ: Prentice Hall.

Wilhelm, J.D. (2001). *Improving comprehension with think-aloud strategies: Modeling what good readers do.* New York: Scholastic.

Wood, K. (1988). Guiding students through informational text. *The Reading Teacher, 41*(9), 912–920.

Wood, K., Lapp, D., Flood, J., & Taylor, D. (2008). *Guiding readers through text: New strategies for new times* (2nd ed.). Newark, DE: International Reading Association.

Wormeli, R. (2005). *Summarization in any subject: 50 techniques to improve students learning.* Alexandria, VA: Association for Supervision and Curriculum Development.

Zwiers, J. (2004). *Developing academic thinking skills in grades 6-12: A handbook of multiple intelligence activities.* Newark, DE: International Reading Association.

Zwiers, J. (2008). *Building academic language: Essential practices for content classrooms.* San Francisco: Jossey-Bass.

Zwiers, J., & Crawford, M. (2009). How to start academic conversations. *Educational Leadership, 66*(7), 70–73.

INDEX

Note. Page numbers followed by *f*, *r*, and *t* indicate figures, reproducibles, and tables, respectively.

reading comprehension: assessment of, 12, 13*t*, 14; challenges for diverse students, 8–9; complexity of, 3, 4, 5*f*; strategies for, 3–4

reading comprehension habits: "academifying," 7–8; definition of, viii; for expository texts, 7; list of, 4; strengthening or pruning branches of key information, 6. *See also* background knowledge; inferences; monitoring comprehension; organization of text information; predictions; questions; word meanings

Reading Habits Bookmark, 175, 190, 199*r*

reciprocal teaching concept, 3, 178

reproducibles, ix–x, xiii

restatements, 142

"right there" questions, 123–124, 131

Robb, L., 16, 17, 187

Roehler, L.R., 99

roots of words, 212–215

Ryder, R.J., 7

S

Salembier, G.B., 158

Sampson, M.B., 80

scaffolding comprehension, 16–17

scaffolds for diverse students, building, 9

schemata, using and developing, 67–68

SCUBA Diving Into Word Meanings, 158, 169*r*

sculpting main idea: components of main idea, 32–34; description of, 31; flexibility and, 34; formula for, 43–45; memory and, 34

Sedita, J., 140

self-assessment and self-monitoring, 12

Self-Selected Vocab Quizzes, 159

semantic context, 144–145

semantic feature analysis, 46

semantic organizers, 45–46

Semantic Webbing, 49–51, 51–52*f*

similar words, using to figure out meaning, 147

Singer, H., 152

Socratic Sessions, 23, 132–133

Sorry, I Lost My Headings, 52–53, 52*f*

sound cards, 49

Stahl, S.A., 146

Stephens, E.C., 23

Sticky Note Snapshots, 85–86, 86*f*

Sticky Symbols and Drawings, 113–114

Stone, C.L., 77

Story Map, 53–54, 63*r*

strategic, being, 15

Student-Created Quizzes and Tests, 133

Students Get to Teach, 54

students teaching students: academic communication and, 22; Jigsaw Summaries, 40–42, 41*f*, 42*f*; Students Get to Teach, 54

suffixes, 211–212

summarizing: categorization component of, 35, 35*f*; classification component of, 36–37, 36*f*; description of, 31; purpose of, 35

Summarizing Training Camp, 54–55

synonyms, 142

syntactic context, 145

T

Taba, H., 156

Talk Show, 133–134

Taylor, B.M., 4, 6, 34

Taylor, D., 39

T+B=I Inference Machines, 114–115, 115*f*, 121*r*

teacher, purpose of, 33–34, 62*r*

Temple, C., 9, 15

Texas Reading Initiative, 148

"text and me" questions, 124

text purpose (Why? component), 33, 62*r*

Text Structure Graphic Organizers, 86–87, 88*t*

textbook reading habits, building, 27

text-to-self inferences, 100–101

text-to-text inferences, 100

text-to-world inferences, 100–101

Theme Possibilities Visual, 56, 64*r*

THIEVES, 87, 89*t*, 96*r*, 97*r*, 175

Think-Aloud Checklist, 190–191, 200*r*

Think-Aloud Hand Signals, 191–192, 192*t*

Think-Aloud Note Grids, 192–193, 201*r*

think-alouds: to figure out multiple meanings, 146; to model comprehension, 16; Read-Aloud Think-Aloud, 187–190, 188*t*

Think-Notes, 193–194, 194*f*

Think-Pair-Share, 89–91, 90*t*

Think-Pair-Square, 91

30-30-30 RATA, 189–190

thoughts, remembering, managing, and prioritizing, 6

Tierney, R.J., 72

toolkit of activities. *See* activities toolkit

topic (What? component), 32

topic sentences, 36

two-column notes, 39

Two-Word Sentence Stickies, 159–160

U

under-the-surface questions, 124, 131, 136*r*, 138*r*, 139*r*

Urquhart, A.H., 8, 20